CHANGING POISON INTO MEDICINE

Sun Lotus Recovery

A Manifesto

of

Spiritual Change

for

The 21st Century

Changing Poison into Medicine

ISBN: 9798724293297

DEDICATION

To my Wife, Mona, whom I love dearly.
Who is my entire life and is the woman who brings out the
best in me and has helped me to become a better,
happier, human being.
Without her support none of this would have been possible.

Changing Poison into Medicine

CONTENTS

1) The Life of Nichiren Daishonin the founder of The   p.2
   Nichiren Shoshu School.

2) Nam Myoho Renge Kyo.   p.17

3) Ten Worlds and Ichinen Sanzen.   p.39

4) The True Object of Worship Dai Gohonzon.   p.60

5) The Recitation of The Lotus Sutra or Gongyo.   p.81

6) Rissho Ankoku Ron.   p.98

   Question One.   p.110

   Question Two.   p.138

   Question Three.   p.153

   Question Four.   p.168

   Question Five.   p.187

   Question Six.   p.201

   Question Seven.   p.211

   Question Eight.   p.231

   Question Nine.   p.241

7) Kechimyaku.   p.270

ACKNOWLEDGEMENTS

The Sun, The Moon & The Stars, Mother Earth and The
Buddha's and Boddhisattva's of The Ten Directions.

Introduction.

Congratulations on completing the twelve sessions of The Sun Lotus Recovery Programme and in meeting The Dai Gohonzon of The Three Great Secret Laws and starting your new life of becoming free from the shackles of your negative karma on this great journey of self-realization and discovery of your true awakened, enlightened self.

Not only are you now beginning to reveal your true self for the first time in your life, which is eternal, pure and absolutely happy, but also through that process of becoming fully awakened to the reality of life and because of your deep inter connection with everything else in the world, you will change not only yourself, your family and society but also Planet Earth and the Universe itself.

This is the limitless and boundless power of the Buddha Nature inherent in all phenomena, inherent in your own life.

This is the second book published by Sun Lotus Recovery and is designed to deepen and enhance belief and understanding of Nichiren Daishonin's Buddhism as taught in The Orthodox Nichiren Shoshu School (The Fuji School) based on The Lotus Sutra, the highest and most profound Dharma of all the eighty eight thousand teachings of Buddhism, known as The True Law or Dharma or The Mystic Law, which is the ultimate truth of life and death.

Through this deeper belief and understanding we can begin the lifelong process of Changing Poison into Medicine through Buddhist Practice for oneself and changing our society and ultimately the whole planet through our practice for others.

This is what this book aims to elucidate and enable you to achieve by understanding in greater depth and to personally experience the power of this amazing practice of radical self transformation with The Gohonzon.

It is also my way of finally expressing and communicating to the world my understanding of Nichiren Daishonin's Buddhism and the great goal of Kosen Rufu or World Peace that has been in my heart for over thirty years to others, in the hope that they will also join me on this great mission in life.

This much needed Spiritual Revolution of The Age.

The Life of Nichiren Daishonin. The Founder of The Nichiren Shoshu School of Buddhism.

Changing Poison into Medicine

Nichiren Daishonin was born on the 16th of February 1222, in Japan eight hundred years ago, in the village of Kominato in Tojo District on the eastern coast of Awa Province (currently Chiba prefecture)
His Father's name was Mikumi no Tayo and his Mother's name was Umegiku Nyo, they made their living by fishing.
In one of his writings called Gosho he writes.

"Nichiren is a child of a Chandala family, from the beaches of Tojo in Awa Japan".

The Chandala are the lowest group in the ancient Indian class system, called the caste system, comprising such professions as fishermen and butchers whose professions involved the killing of animals, and Nichiren Daishonin is acknowledging that his origins were of the humblest kind.
He was given the childhood name Zennichi maro which translated means "Splendid Sun" or "Virtuous Sun Boy".
There were various omens surrounding the child's birth, as his Mother was recorded to have said that she had a dream before his birth in which she saw herself seated on Mount Hei, the place where the Head Temple of The Tendai School (The most powerful Buddhist School in Japan of that time) was located, and she was washing her hands in the waters of Lake Biwa, as the Sun rose out of the east from behind Mount Fuji, she cradled the Sun (Japanese- Nichi) in her arms.
Startled by this dream she awoke and told it to her husband.
He too had an unusual dream in which Bodhisattva Space Repository (Kokuzo) who represents the wisdom of the universe, appeared before him.
On his shoulder the Bodhisattva carried a handsome boy, he told the Daishonin's Father that this child was Bodhisattva Jogyo and was destined to become a great leader that would save all people.
Boddhisattva Space Repository said, "I will grant this lovely boy to you" and disappeared.

Shortly after Umegiku nyo realised she was pregnant.
Umegiku nyo had another dream the night before the Daishonin's birth in which a blue lotus (Japanese-ren) flower blossomed with pure water springing forth from it.
A baby was inside the lotus flower taking its first bath.
The water which sparkled with a golden colour, spilled out onto the ground and the grasses shone as trees blossomed and bore fruit.
These symbolic dreams foretold the advent of the True Buddha of The Latter Day of The Law.
To put the Daishonin's birth date into context in terms of Buddhist chronology here is an explanation of The Three Periods of Buddhism.

Changing Poison into Medicine

In Buddhism the time following the death of Shakyamuni Buddha is divided into three periods that relate to the effectiveness of his teachings.

The first thousand years after his death are called The Former Day of The Law (Jap- Shobo) and during this period Shakyamuni's Buddhism prevailed and human beings could attain enlightenment through his teachings and practices.

The second thousand years are called The Middle Day of The Law (Jap-Zobo) where the efficacy of Shakyamuni's teachings began to decline and although Buddhism was well established in society it gradually lapsed into formality.

The third period called The Latter Day of The Law (Jap-Mappo) begins two thousand years after the death of Shakyamuni Buddha and extends for ten thousand years and on into the infinite future.

It is in this age of Mappo which corresponds to our western concept of The Anthropocene Age, Shakyamuni's teachings and practices lose their power to lead human beings to enlightenment.

In the age of Mappo the lives of human beings become defiled by what Buddhism calls The Three Poisons which arise from fundamental darkness and are categorised as Greed, Anger and Ignorance or Stupidity causing the world to be filled with conflict and corruption.

Nichiren Daishonin was born into the age of Mappo which corresponds to today's Anthropocene Age into which we were also born.

The date of Nichiren Daishonin's birth, has a mystic connection with Shakyamuni's Buddhism because Shakyamuni died on February 15th, this indicates that The Daishonin's Buddhism began at the point where the power of Shakyamuni's Buddhism ceased.

In 1233 at the age of twelve Zennichimaro climbed to an historic old Temple called Seicho-Ji on Mount Seicho near Kominato, which belonged to The Tendai school, where he began his Buddhist study under the tutelage of The Chief Priest of Seicho-Ji called Dozen-bo.

The Japanese world of Buddhism at that time fully manifested the characteristics of The Latter Day of The Law when The Great Pure Law had been lost.

Although all of the predominate Buddhist schools of Japan in those days such as the Nembutsu School, Zen School, Shingon School, Ritsu School and Tendai School all derived from Shakyamuni's teachings, it was not clear which Buddhist school was the correct teaching and practice and which was incorrect.

Amidst such confusion and chaos in the Buddhist world of Japan and whilst pursuing his studies, he wished to resolve these conflicts within the Buddhist world, and to solve the fundamental problems of life, and as he later wrote in.

Reply to Myoho-ama.

Changing Poison into Medicine

"Ever since my childhood, I have studied Buddhism with one thought in mind.
Life as a Human Being is pathetically fleeting.
A man exhales his last breath with no hope to draw another.
Not even dew borne by the wind suffices to describe this transience.
No one, wise or foolish, young or old, can escape death.
My sole wish has therefore been to solve this eternal mystery.
All else has been secondary".

Motivated by this great desire to liberate all human beings from their illusions and sufferings, in this way, he sought the truth of Buddhism.
In the Temple Hall of worship in Seicho-ji there was a statue of Boddhisattva Kokuzo (Sanskrit-Akasagharba) and from the time he first entered the Temple at the age of twelve, Nichiren Daishonin studied and meditated.
In later years he wrote of that time.

"Having sought learning since my childhood, at the age of twelve I prayed before Boddhisattva Kokuzo to become the wisest person in all Japan".

He added that Boddhisattva Kokuzo bestowed upon him,

"A jewel of wisdom"
That is, he awakened to the ultimate reality of life and the universe but in order to reveal this enlightenment to the people of The Latter Day of The Law he had to systematise his ideas.
As he studied Buddhism, he was especially concerned about the bewildering multiplicity of Buddhist sects and the doctrinal contradictions within The Buddhist Canon.
He was convinced that there must be one among the many sutras that represented the highest truth of Buddhism.
At the age of sixteen, he resolved to be ordained and took the religious name Zesho-bo Rencho.
Rencho meaning Lotus growth.
Sometime later he took leave of his teacher Dozen-bo and travelled to Kamakura to further his studies.
There he delved into the teachings of The Jodo and Zen sects, but Kamakura was still a relatively new capitol city with a limited tradition of Buddhism, so after four years of study there Nichiren Daishonin returned to Seicho-Ji briefly in 1243 and in the same year left for the old capital of Imperial Japan, Kyoto and to Mount Hiei the centre of The Tendai (Chinese-T'ien T'ai) sect, of which his Temple Seicho-Ji was a branch Temple, and later to Mount Koya the headquarters of The Shingon sect as well as all the other important Temples in the Kyoto and Nara areas.

Changing Poison into Medicine

After some ten years of study at Mount Hiei and elsewhere, he concluded that the true teachings of Buddhism are to be found only in The Lotus Sutra.
The Lotus Sutra represents the very heart of The Buddha Shakyamuni's enlightenment, all the other sutras are mere expedients leading up to The Lotus Sutra.
After thoroughly mastering all the doctrines of Buddhism known as The Dharma, Rencho, as he was still named, returned to his home Temple Seicho-Ji in early 1253 and on the morning of April 28th, 1253, he climbed to the top of Kasagamori Peak on Mount Seicho where he powerfully chanted Nam Myoho Renge Kyo for the first time to the rising sun as it appeared at dawn.

With this he declared The Establishment of True Buddhism to the Universe and thereby providing the key for all future generations to unlock the treasure of enlightenment in their hearts.
At this time, he also changed his name to Nichiren.
(Sun Lotus)

After he climbed down the mountain, he delivered his first sermon at noon that same day to his parents, and his older fellow disciples, Gijo-bo, Joken-bo and Joen-bo at the Jibutsu-do hall of Dozen-bo's lodging Temple called, Shobutsu-bo at Seicho-Ji Temple.

Changing Poison into Medicine

At that sermon he declared that none of the pre-Lotus Sutra teachings revealed the Buddha's enlightenment and that all the sects based on those teachings were misguided.

He then made this clear by citing documentary proofs, that the Nembutsu, Zen and the other sects prevalent at that time, were erroneous teachings, that go against the true intention of Shakyamuni Buddha.

He stated that The Lotus Sutra was supreme and that Nam Myoho Renge Kyo, the essence of The Lotus Sutra, is the only Buddhist teaching that can lead human beings in The Latter Day of The Law to enlightenment.

Few in the audience could understand the meaning of The Daishonin's first sermon.

They responded with anger, since it appeared to them as an attack on their own religious beliefs because his teaching refuted the popular sects of Buddhism of that time which would potentially antagonise the secular authorities who adhered to them.

The Daishonin's parents became fearful for their son and pleaded with him to reconsider his views.

The Daishonin, however, taught and guided his parents patiently until they finally became the first believers to take faith in True Buddhism.

Changing Poison into Medicine

On May 28th exactly one month after his first sermon, The Daishonin once again took the master's seat to present his doctrines, facing the south side of the Jibutsu-do hall of Shobutsu-bo at Seicho-Ji Temple, where a very great number of people had now gathered, due to the reputation he had already gained due to his first sermon.
In this sermon he called himself "Nichiren, The Votary of The Lotus Sutra" and addressed his audience once again.
The contents of his presentation shocked the religious world of his day and had a huge impact on the people who were gathered there.
He immediately became the target of Tojo Kagenobu, the Steward of the region and a staunch believer of the Nembutsu sect who on that day made the very first attempt on The Daishonin's life, but with the help of his fellow Priests, Joken-bo and Gijo-bo, he managed to escape the crisis.
Since The Daishonin fully expected to meet this kind of great persecution, his great compassion and desire to save all people and commitment to propagate True Buddhism never wavered for a moment.
On the contrary, The Daishonin determined that further propagation activities should be take place in the capitol Kamakura, the political seat and centre of power in Japan at that time in order to save the entire Japanese nation.
In August on 1253 he settled in a small cottage at a place called Matsubagayatsu in the southeast area of the City of Kamakura, the new capital of Japan.
At his cottage and at the homes of supporters, he began to sow the seeds of his spiritual revolution and the reformation of Japanese Buddhism, where he began to tell the people about the teachings of The Lotus Sutra and Nam Myoho Renge Kyo.
On occasion, he visited Temples in the city to debate with their Chief Priests.
He denounced the beliefs of the Jodo sect, one of the most powerful schools in Japan at that time, which teaches that salvation can be gained merely by invoking the name of Amida Buddha and he also attacked the Zen sect for its rejection of the sutras.
His attacks angered not only the religious leaders but the government authorities of the Shogun as well, since the latter were in many cases ardent patrons of the Jodo and Zen sects.
Soon he was faced with fierce opposition, though he continued his efforts to win converts.
It was in these early years of propagation that such major disciples as Shijo Kingo, Toki Jonin, Kudo Yoshitaka and Ikegami Munenaka were converted and many of The Daishonin's letters of spiritual guidance and encouragement to them are still extant.
Beginning in 1256, Japan suffered a series of calamities.

Changing Poison into Medicine

Storms, floods, droughts, earthquakes, epidemics, inflicted great suffering and hardships upon the nation.
In 1257 a particularly severe earthquake destroyed many Temples, government buildings and homes in Kamakura, while in 1259 and 1260 severe famine and plague ravaged the population.
Nichiren Daishonin believed that the time had come for him to explain the basic cause of these calamities.
In 1258 he went to Jisso-ji Temple in Iwamoto in present day Shizuoka prefecture to consult a copy of The Buddhist Canon and assemble incontrovertible proof of the real cause of the disasters.
During his stay there, he met a thirteen year old acolyte, Hoki-bo, who was so impressed by the demeanour and wisdom of The Daishonin that he immediately requested permission from the chief priest to become his disciple.
Hoki-bo was later to become The Daishonin's legitimate successor and the second High Priest of Nichiren Shoshu, Nikko Shonin.
Having heard the pain filled outcry of the people, The Daishonin poured his entire soul into one of his, if not the most famous of his writings or treatise, called Rissho Ankou Ron (On Securing the Peace of The Land Through the Propagation of True Buddhism) to clarify the causes of Japan's misery.
It is this famous and most important treatise that we will study in greater detail later in this publication.
The gist of the writing is that the fundamental cause of the disasters lay with the sovereign and the people's adherence to heretical sects and false doctrines, or slander of The True Law, their worship of Amida Buddha, he asserted was the source of such slander and was in opposition to orthodox Buddhism.
He stated that if the people did not convert to The True Dharma and discard their attachments to erroneous teachings, the Nation would know no relief from suffering.
Quotes from the Konkomyo, (Golden Light Sutra) Yakushi, (The Medicine King Sutra) Ninno (Benevolent Kings Sutra) and Daijuku (the Sutra of The Great Assembly) Sutras were given to substantiate these assertions.
These sutras mention seven calamities that will befall any nation inimical to True Buddhism.
Of the seven, five had already struck Japan.
The Daishonin predicted that if the authorities persisted in turning their backs on The True Dharma the two additional disasters, internal strife, and foreign invasion, would occur without fail.
Resolutely taking his stand and explaining his reason for submitting his bold warning to the government, The Daishonin said.

"I am saying this entirely for the sake of the Nation, the sake of The Dharma, for the sake of the people and not for the sake of myself".

9

Changing Poison into Medicine

On July 16th, 1260, the Rissho Ankoku Ron was submitted to the most powerful man in the country at that time, who was Hojo Tokiyori, a former regent of the Kamakura Shogunate who had retired to a Zen temple, through the offices of Yadoya Saemon Nyudo, an official of the Kamakura government.

The Daishonin was 39 at the time of this first remonstration with the government.

Tokiyori and the shogunate officials appear to have taken no notice of the treatise.

When word of its contents reached the followers of the Jodo sect, they were incensed.

A band of them swarmed down on The Daishonin's cottage at Matsubagayatsu on August 27th, to take his life.

The Daishonin once again escaped his persecutors with a few disciples to Shimosa province, where he stayed for a time at the home of Toki Jonin, his follower and an influential lord.

His sense of mission would not allow him to remain there long, in less than a year he was back in Kamakura to resume his preaching campaign.

The Jodo priests alarmed at his success in attracting followers, contrived to have charges brought against him before the Kamakura government.

The Regent at that time was Hojo Nagatoki, the son of Shigetoki, the latter a confirmed enemy of The Daishonin.

Without investigation or trial Nagatoki accepted the charges and on May 12, 1261, ordered Nichiren Daishonin banished to the desolate coast of Izu Peninsula.

This was the first government persecution suffered by The Daishonin. Izu was a stronghold of the Jodo sect, and exile there promised to place The Daishonin in great personal danger.

Fortunately, however, he was taken in by Funamori Yasaburo, a leader of the fishermen in the area, and he was treated with great kindness by this man.

In time, the shogunate, apparently at the instigation of the former regent Hojo Tokiyori, issued a pardon, and Nichiren Daishonin returned to Kamakura in February 1263.

In August of 1264, Nichiren Daishonin, concerned about his aged mother, returned to his home in Awa.

He found his Mother to be critically ill, his Father had died earlier, but he prayed for her recovery, and she was able to overcome her illness and live another four years.

Unfortunately, word of his return reached Lord Tojo Kagenobu. When The Daishonin and a group of his followers set out to visit a supporter in the area, they were attacked by Tojo and his soldiers in a place called Komutsubara.

Although The Daishonin escaped death, he received a sword wound on his forehead and his left hand was broken.

In 1268, the foreign invasion that Nichiren Daishonin had predicted seemed about to materialise.

That year, as mentioned earlier, a letter from the Mongols arrived at Kamakura to demand that Japan acknowledge fealty to Khubilai Khan.

The Japanese leaders realised that the nation faced grave danger. Construction of defensive fortifications was immediately undertaken in Kyushu on the coasts facing Korea, and every Temple and shrine in the country was ordered to offer prayers for the defeat of the enemy.

Nichiren Daishonin who had returned to Kamakura, became convinced that it was time for him to act.

He sent eleven letters of remonstration to top ranking officials, including the regent Hojo Tokimune, the deputy chief of military police, Hei no Saemon and the two most influential priests in Kamakura at the time.

These letters briefly restated the declaration in The Rissho Ankoku Ron, that unless the government embraced The True Dharma, the country would suffer the final two disasters predicted in The Sutras.

All eleven men chose to ignore The Daishonin's warning.

In 1271, the country was troubled by persistent drought.

The government, fearful of famine, ordered Ryokan, the famous and respected priest of the Ritsu sect to whom Nichiren Daishonin had earlier addressed one of his letters, to pray for rain.

When The Daishonin learnt of the request, he sent a challenge to Ryokan offering to become his disciple if the latter succeeded in bringing rain.

If he failed, however, Ryokan was to become The Daishonin's follower. Roykan accepted the challenge, but in spite of his prayers and those of hundreds of assistant priests, no rain fell.

Instead, Kamakura was struck by fierce gales.

Ryokan, needless to say, did not become a disciple of The Daishonin. On the contrary, he began to plot against him in collusion with Hei no Saemon, the deputy chief of the military police.

Ryokan, and the Zen priest Doryu both headed Temples that had been founded by high officials of the Hojo Family.

Though the founders had died, their wives still exercised strong influence within the government.

Ryokan and Doryu aroused the anger of the wives by telling them that The Daishonin in his earlier letters of remonstrance had spoken disrespectfully of their deceased husbands.

Eventually, as a result of their machinations, a lot of charges against The Daishonin was submitted to the government.

On September 10th, 1271, Hei no Saemon ordered Nichiren Daishonin to appear in court to answer the charges.

This marked the beginning of the second phase of official persecution.

Changing Poison into Medicine

The Daishonin eloquently refuted the charges and repeated his predictions of foreign invasion and strife within the ruling clan.
Two days after the investigation, Hei no Saemon and his soldiers burst into Nichiren Daishonin's dwelling.
Though innocent of all wrongdoing, The Daishonin was arrested like a common criminal and sentenced to banishment on the distant island of Sado.
Hei no Saemon, however was determined to have him beheaded at the execution ground in Tatsunokuchi.

Nichiren Daishonin and his followers believed his death was at hand, but at the last moment the sudden appearance of a luminous object in the sky, so terrified the officials that they called off the execution.
There after The Daishonin regarded himself as having been reborn to a new life.
A detailed description of these dramatic events in the Daishonin's own words will be found in the work or Gosho entitled "On The Buddha's Behaviour".
In October 1271, Nichiren Daishonin, accompanied by warrior escorts, sailed across the Sea of Japan to Sado, his place of exile.

Changing Poison into Medicine

The only friendly person to go with him was his faithful follower Nikko Shonin.
The two of them were quartered in a dilapidated hut in an area where corpses of paupers and criminals were abandoned.
They were short of food and clothing and had no fire to keep them warm.
Huddling in skins and straw mantles, they somehow managed to survive the first bitterly cold winter.
In time the situation improved somewhat as The Daishonin began to receive gifts of food and clothing from local supporters, even though he was faced by great hostility from the Jodo priests on the island.
His time was devoted mainly to preaching and writing.
Many of his most important works, including "The True Object of Worship" and "The Opening of The Eyes" date from this period in his life.
On February 18th, 1272, a ship reached Sado, bringing news that fighting had broken out in Kamakura and Kyoto as a result of a power struggle within the ruling Hojo clan.
The Daishonin's prophecy of dissention within the ruling clan had come true, and before long, the second disaster he had prophesised, foreign invasion, became increasingly likely as The Mongols continued to send envoys demanding submission.
At the beginning of 1274, the regent Hojo Tokimune, who had never completely agreed with the severe treatment accorded to The Daishonin, revoked the act of banishment.
Two years and five months after he had been exiled, Nichiren Daishonin was pardoned and returned to Kamakura on March 26th.
On April 8th, Nichiren Daishonin was ordered to appear before the military tribunal. Hei no Saemon was the presiding official, as he had been three years earlier when charges had been brought against The Daishonin, though this time he behaved with reserve and politeness.
In reply to questioning concerning the possibility of a Mongol attack, The Daishonin stated that he feared an invasion within the year.
He added that the government should not ask the Shingon priests to pray for the destruction of The Mongols, since their prayers would only aggravate the situation.
As an old Chinese maxim states, "If a sage warns his sovereign three times and still is not heeded, he should depart the country".
Nichiren Daishonin had three times predicted crisis, once when he presented "The Rissho Ankoku Ron" again at the time of his arrest and near execution at Tatsunokuchi, and once more on his return from Sado Island.
Convinced that the government would never heed his warnings, he left Kamakura on May 12th, 1274, for a life of retirement.
He settled about thirty kilometres west of Mount Fuji, in a small dwelling at the foot of Mount Minobu in the province of Kai.

Changing Poison into Medicine

Because of the remoteness of the region, his life at Minobu was far from easy.

His followers in Kamakura sent him money, food, and cloth for clothing and occasionally went in groups to receive instruction from him.

He devoted much of his time to writing, nearly half of his extant writings date from this period.

He also spent much time lecturing and training his disciples.

His lectures on The Lotus Sutra delivered at this time were compiled by Nikko Shonin to form the work known as The Ongi Kuden.

In October 1274, five months after The Daishonin entered retirement, The Mongols launched their attack.

In a letter to one of his followers The Daishonin expressed his bitter disappointment that his advice had been ignored, for he was convinced that the nation might have been spared this suffering if it had been heeded.

During this period, Nikko Shonin was successful in making a number of converts among the priests and laymen of the nearby area of Atsuhara.

The priests of a Tendai Temple in the area, angered by his success, began harassing the converts.

Eventually, in a quarrel over land rights, they sent a band of warriors to attack a number of unarmed farmers of the convert group.

Twenty of the farmers were arrested by the government authorities and tortured, and three were eventually beheaded.

This incident, known as The Atsuhara Persecution, was significant because, whereas earlier persecutions had been aimed mainly at The Daishonin, it was innocent followers who were the victims this time.

The farmers, however, persisted in their faith in spite of the threats from the authorities.

Nichiren Daishonin was convinced that his disciples and followers had now grown strong enough in their faith to risk their lives to embrace The Mystic Law.

This motivated him to inscribe The Dai Gohonzon, The True Object of Worship for the happiness and enlightenment of all living beings.

The date was October 12th, 1279, twenty seven years after he first chanted Nam Myoho Renge Kyo.

By his sixty first year The Daishonin was in failing health.
Feeling that his death was near, he designated Nikko Shonin as his
legitimate successor.
On September 8th, 1282, he left Minobu intending to visit a hot spring in
Hitachi for his health.
When he reached the residence of the Ikegami brothers in what is
today part of the city of Tokyo, he found he was too ill to continue.
Many of his followers hearing of his arrival, gathered at Ikegami to see
him and early on the morning of October 13th, 1282, surrounded by his
disciples reverently chanting Nam Myoho Renge Kyo, he passed away
peacefully.

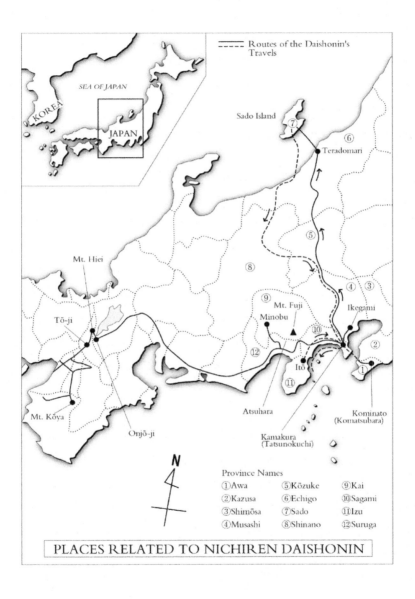

PLACES RELATED TO NICHIREN DAISHONIN

Nam Myoho Renge Kyo.

The chanting of Nam Myoho Renge Kyo is the core of the practice of Nichiren Shoshu Buddhism.

It is a very vital subject but also an exceedingly difficult subject to explain because Nam Myoho Renge Kyo, being virtually an unseen force, defining it absolutely clearly, is an extremely hard thing to do.

I hope by the time you have read this explanation you will have some idea of what Nam Myoho Renge Kyo really is.

First, let us explain that Myoho Renge Kyo without the Nam, is the force of life, or life itself.

The dynamically creative force, which at the same time is entirely harmonious.

This dynamically creative life force produces all the phenomena that we see around us in the whole universe.

From the stars to the trees, to the ebb and flow of the tides, to the seasons, and plants, and of course us human beings.

That immediately makes it clear that through observing nature, we can be sure that this force of life is essentially dynamic and progressive, yet at the same time it is completely and totally harmonious.

Nature, when you look at it has a perfect balance, it is only due to the influence of humanity at this time in the history of our species that has caused nature to become imbalanced and out of kilter, upset, but left to itself the life force of Myoho Renge Kyo is the most beautiful harmonious and integrated thing that you could possibly imagine.

It is life in all its amazing glory.

The life that we see manifested in phenomena that are quite unbelievable in their variety, a myriad different varieties of phenomena arising out of this creative force of Myoho Renge Kyo.

In The Sun Lotus Recovery Programme, we have previously studied The Ten Worlds Teaching, or the ten states of life, that is Hell, Hunger, Anger, Animality, Tranquillity, Rapture (Heaven), Learning, Realization (Partial Enlightenment), Bodhisattva and Buddhahood and from that previous study in session four of the programme, you have understood that hell and heaven and the state of Buddhahood are to be found nowhere else but within your own life.

This is one of Nichiren Shoshu Buddhism's strongest teachings, and I am sure that you have, like me, had the experience of hell in this lifetime and sometimes you have also experienced the rapture of heaven.

Changing Poison into Medicine

The Ten Worlds or these ten basic conditions of life that we revolve through at every moment of the day and night, are the ingredients of this creative force of life, Myoho Renge Kyo.

As far as us human beings are concerned, we have the treasure and sometimes the disadvantage of a thinking, discerning mind. Through that thinking mind we also have the free will to decide which way to go, what to do, what action we can take.

Not spontaneously and instinctively like an animal but where necessary through judgement arising from deep thought.

Those Ten Worlds that we studied, work either negatively and destructively, or positively and creatively in our lives and because of our thinking mind, the human being can make a choice.

We can either go through life basing our actions on the negative side of the ten states of life or on the positive enlightened and creative side.

We learnt also that as far as those six lower worlds are concerned, Hell, Hunger, Anger, Animality, Tranquillity and Rapture, the human being passes through these worlds without any effort whatsoever.

We are pushed into them through our reaction to happenings in our environment.

On the other hand, in order to get into the four higher worlds of Learning, Realization, Bodhisattva and Buddhahood we have to make great effort.

The human being has the choice of being swayed by the environment, to be at the mercy of the environment, or through a great effort we can live a creative and harmonious life by using The Ten Worlds in a positive way, not just in a negative way.

Nam of Nam Myoho Renge Kyo, is that great effort.

This great effort or Nam is the effort needed to put yourself in rhythm with Myoho Renge Kyo, the natural, creative, and harmonious force of life itself, or the Universal Life.

Nam Myoho Renge Kyo, which is what we chant, has the power to turn every one of those ten conditions of life into positive, creative, and harmonious action in its fullest sense.

Nam Myoho Renge Kyo is the Buddha state.

The highest enlightened state of life in which a human being is totally awakened to the ultimate truth and can live totally creatively, totally progressively and yet despite that creative and dynamic urge to progress, can now live harmoniously with our environment, which is our home Planet Earth.

When we look at the world today we see that we have a great problem, which is that humanity wants to live dynamically and progressively and this is a natural instinct, but we continuously fail to live harmoniously either with our fellow human beings or with the natural environment in which we dwell.

Likewise, you get some thoughtful people who wish to live harmoniously, yet sadly all they succeed in creating is a compromise which is weak and usually collapses and fails in the end.

Nam Myoho Renge Kyo is essentially, dynamically progressive and immensely creative, yet at the same time totally harmonious.

Nam means to be in rhythm with the natural law of life of the whole universe or Myoho Renge Kyo.

Already you can see that in contemplating Nam Myoho Renge Kyo, you are contemplating something that is simply boundless, infinite, and eternal and something which is also incredibly powerful yet incredibly beautiful.

It is the natural law of life itself.

It was Nichiren Daishonin who was born on the 16th February 1222, in Japan who declared not only that Humanity can live in rhythm with this incredible universal life force if we chant Nam Myoho Renge Kyo, but also revealed his understanding of exactly how that incredible life force works.

This understanding of how this universal life force works is the philosophy or Dharma of Nichiren Shoshu Buddhism.

This profound Dharma is often called 'The Philosophy of Life,' and the chanting of Nam Myoho Renge Kyo is its practice.

A practice that enables you to actually live this great philosophy throughout your whole life.

There are many philosophies in this world, many that are great and noble thinking, but the problem has always been that humanity cannot live them.

The beauty of Nichiren Daishonin's teachings is that he not only gave a great, complete, and all embracing philosophy of life but he also gave one with a practice to actually live it continuously, day in and day out for the whole of one's lifetime.

Nichiren Daishonin spent a great many years studying as many teachings as possible of Buddhism that he possibly could in Japan's various Buddhist schools of his day.

As a young boy, like many intelligent young boys in Japan at that time, he went to his local Buddhist temple to be educated and as a result of living in this temple he decided to become a priest.

After being accepted into the priesthood as a teenager he then set about his studies.

Later in his life when he was talking about his childhood, he described to some extent how it was that he came to be enlightened.

He didn't set out to study all the Buddhist teachings in Japan to become enlightened, he became enlightened before he did that.

The purpose of him setting out to study the teachings of Buddhism wherever he could lay his hands on them, was in order to prove through historical or literary proof the validity of his enlightenment in the flow of the history of Buddhism as a whole.

He wished to relate his enlightenment to the enlightenment of Shakyamuni Buddha two thousand years previously and this he absolutely succeeded in doing.

His teaching contains all the necessary facts in order to establish the crystal clear flow of Buddhism from the days of Shakyamuni through the two thousand years to the days when he himself was teaching.

He described his enlightenment as a great jewel, as brilliant as a star, that he was given and that he tucked this jewel into the right sleeve of his priestly robe.

Nichiren Daishonin was enlightened not through the teaching of anybody else but through the natural processes within his own life and it is his enlightenment that enabled him to provide us living today with this philosophy and practice which if we follow it, enables us to live in rhythm and harmony with the natural law of life.

After sixteen years of study, in which he justified in an historical and literal sense, everything that was involved in his teachings, he returned to the same temple of his childhood and on the 28th April 1253, he asked the priests and lay persons of the community in which his temple was situated, to come and listen to a lecture.

At that lecture what he said simply shocked everyone to the very core of their being and shook the very foundations of their lives.

At that time Japan was suffering many incredible natural disasters.

These were the worst in all the recorded history of Japan up to that time.

There were earthquakes, typhoons, famines and epidemics.

It was the most incredible era of forty years in Japan's history from the point of view of natural disasters.

He said in his lecture that the reason why the country is suffering from these terrible calamities and disasters is because everybody has failed to follow the teachings of Shakyamuni Buddha correctly.

That in itself made people really sit up straight and listen intently.

He then began to expound the teaching of Nam Myoho Renge Kyo.

He pointed out to them all, that two thousand years previously, Shakyamuni Buddha had clearly said that during the two thousand years since his passing his original teachings would decline and in the end be of no value to people or be able to bring happiness and enlightenment to the people of that later age.

Shakyamuni had said when that period of two thousand years after his death begins, the world would be in a continual state of chaos, and he listed many of the disasters that would be occurring at that time.

He then said that the only teaching which will be powerful enough and able to bring the people happiness and enlightenment in that age which he called 'Mappo' is The Lotus Sutra, and the title of The Lotus Sutra is Myoho Renge Kyo.

Nichiren Daishonin explained this to everybody and there was an absolute uproar when he finished talking.

From that time onwards, throughout the whole of the rest of his life, he was savagely persecuted.

This is not surprising, it is exceedingly difficult to visualise today what the situation was like then.

The fact was that the people of Japan had been following the earlier sutras of Shakyamuni for hundreds of years.

Priests had vested interests in their jobs in temples, Emperors and Shoguns followed one or another of a particular Buddhist school based on the early teachings or sutras and by suddenly refuting them all he brought the fury of the nation down upon his head.

Who was this upstart, this ordinary common priest who had the nerve to stand up and say that we are all wrong and deluded? Nevertheless he lived his whole life naturally, despite the ongoing persecutions and threats on his life, and during the course of it firmly established these teachings and the practice that we are doing today.

The Lotus Sutra was taught by Shakyamuni Buddha in the last eight years of his life and by that time he had been teaching for forty years.

He had reached the point in his teaching where he felt his disciples were ready to hear his supreme teaching which is the ultimate conclusion of his own enlightenment and his lifetime of teaching and the purpose of his advent in this world.

He told his students that if you want to understand and comprehend this teaching you must discard all my previous teachings, which were only partial, incomplete or provisional.

Shakyamuni also said that only a few will understand The Lotus Sutra in his day, but he also said that two thousand years later

22

after his passing, the people will then have the intellectual capacity to be able to understand it and live by its teachings.

The Lotus Sutra as originally taught by Shakyamuni Buddha nearly three thousand years ago was recorded in Sanskrit as Sadharma Pundarika Sutra.

Gradually as the centuries passed after the death of Shakyamuni Buddha, this teaching travelled from India into China.

It was translated into what is now the ancient Chinese language by a great scholar and translator called Kumarajiva and its name or title in ancient Chinese is Miao-Fa Lien-Hua Ching.

So how do we then get to Myoho Renge Kyo?

To understand this, it is necessary to realise that Chinese characters were imported into Japan by the Japanese because they are the most amazing and economical way of expressing an enormous amount of knowledge and information in a single character.

One character of the ancient Chinese language can supply you with enough information to write a book.

The Japanese were incredibly wise to adopt these characters but of course they had a different language, so therefore Myoho Renge Kyo is the meaning of those Chinese characters expressed or rather the sound of those Chinese characters expressed in Japanese phonetics.

Myoho Renge Kyo is the phonetics in Japanese of these ancient Chinese characters, which in turn were a translation of the original Sanskrit.

It is just as difficult for a Japanese person to understand the meaning when they look at the characters of Myoho Renge Kyo as it is for us or for any other nationality, so in that sense everybody universally or internationally who practices Nam Myoho Renge Kyo starts at square one with no advantage whatsoever.

Even a Chinese person who looks at those characters, though they may be able to pronounce the sound Maio-Fa Lien-Hua Ching, cannot for the life of them understand the depths of the meaning, because these characters are ancient and no longer in general use.

The meaning of Myoho Renge Kyo could be literally translated as The Wonderful Law of The Lotus, or The Teaching of The Perfect Law of The Lotus Flower.

That is its literal meaning but as you must be already realising, Myoho Renge Kyo in fact is not only the title of The Sutra, but it is also the very essence of what The Lotus Sutra teaches.

Changing Poison into Medicine

The five characters of Myoho Renge Kyo in fact describe the mechanics and the ingredients and the workings of life, the natural law or rhythm of universal life.

Although this is exceedingly difficult to explain, it has a great practical advantage from the point of view of practice.

It means that on what we call our object of devotion or The Gohonzon, we can put the whole essence of all The Buddhist Teachings on a small scroll and in those characters in fact everything is contained.

Shakyamuni Buddha, when he taught The Lotus Sutra, said this sutra contains the essence of all that I have taught over all the forty two years of my teaching life.

This was further explained and defined and distilled down to two main chapters of the twenty eight chapters of The Lotus Sutra, and it is those two main chapters that we recite in our daily practice of Gongyo, called the Hoben pon and the Juryo hon.

These two chapters contain the essence of the whole of The Lotus Sutra and Nichiren Daishonin pointed out that in the normal customary way with all Buddhist teachings, that the title of the sutra itself contains the essence of everything and that essence or essential teaching was Myoho Renge Kyo.

This is understandable when you think that if someone says to you England.

England will convey in that one word everything that you can think of about England.

The people, the towns, the cities, the weather, the problems, Brexit, every single aspect of England is contained in that one word.

Myoho Renge Kyo similarly contains everything.

The only difference is that we have never understood Myoho Renge Kyo, whereas we have grown up to understand England.

The purpose of the Buddhist teachings is to enable us to understand Myoho Renge Kyo and to prove their validity in our daily lives.

In the Gosho, which are the writings of Nichiren Daishonin, he wrote this in a famous Gosho called,

On Attaining Buddhahood.

"This truth is Myoho Renge Kyo, chanting Myoho Renge Kyo will therefore enable you to grasp The Mystic Truth within you.

Myoho Renge Kyo is The King of The Sutras, flawless in both letters and principles, its words are the reality of life, and the reality of life is The Mystic Law, Myoho".

He prefaced that by saying.

Changing Poison into Medicine

"If you wish to free yourself from the sufferings of birth and death, which you have endured throughout eternity, and attain supreme enlightenment in this lifetime, you must awaken to the mystic truth which has always been inherent within your own life, this truth is Myoho Renge Kyo."

In other words, the truth of life is expressed in the words or characters Myoho Renge Kyo and Myoho Renge Kyo exists in us and in the whole Universe but unfortunately, we have never understood that.
Now let us take each word or character and explain what they mean.
We will not start with Nam; we will come back to that last of all.

First let us look at Myoho.

Myoho as it says in the excerpt from the Gosho means The Mystic Law.
Mystic means something that is difficult to understand.
Sometimes we mistake mystic to mean magic but that is not the true meaning of mystic.
Mystic is something awkward or difficult to understand or comprehend.
The words Myoho which mean Mystic Law and these characters can be translated in many different ways.
They can mean darkness and light, Myo being darkness and Ho being light.
Myo is also Mystic and difficult to understand and Ho means Law.
It can also mean Myo, unseen and Ho, seen.
It can also mean Myo, latent, Ho, manifest.

Changing Poison into Medicine

Even with these various definitions of the characters Myoho you may be starting to get a picture of what it is these characters are trying to describe.
Something that can be both, unseen and seen, something that can be both dark and yet also light, something that can be latent and also manifest or active.
Myoho, Mystic, Law, Dark, Light, Seen, Unseen, Latent, Manifest.
Nichiren Daishonin went on to point out that if you really look at life, this is exactly what you find that it is like.
If we look at the surface of life, we only see the phenomena around us.
If we look at ourselves, or I look at you, on the surface I see your shape, your body, and the clothes you are wearing but in everything there is something else that can be called the spiritual side of life or the unseen side of life.
We know there is this unseen part of life.
All we can see is the seen part, but we know there is an unseen aspect because we see it in action so often.
We know that we can produce anger.
We know that when we are angry, we have a red face and staring eyes but where does anger come from and where does it go to?
We can be angry for a moment and yet we can be happy in the next moment, so where has anger gone?
It has not left our lives because something else can happen and we can become angry again.
Anger in other words is latent in our lives, unseen, yet when something triggers it off in the environment it is very much seen.
All the other emotions we can think of are the same.
Joy, sadness, all existing in our life, latent until something draws it out.
The red face and the staring eyes are just the tip of the iceberg, what is really something is anger itself, that unseen force which expresses itself in a red face and staring eyes and angry words.
This is Myoho, anger which can be seen, yet unseen.
Myoho can also be life and death.
Myo, Death. Ho, Life.
Life we can see all around us but how is it that this manifestation of life can actually appear, where did it come from?
You may say that in our case we are conceived and born in and from our Mothers womb and there are all sorts of complicated things like genes and all the rest of it which do it, but this is not so is it?
Even the genes are a manifestation of life.
What about the force that created them?

What about the force that creates a typhoon?
What about the force that makes thunder?
What about the force that creates earthquakes?
This is Myo, the unseen incredibly powerful force of life.
The force that can create such a myriad different, infinite,
manifestations of itself.
Myoho, life and death.
This is an incredibly significant point because Buddhism points out
that this is the rhythm of life.
That life itself in all of its various manifestations, is going through
the movement of Myoho.
From latency to manifest and back to latency again and then
manifest again.
Buddhism points out that this is one of the great rhythms of life,
that everything is going through a cycle of Myoho, manifest and
latent and manifest again and then latent again.
Buddhism points out that this universal rhythm of life and death,
Myo and Ho is vital because only through the state of death
which has such a horrible ring to our ears, yet in fact it is only
through the state of death or latency that an entity of life, which
maybe ourselves, or a beetle, or whatever form of life, can
regenerate sufficient energy to take on another life, another seen
form.
Therefore, this rhythm of Myo and Ho, life and death is vital, just
like it is vital for us to sleep every night in order to sustain and
maintain the physical form that we have now.
All physical things must decay, this is in the very nature of anything
that is physical or material but the life entity or the life that exists in
it is indestructible.
You can shoot someone through the heart or the head, but you
cannot destroy that person's actual life.
You can destroy the physical self, the manifestation of life but not
life itself.
Myo and ho are one part of the explanation of life and death
and I hope now that has some meaning for you.

Changing Poison into Medicine

Let us move on now to Renge.

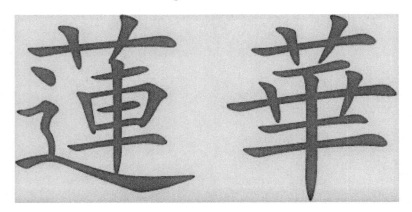

Renge literally means Lotus Flower.
That is why the teaching in its original form by Shakyamuni
Buddha was called 'The Wonderful Law of The Lotus.'
The lotus flower produces its flower and its seed at the identical
same time, and it is the only plant or flower that does such a
thing.
Normally of course, the seed follows the flower, and this
represents the simultaneity of cause and effect.
This is the second aspect of this incredible Law of Life.
The law of cause and effect.
The law which makes it clear that whatever you do, whatever
action you make, every minute and second of the day will have
an effect which will manifest itself in your life at some time when
the time and conditions and circumstances are right.
You can think of times when you have made a cause and the
effect has been absolutely immediate.
If you are really angry with someone and hurl insulting words at
them, the effect might be very, very quick.
That person may come at you and take a swing for you, or they
may hurl even more insulting words back at you.
Cause and effect there is almost instantaneous, but that is not
always so.
Even if you take that same example, you could get a case where
you hurl insulting words at someone and that person does nothing
at that moment, they may go away smouldering and upset,
revengeful, and five years later when you meet them as you walk
around the corner, everything comes back to them and then
they may take a swing at you!

The point of that rather silly story is that the effect was immediately built into their life.

The person who was insulted and also in the life of the person who called out those insulting words and it appeared when the time and circumstances were right.

Scientists know about cause and effect as all their analysis and research is based on an understanding of cause and effect.

What science doesn't entirely understand is that the effect is instantaneous.

What Buddhism teaches is that there is an inherent cause/latent effect created each time we think, speak and act created deep in our lives which produces a manifest effect when triggered by an external cause through our relation with the environment.

We will look further at this teaching in the next chapter.

The most important point being that the two are entirely instantaneous.

The moment you do something, the moment you say rude words to somebody the effect is in your life immediately and in the life of the other person.

What Buddhism is pointing out is that the motivation for our lives is founded on this cause and effect.

Nichiren Daishonin said that if you want to understand what has happened to you in the past, look at what is happening in your life right now at this very moment because what is happening in your life right now at this very moment, is the effects of the causes you made yesterday, the day before, last year, forty years ago, and even in a previous lifetime.

If you want to know what your future is going to be like, look at the causes that you are making right now and the causes you make tomorrow and the next day and so on.

This law of cause and effect is extremely strict.

You made the causes, therefore the only way to change your circumstances is to recognize this and to start making great causes from this moment on.

The tragedy of this world is that everyone is hitting out and blaming everyone else wherever you go.

This is why there is no harmony.

This is why there are wars.

This is why there is violence.

This is why there is greed and competitiveness because everyone is blaming everybody else for what they are suffering from.

In fact it is us, no one else is to blame, we made the causes to suffer as we are suffering maybe at this very moment.

The more you think about this, the more this principle really lives, and the more you actually see it working in your life.

Changing Poison into Medicine

You may do something tomorrow and the next day you may get the effect.

You can prove it all over the place, so the law of cause and effect is extremely strict.

It is the law of life, it is as much a part of the law of life as the law of gravity, which is also part of the law of life.

We know gravity exists, we do not know how it works exactly and we certainly cannot see it, except in its manifestation, but we know that law is there.

The more your eyes and mind become open to the law of cause and effect, the more clearly it exists.

You cannot escape the fact and it is no good complaining and moaning about it because it is undoubtedly there.

Therefore, the best thing to do is recognise it and to start to harmonise your life with this aspect of the law of life by making great causes.

Fortunately the power of Buddhist practice gives you the strength to sustain such a difficult course and to continue to make great causes everyday throughout the course of your life.

Myoho, which is the cycle of life and death and Renge is the law of cause and effect which runs through it, just like the warp and weave of a cloth, this is the rhythm or pattern, the very ingredients of life.

Finally, we have Kyo.

Kyo translated literally means again a number of different things.

It can mean teaching or sutra, or communication, or vibration, or sound.

Everything to do with Kyo is sound or vibration.

The human voice communicates through sound.

Everything we do every day which relates to something else in our environment is related through sound.

Sound is the link that exists between all the myriad manifestations of Myoho Renge the Law of Life.

Not only do we communicate by sound but also porpoises and dolphins do under the sea by making clicks and bleeping noises, there are sounds we cannot even hear.

Humankind has invented whistles that will call a certain bird or insect or animal that you cannot hear with your normal hearing.

Sound is an incredible thing, wavelengths on the radio are conveying sound.

Sound ripples out from me or you, out into the boundless universe. Nothing can actually stop sound, sound can penetrate walls, waves of sound can go on for ever.

This fundamental principle is used in the science of astrophysics where they can use instruments to hear the background sound of the big bang from billions and billions of years ago.

Since we communicate everything we do, every pulse and vibration of our life by sound, we can see that connection that we have with everything around us has no limit, has no boundary.

We do not know what happens to sound waves when they go beyond the distance that humanity can perceive and measure. Buddhism says they are going out and further out but of course they are also going in and into us.

Kyo is the life link.

The link that binds every living thing and all phenomena together. Kyo is what binds a human with an insect or with a tree, plant, everything that you can see and think about.

Kyo is also the foundation of a great Buddhist principle called Esho Funi which translates as the oneness of the self and the environment.

Everything that we do is affecting our environment and our environment is reacting to that effect and we are then reacting to that.

The whole of life is like a series of acting and reacting sounds or waves or vibrations.

Kyo is vitally important to understand the link of life that connects us all with everything else and everybody else, weaving a limitless, intricate and interconnected tapestry of the myriad vibrations of life in this universe.

One action leads to a reaction, which leads to a further reaction. You may get up from reading this book and go out to a café and you may discuss with a friend what you have just read, someone may overhear you and through that discussion you understand even more.

You then talk more to somebody else and that person who heard may talk to somebody else or they may say, "what is that nonsense you are talking about?" and that will have a further effect on everyone around them.

The actions and reactions, these interactions flow outwards like a pebble in a pond with the ripples moving out until it reaches the very edge, but we do not know where the edge of the universe is. As far as we know it is boundless, so the ripples go on and on and on.

Everything we do is affecting not just our environment but the whole universe.

Everything that we do, though it is difficult to perceive and therefore believe, is affecting not only other people but all the things that grow around us, the weather, even the behaviour of the climate.

This why Nichiren Daishonin said in Japan at that time, the reason why the people were suffering so intensely, is because the whole of the population were basing their lives on what was in fact a wrong, incorrect, incomplete and negative philosophy or world view and the effect of this goes outwards from their bodies and minds into everything in the environment.

I do not expect you to take that in or begin to believe it in one go, but the more you think about it, the more you observe, the more you ponder over things like pollution, and destruction of the environment, global warming, and the current climate crisis, the more you realise this is true.

What is the difference between a wise farmer and a stupid farmer?

Everything that they do, in the wise farmers case, will produce good results, richness of soil and a richness of plants, fruit and vegetables and bumper harvests.

The stupid farmer who has no wisdom and sows their seeds at not quite the right moment and fails to fertilise the crop at the right time, who fails to prune their trees at the right time of year, will produce a result which is less rich, according to the degree of their stupidity.

We may say it was bad luck, but Nichiren Shoshu Buddhism would say that this is cause and effect.

If a person makes wise causes, then they will reap rich rewards or effects.

Finally let us now return to Nam.

Nam is the effort you have to make to put yourself in rhythm or in harmony with Myoho Renge Kyo, the law of life and the universe itself.

Namu is derived from Namus, a Sanskrit word which means in its literal translation devotion.

When the Japanese language is spoken many words have an 'U' or an 'Ah' on the end of it, but it is not pronounced or sounded in normal conversation, so we do not say Namu we say Nam.

This word means not just devotion in a literal shallow sense but the devotion of your whole life, your body and spirit, your entire being.

The seen and the unseen, every part of you, devoting itself, to making that great effort to be in harmony with the natural rhythm of the law of life and the universe, Nam Myoho Renge Kyo, Nam Myoho Renge Kyo, Nam Myoho Renge Kyo.

We do this through the Buddhist practice of Gongyo & Shodai. Every day, twice a day, and if you wish even more than that. It is entirely up to you and your life state and desires at any given moment.

You take the trouble to spare a little time to struggle, to make effort to put your life in rhythm with the natural law of life itself or 'Universal Life' by following the teachings of The Original Buddha Nichiren Daishonin.

Those teachings are to chant Nam Myoho Renge Kyo and also to recite those certain vital chapters of The Lotus Sutra and to express your determination to continue to make effort day in and day, week in and week out, to keep yourself on the road, the direct path to your own awakening, enlightenment and absolute happiness.

Changing Poison into Medicine

This is of course very mystic.
It is very difficult to believe that just by chanting those few words
you can achieve such an incredible result.
But the fact is that you do.
I do not think anyone would continue to practice unless they got
the actual proof that they were on the correct path.
It is true that those who sometimes decide to stop practicing can
see that they have come off the road and are bumping along
the curb side, into all the vegetation and rubbish and detritus that
is there.
The only reason that you can continue to do this practice, which
whilst it is not really difficult, is difficult enough to require constant
daily effort, is that they see the actual proof of the benefits that it
brings to their daily lives.
Day in and day out I have now practiced for over thirty years.
Never in the whole world would I have been able to keep going
without seeing the results.
Incredibly enough when you first start to chant you wonder what
on earth you are doing.
Sitting or kneeling in your room saying these extraordinary words
that you don't really understand at all.
But the fact is if you keep going for a month or two, even if you
keep going for one week, you will see and feel the result in your
life without fail.
Perhaps at first you don't believe it.
You say, this is just coincidence, but something has touched your
life, that discovery of a whole new dimension to your being.
Deep in your life something feels that this extraordinary thing is
important, and you decide to go on, to continue.
Perhaps you have a friend you can trust who says please keep
going a bit longer and for one reason or another you do, and you
get the proof.
There is not one person that I have ever heard of who chanted
Nam Myoho Renge Kyo for as long as three months who did not
get clear, absolute, actual proof that what this man Nichiren
Daishonin was teaching is absolutely valid and true.
This is so incredible, and it gives me so much joy to be able to say
that with absolute total conviction.
The whole purpose of this practice of chanting Nam Myoho
Renge Kyo to keep yourself in rhythm, is to make great causes,
good causes, positive causes and to make sure that you do not
revert to making bad causes, miserable causes ever again and
you know all too well what they are and what the consequences
of those negative actions entail.
Of course, it does not happen overnight.

Changing Poison into Medicine

You have really got to discover yourself in order to overcome those weak points in your life, in your karma, which made you make those bad causes, miserable causes, time and time again in the first place.
Through the practice you see this more and more.
The desire to make great causes then becomes stronger and stronger within you.
This is why Nichiren Shoshu Buddhism is called True Buddhism.
There is a principle in Nichiren Shoshu Buddhism called Honin myo, which means the principle of the True Cause.
There is another matching principle, which is the other side of the coin called Honga myo which is the principle of the True Effect.
What Nichiren Shoshu Buddhism is saying is that the most important thing is to make these great and good causes and to base your life on that.
Though you have a karma now that manifests itself in this way at this particular moment, what is going to reshape it is the causes that you make from now on.
You cannot do anything about what you see your life is at this very moment because the causes were made long ago or yesterday, or an hour ago and you cannot undo them.
Therefore there is no point being guilty and feeling miserable and moaning and groaning about one's lot in life because nothing is going to change those causes that you and only you have made before.
The best thing you can do according to Nichiren Shoshu Buddhism is to make great causes from now on.
From this moment on and tomorrow and the next day and the next day and if you follow this practice exactly as it is taught then you will generate and have the power to do it.
Honga myo, the True Effect is something we should try to fight to avoid.
When you think about the meaning of Honga myo you may realise that you have been living a life based on that principle of the true effect for years.
The principle of the true effect, Honga myo, manifests itself every time you say, "well they can do it, but I don't think I can," or "It's all right for them, but I know me, it's not possible for me," or "they can find recovery, but I don't think I have got a chance" that is Honga myo.
Living a life based on the principle of the True Effect, the true effect of thinking in this way, making these negative causes in your life is to be stuck in your negative karma, overwhelmed by your circumstances, disempowered, going nowhere, totally stuck.

Changing Poison into Medicine

The whole of this practice, the whole of this teaching is founded on the teaching of The True Cause.
Guilt is impossible if you practice Nichiren Shoshu Buddhism correctly.
You may still feel guilty at the beginning as it is so deeply ingrained in us westerners through the philosophies and traditions of religions we have been brought up into which permeate our culture.
Sometimes it takes a long time to iron it out of ourselves, but in the end through this wonderful practice, you can rid yourself of it and the sooner the better.
Once and for all.
Guilt is pointless and not only is it pointless it is destructive.
It also saps one's very life, saps one's energy, saps one's will to do great things.
Guilt is disgusting and it is horrible.
Guilt is really one of the great problems in this world.
Living the principle of the True Cause brings about a fantastic, liberating change in the deepest most fundamental level of your being or life.
Not only does the practice of chanting Nam Myoho Renge Kyo change you because it brings its rewards or benefits, but the fact is that you are no longer living in that miserable, stuck, Honga myo victims experience or existence.
The fact is that now you can turn everything into positives.
This means that all the sufferings and difficulties and problems you experience, no matter how complex and difficult they may seem, you start to realise that the more you practice, that you actually can and do have the power to overcome them.
The more you change your own poison into medicine, the more the spirit of Honga myo gradually dwindles and disappears from your life.
This is why Nichiren Shoshu Buddhism is called True Buddhism because it reveals The True Cause to attain Buddhahood or your own awakening and enlightenment in this lifetime.
It is in no way denigrating Shakyamuni's Buddhism as some people seem to think.
This is a description of the Buddhism that we are practicing.
Nichiren Daishonin was enlightened to this law of life, and he was the person who had the task of first discovering this.
There is nothing unusual in that.
Newton was the first person to discover the law of gravity.
The law of gravity had always existed but Newton with his seeking mind, naturally, just by watching a falling apple from a tree, perceived and realised the law of gravity.

Changing Poison into Medicine

Nichiren Daishonin as a young man through his seeking mind and the enlightened nature of his life perceived and realised the law of Nam Myoho Renge Kyo.
His purpose, his task in life was to be the first one.
Shakyamuni Buddha and The Lotus Sutra only explained his experience of enlightenment.
He gave clues and hints, but Shakyamuni Buddha could not teach us how we could become enlightened ourselves.
This was not anything to do with Shakyamuni's ability or the nature of his enlightenment.
Shakyamuni totally understood Nam Myoho Renge Kyo, but it was not the age or the time when people could have possibly practiced it.
Nichiren Daishonin was born in this age of Mappo just exactly as Shakyamuni had predicted and he was able to teach us in such a way that we can follow this practice today.
We chant sitting up straight, with our eyes open and when we have understood and got our proof of the practice, we want to receive The Gohonzon, or The Great Mandala, which is another teaching which will be covered in a later chapter of this book.
The actual true object of devotion and we chant Nam Myoho Renge Kyo and as we say these words we express our desires and wishes.
Nichiren Daishonin said when you chant Nam Myoho Renge Kyo it is important to have a single mind.
In the Gosho he said anyone in two minds will never achieve anything remarkable.
We chant with a single mind confident of the fact that because Nam Myoho Renge Kyo is the law of the universe, the force of life itself, it can only work creatively and harmoniously.
In other words if whatever we are chanting for is not right for our happiness and enlightenment, we will quite soon discover that for ourselves.
Absolutely clearly and to our full satisfaction.
Nam Myoho Renge Kyo can only be creative and harmonious and never destructive and chaotic.
Even if you chanted for something that was positively wicked, in no time at all in some way or another, with your whole life you would be made to realise that, in other words it would rebound on you.
There is an experience of a young American practitioner who met the practice whilst still in addiction and he had been told by his doctor that if he continued in the way he was doing he was going to die within that year and so he tried to get help.

Changing Poison into Medicine

He was wandering on the beach in San Francisco, and he met a girl who he knew on the street and said can you give me a roof for the night and the girl said yes on one condition, that you chant.
He was furious at this, but he wanted that shelter, and he was already very ill, and so he sat in front of her Gohonzon and ridiculed it.
But because he wanted to stay there, as the roof over his head was so important, he told her that he would chant but he did it with his tongue firmly in his cheek.
He chanted for more drugs and two days later there was a knock on the door and a using friend asked him to take this suitcase from him, quickly, as the police were chasing him.
The suitcase was full of drugs, and he used the lot in the following month and became even more desperately ill, just as the doctor had predicted and he knew he was going to die.
For the first time, because of the strongest desire in him to survive and not to die, he began to chant seriously.
Chanting as if his very life depended on it and he survived and is now still alive and has become a great practitioner of Nichiren Shoshu Buddhism in America.
Nam Myoho Renge Kyo can only work for enlightenment, happiness, creativity and harmony and in no other way, and through practicing you can prove that very strongly for yourself.
I hope this section of the book has given you an understanding of what Nam Myoho Renge Kyo actually is.
It is impossible to define it exactly but when you try to chant at the suggestion of your friend, at least you will now have some feeling of the incredible depth and height and length and width of what you are now doing.

The Ten Worlds and Ichinen Sanzen.

Changing Poison into Medicine

The Ten Worlds teaching is part of another teaching from The Lotus Sutra, which is called in Japanese, 'Ichinen Sanzen.' This translates as 'Three Thousand Realms in a Single Moment of Life,' or existence and we will be touching on that principle also. The Ten Worlds, starting with the worst or lowest, are Hell, Hunger, Animality, Anger, Tranquillity, Rapture (Heaven), Learning, Realisation (Absorption), Boddhisattva and Buddhahood, which is the best.

In early Buddhism, or in the teachings of Shakyamuni Buddha before he taught his ultimate teaching of The Lotus Sutra, in those earlier pre Lotus Sutra teachings he taught The Ten Worlds, but not as an entity in themselves.

Each world was taught separately, and people were categorised according to what world they might be in, in this particular lifetime.

They were encouraged to improve their life condition and the causes they were making in order to climb out of that world into a better world or higher state of existence.

This was thought to take aeons or lifetimes in order to achieve. If that persons karma was unfortunate then the slower they would be from moving from one world to the next.

In early Buddhism (Theravada) The Ten Worlds were like a ladder of progress.

You progressed out of hell, which was the worst, through the other worlds and into the worlds of learning and absorption, bodhisattva and ultimately after aeons and aeons of lifetime after lifetime, you may be fortunate enough to be able to sustain the Buddha state as the main tendency of your life.

These were the teachings before The Lotus Sutra, known as his pre Lotus Sutra teachings.

Shakyamuni Buddha taught for more than forty years, which is a very long time, and eight years before he died he taught The Lotus Sutra or as it is sometimes known, 'The Sutra of The Wonderful Law of The Lotus,' which he declared at that time to be his supreme teaching and furthermore he said that all his previous teachings should be discarded because The Lotus Sutra also contained everything that he had taught so far.

What did The Lotus Sutra say which his previous teachings did not say?

It said, first of all and to everyone's absolute amazement at the time, that everyone had Buddhahood or Buddha Nature inherently in their lives and that it was potentially there all the time.

Previously people looked upon Buddhahood as virtually unobtainable.

Changing Poison into Medicine

Shakyamuni himself was extremely wealthy and handsome.
He was a prince of noble birth, he had wonderful qualities, and
great eloquence.
In those very early times nearly three thousand years ago in a
feudal system in India, where all the ordinary people were
peasants or serfs, it was thought that no ordinary person could
have possibly imagined that they could be and have the same
qualities as The Buddha himself.
Even when Shakyamuni said that himself, at that time in
humanities evolution, it simply would not have penetrated
people's intellects.
In The Lotus Sutra, Shakyamuni clearly states that Buddha Nature
was inherent in everybody, and everybody could potentially
attain Buddhahood.
Most people either could not understand that or if they had an
inkling of understanding, they certainly could not believe it at that
particular time.
In fact he said that The Lotus Sutra would not be understood by
many people of that era.
This would be the teaching for the later age to come, our age,
the age of Mappo.
Mappo, he said, would begin two thousand years after he had
died.
He said that only then people would have the intellectual
capacity to be able to understand The Lotus Sutra and practice
it.
Furthermore he also said that another Buddha would appear at
that time in order to teach the people The Correct Dharma.
The other important point which The Lotus Sutra taught was that
these Ten Worlds could be expressed with absolute consistency
from your entire life.
Whatever world or state of life you were in, it would be expressed
totally and consistently in every possible way from that life.
In the principle of Three Thousand Realms in a Single Moment of
Life, Shakyamuni Buddha taught that since Buddha Nature is
within everybody and since people are in all sorts of different
worlds or life conditions in their daily lives, this must mean that the
other nine worlds are also contained in each of those Ten Worlds.
This is known as the principle of The Mutual Possession of The Ten
Worlds, which means even The Buddha has hell, hunger,
animality, anger and all the other worlds contained or existing in
his life.
This is a very important principle because it meant that The
Buddha is in fact an ordinary human being but a human being

who is truly awakened and enlightened to the true nature of life, the ultimate truth of the universe.

This was vitally important especially in those early days because many people looked upon Shakyamuni almost as a superhuman, almost as a god and this is why so many temples contain statues of Shakyamuni Buddha in various positions, to which people would devote their prayers.

In The Lotus Sutra, a sutra which was so difficult to understand for the people of that age, he pointed out that everyone could be Buddha and that this Buddha state had within it all those other nine worlds.

This is a clear statement that Buddha is a human being and furthermore a human being in which all the other nine worlds are capable of working, just like us.

Likewise, anybody who is in hell state also has Buddha within their life.

This is an extremely important point because it means that no matter what your sufferings, no matter what awful things you may have done in the past, you too, can attain Buddhahood.

Buddhahood or enlightenment is obtainable to anybody whatever their past, whatever their sufferings and whatever miserable state they may be experiencing at this particular moment in time.

This is The Mutual Possession of The Ten Worlds in a single moment.

10 x 10 worlds equals 100 worlds, simple arithmetic.

Going on from there The Buddha then expounded a principle known as The Ten Factors of Life.

These concern the way in which we can express any one of these Ten Worlds from our life into our environment and also within the whole of our life itself.

The Ten Factors of Life we recite every day in Gongyo at the end of the Hoben pon chapter, and we recite them three times over. Each one is a factor of life, and this is how these worlds, or any particular world, you are in at this moment are expressed from your life.

Let us now look at each factor's meaning.

Changing Poison into Medicine

1) Nyo ze so, (Appearance) is the physical aspect of your life, you express whatever world you are in, hell, hunger, anger or Buddhahood, through the physical aspect of your life and also through the next factor.

2) Nyo ze sho, (Nature) through the spiritual or unseen aspect of your life.

3) Nyo ze tai, (Entity) is the very core or entity of your being or life itself which integrates appearance and nature.

If you are in the state of anger, even the entity of your life is wholly in that state of anger.

4) Nyo ze riki, (Power) the power which is inherent in the entity which expresses that life state or world.

5) Nyo ze sa (Influence) is the influence that you create as an entity around you through being in that life state, when the power is activated and expressed through thought, speech and action. Anger is an easy example of how your anger can have such an effect in any room that you walk into.

If you walk in full of smiles radiating warmth, that has a very different effect to walking into a room with a grim face obviously seething with anger of some sort, even without opening your mouth people can feel it in the room, that is Nyo ze sa, the influence of the power of your life wherever you may be.

6) Nyo ze in, (Inherent cause) is the inherent cause, that is created through thought, speech and action, because of your anger you are bound to make causes through thoughts, speech and physical actions inherently in your life which will then express themselves externally at some point which is,

7) Nyo ze en, (Latent effect) or the unseen effect which is simultaneously created with the inherent cause.

8) Nyo ze ka (relation/external cause) this is the factor that links the internal world with the external environment.

This relationship is Nyo ze ka and in that environment there are external causes that trigger the latent effect to produce,

9) Nyo ze ho, (Manifest effect) hurling verbal abuse or physical violence and the final factor.

10) Nyo ze honmak kukyo to, (Consistency from beginning to end) whatever world or state of life you may be in, you will express it in those ten different ways, and they will be absolutely consistent.

If you are in anger you really can't hide it because it will radiate from you physically, spiritually from the entity of your life itself, through the power of your actions and the influence that they create, through causes and effects, absolutely consistently from beginning to end, anger from the inherent cause through to anger as the manifest effect.

Changing Poison into Medicine

This is an amazing teaching, such an incredible enlightenment as to the mechanics of life itself and when Shakyamuni Buddha taught it, most of the people could not understand it at all.
He understood this.
He knew they would not understand because actually he was teaching this Dharma for the people in our present age Mappo, an age that began two thousand years after he died, which is approximately 1000 A.D. or the eleventh century.
No one knows exactly the date of Shakyamuni's death and the scholars are still arguing about it to this day, but it is roughly around about 900-1000 B.C.
So the eleventh century was when Shakyamuni said that this age would begin and there would be a great deal of unhappiness and chaos in the world.
He predicted that in this age there would be misery, epidemics, famine, natural disasters and wars.
This is our present age that we, who are all alive today, have been born into.
He said that this latter age would continue for ten thousand years and on into eternity.
The Buddha did not say that the whole of the age of Mappo would be unhappy and chaotic and full of misery for many.
He said that only the early part of Mappo would be like this and at this time the teachings of The Lotus Sutra would be required to be practiced by the people to sustain and feed their happiness and enlightenment enabling them to create a peaceful and harmonious Planet in this current age.
There is one more step in this amazing theory of Ichinen Sanzen.
Something that is called 'The Three Realms of Existence,' which are very simple really.
We have now explained the hundred realms of the mutual possession of The Ten Worlds and the thousand realms by adding The Ten Factors, 10 x 10 x 10 = 1000 and this next step brings us to 10 x 10 x 10 x 3 to bring the total to three thousand realms (potentials) of being in a single moment of existence or life.
They are the realm of your inner self or the realm of yourself, and then the realm, were we coexist with others of our species, which we call society, and then the third and final realm, which is the environment or the land itself.
The actual land in which you live, which is on our Planet Earth, which is intimately connected to the Solar System, which in turn is intimately connected to our Galaxy, which in turn is intimately linked to the rest of The Universe.

Each of those Ten Worlds, which everyone is in and experiencing, will be expressed through the Ten Factors out into The Three Realms of Existence.

Going back to the example of anger.

That anger will be expressed of course within your own life and will also be felt and create influence and causes and effects in society and also on into the land or environment itself.

Let us use the farming analogy once more.

If a farmer is in the life state or world of anger, their wisdom is unlikely to work, and they will make a mess of their land in the process.

In every possible way, the state of life you are in or experiencing, emanates from you, from your entire being, into the other two realms of existence, that of society and the environment in these three thousand different ways, which encompasses not only yourself but also the entire universe.

One of the things you can understand from this amazing theory is how incredibly powerful your life is.

This is the incredibly crucial point that most of us are completely ignorant of, we are totally unaware and do not appreciate this truth or reality in any way shape or form, whatsoever.

We have this term in Buddhism called 'Ichinen' which arises from this theory, which means your determination with your whole life, your life's determination, or driving force.

Whatever life state you are in, whatever your driving force is will be expressed in those three thousand different ways, out into the universe itself.

Any determination that arises out of the various worlds will obviously be expressed in the same way.

If your living in the world of hunger, which is a strong desire to possess things or crave things, then that desire will express itself in those three thousand realms and if your living in the world of anger and you wish to dominate others, then it will be expressed in the same way very strongly.

For this reason the world of anger can create a state of war, but also most important of all from this Buddhist principle, if Buddha or Buddhahood is your state of life, then Buddhahood and enlightenment will be expressed from your life, powerfully in these three thousand realms of existence.

This is why benefits arise from this practice.

The purpose of the practice of Nichiren Shoshu Buddhism is to elevate your life condition into the Buddha or enlightened and awakened state of human life.

Then the emanations from that Buddha state of life are radiating out of your life in all of these three thousand different ways out

45

into the environment, then the environment will begin to work with you because of the influence of the Buddha state emanating from you and in that way benefit comes in all sorts of different ways.

This is quite a difficult theory to understand, and this is just a brief outline but as you pursue your Buddhist practice and study Nichiren Shoshu Buddhism the realism of this theory becomes more and more apparent and a living thing to you.

You really begin to see it working in your life.

Even now, those of you that are reading this for the first time, if you think about the ten states of life or The Ten Worlds which are the basis of this theory, you will begin to recognise all these worlds in your life, and maybe, if you are anything like me, you will start to see if Buddhism is really right and correct.

"Can I think of any other worlds? I am sure there must be other worlds beyond just those ten that my life can be in?"

I will bet you that no matter how hard you think, you will not be able to find one that is outside the ten that we have named.

This is the wonderful and complete teaching or theory of Ichinen Sanzen, and I have explained it as best I can and it is vitally important to understand that the effect of being in any of these worlds is tremendous and as we go through each world and study it, you can probably think of times in your life where your anger or your yearning hunger and craving or even if you were in hell has affected your life far beyond your inner self and out into your environment.

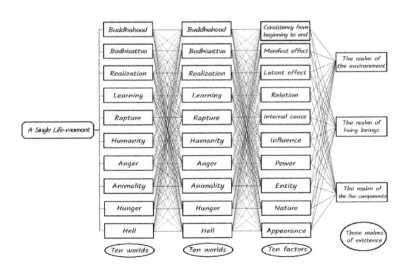

The title of The Lotus Sutra that Shakyamuni taught was called in Chinese characters Myoho Renge Kyo and we come to the vital part that Nichiren Daishonin played.

He was born in 1222, just after the beginning of this age of Mappo.

He was the person who taught us how to apply the teachings of The Lotus Sutra into our daily lives and by doing this he fulfilled the predictions of Shakyamuni Buddha in The Lotus Sutra itself.

He was the person who took The Lotus Sutra, dissected it and took from its heart and essence the way to practice it.

The way to practice it, he said, was to chant over and over again to your hearts content, Nam Myoho Renge Kyo to The Gohonzon. Nam meaning to devote your life to the Myoho Renge Kyo which is The Law of Life itself, which we have discussed in depth earlier in this book.

Furthermore he devised, in his wisdom, the object of devotion to which you should concentrate your mind on as you chant Nam Myoho Renge Kyo, to what we call The Gohonzon.

Both Nam Myoho Renge Kyo and The Gohonzon are the key to our practice and to the attainment of Buddhahood in this lifetime. Nichiren Daishonin also pointed out through explanations taken from The Lotus Sutra itself, that Buddhahood and the attainment of it in this age of Mappo, is not a matter of practicing lifetime after lifetime after lifetime, but on the contrary, through The Lotus Sutra it was apparent that Buddhahood or enlightenment could be attained in one single lifetime.

The seed to be sown within your life in order to achieve this, was Nam Myoho Renge Kyo.

This was a revolutionary teaching in the Japanese Buddhist world at that time and because of this Nichiren Daishonin was persecuted for his entire lifetime.

This too Shakyamuni had predicted in some detail in The Lotus Sutra, and because it was totally revolutionary in that day, it challenged the religious beliefs of everybody in Japan at that time.

I hope that gives you an inkling of understanding into the theory and practice which is behind this incredible teaching called The Ten Worlds and Ichinen Sanzen.

Let us now look at The Ten Worlds individually, and as we do so, maybe you could think of your life and the times when you have been in one of these worlds.

The first six worlds that of hell, hunger, animality, anger, tranquillity and rapture or heaven, are known as the six lower worlds and the remaining four, learning, absorption/realisation, bodhisattva and

Buddhahood are called The Four Noble Paths or Higher Worlds, that is, six lower worlds and four higher worlds.

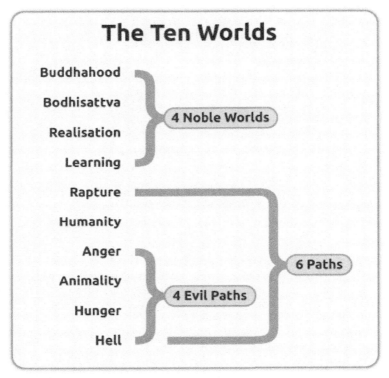

The Ten Worlds

Buddhahood

Bodhisattva

Realisation   4 Noble Worlds

Learning

Rapture

Humanity

Anger   6 Paths

Animality   4 Evil Paths

Hunger

Hell

Why are they called that?

The answer is that you move through the six lower worlds according to influences from your environment.

Almost helplessly you can move from anger to hell to hunger according to what the environment is presenting your life with, what you are experiencing at that moment.

For example, you can get a fantastic letter from your partner, and you are in total rapture and the next minute the telephone rings and you hear you have been made redundant from your job and now you are in hell, and then you put on the kettle and the television to console yourself and find yourself feeling less stressed and a bit warmer and perhaps you find yourself getting into the world of tranquillity for a few moments until somebody knocks on the door and drops a bill that you cannot afford to pay and your back in the world of hell again and so on.

This is how you revolve through these six lower worlds through the influence of the environment.

The Four Noble or Higher Worlds are called that because you have to make great effort to enter them.

To learn something or master a craft or to be creative or to help others, which is the world of bodhisattva, and certainly to attain Buddhahood you have got to make great deal of effort, personally and individually, in order to do so.

I hope that has made clear why they are called the Six Lower Worlds and The Four Higher Worlds and in The Six Lower Worlds there lie what is known as The Three Evil Paths which are the first three, Hell, Hunger and Animality, sometimes they are called The Four Evil Paths and include Anger.

These first four are the most difficult worlds that we have to cope with daily in our lives and Nichiren Shoshu Buddhism is teaching us that every single living thing has these worlds within them and it is especially evident in the human being who is a conscious thinking creature.

Let us now look at the world of Hell.

Buddhism teaches that heaven and hell exist nowhere else but in this world.

In many religions it is taught that hell was somewhere else and often it was described as underground in some fearful pit.

This is quite a reasonable description which was made in those very early days when such descriptions were given to people because actually when you are in the state of hell, if you have ever been in there and I certainly have, you feel oppressed, you feel really weighed down, it is as if you cannot get your head up. The problems you are surrounded with seem so great and overwhelming.

Even the light seems darker, everything is heavy, but this is why very graphically, in the olden days, that hell was described as underground.

It is a state where you are totally oppressed and imprisoned by the circumstances in your environment.

It could be imminent death, it could be toothache, it could be the loss of someone you dearly love, there are many different reasons but whatever happens you feel totally downcast by it, so downcast that you cannot see the light, you cannot see any way out of the problem.

This is the torture of being in hell.

There are many different states of hell and Buddhism classifies each one.

Changing Poison into Medicine

There are icy cold hells and very hot hells, there are slimy hells, smelly hells, bloody hells, every sort of hell.
There are actually about fifteen of them described in The Buddhist Canon, but they are all really true.
Maybe you can remember being in an icy hell or a hot hell.
In the sutras there are very vivid descriptions of the various types of hell that you can find yourself in depending on the cause for you being there.
They are hell because you are battened down and oppressed and can see no way out which is a role of frustrated anger, an anger which seethes and smoulders inside.
It is not a demonstrative anger, there is no way you can be demonstrative, but it is seething and bubbling and smouldering inside you.
There is of course a separate world of anger but that is the world of dominance and domination.
This is a different sort of anger, a smouldering resentment and frustration.
Fortunately, in the world of hell, there are means of getting out of it.
Buddhism in its early days, in its very colourful language, described this means as the 'Hell Hounds.'
The Hell Hounds are of course imaginary creatures who snap and snarl and bite and menace you so much that even though you are oppressed in your fear and hate of the place that you are in, your determination is to get out as things seem to get worse and worse and as your cornered more and more, you have to make an immense effort and you then get yourself out of hell.
Buddhism describes this as the hell hounds biting at your backside.
Fortunately hell is so miserable and so awful that even though you feel oppressed for a time that feels like eternity, in the end your human spirit and your desire to be free, causes you to make some colossal effort to get out of your situation.
The sooner the better and if you are in now in recovery, you will understand exactly what I am talking about.
Believe it or not there is a positive side to every one of these worlds and in particularly there is a positive side to The Three Evil Paths.
Nothing is without a positive side in life.
There is a positive in hell and the positive aspect is that unless you knew it you would not know what happiness is.
Sounds strange but it is really true.

Those of you who have experienced incredible suffering in your addiction will remember the joy and happiness when you climbed out of it and possibly that joy and happiness has remained a marvellous memory that you can feed on, it can feed your spirit for your entire lifetime.

Without hell we could not know true happiness, so even hell has a purpose.

Additionally the fear of hell is what makes people to really try hard to live a life that will not lead them into hell again.

In other words, we make effort to make positive causes in our lives because we do not want to go back into hell and certainly this is one of the reasons that people begin to practice Nichiren Shoshu Buddhism.

Buddhism is very important because it elevates your state of life and leads you to the highest awakening and enlightenment.

Hell in every way is an important thing.

Without hell to drive us forward we would very easily become complacent, idle, and useless.

Let us now look at the second of The Three Evil Paths, that is the world of Hunger.

Hunger, meaning greed.

Hunger is a state where there seems to be within you an inexhaustible desire to possess, use or to achieve something, to satisfy your desires.

There are waves of yearning and action to perhaps possess material possessions or for money, or for sex, or for drugs and alcohol, even for sleep, for food, for power, or honour.

A yearning even to preserve yourself at all costs, against all odds, hungering after life in many different ways, hungering after your desires, this is the world of hunger.

It is a world that can very easily possess you because the peculiar thing is the moment you obtain your desire through the driving force of hunger, you find that you are not satisfied and want something more.

This is the world of hunger at work.

Always yearning for something and when you get it yearning for something else.

Hunger is instinctive and can have a very bad effect on your life if it takes power over you, because your life is then following a very narrow, selfish path which is only for your own self-satisfaction but like all the lower worlds it has a purpose, it has a positive side and that is it is a driving force.

Your desires are a driving force.

Changing Poison into Medicine

Nichiren Shoshu Buddhism is amazing in that respect because one of its main principles or teachings is to turn desires into enlightenment.

Through Buddhist practice you chant for your desires, but the process of chanting is so strong that it will then lead you to what you really need for your happiness and enlightenment or what you really need to develop your life.

Nichiren Shoshu Buddhism or the teachings of Nichiren Daishonin does not in any sense deny your desire.

Many religions have tried and do try to deny desire.

It is impossible, desires are a part of your life, if you repress desire in the end it will bounce back and bite you.

You cannot remove desire, but this Buddhism gives you a practice that is so powerful and strong that it can turn your desires into enlightenment.

You can chant even for something that might appear to be shallow but always the power of the practice will lead you in another step towards enlightenment because you are actually doing the practice of chanting and quite easily the world of hunger can be turned, over a period of time, into another world or even towards the world of Buddhahood.

Hunger in its positive sense is a driving force for peace or fair play or justice, for Kosen Rufu.

People can yearn for it, hunger for it and that is hunger working in a positive way.

Everyone has a main tendency in their life, this is their karma, the main tendency being the state they move into more often than any other.

For some it may be anger, for others it may be hunger, for others it may be tranquillity, for others even hell, some people yearn for hell in a peculiar way, they feel protected in hell, or feel that they deserve it, even though they do not like it and are always longing to get out of it.

The purpose of our daily practice is to create the karma where the life condition of Buddhahood or enlightenment becomes the main driving force of our life.

The goal or our determination is to raise our predominant life condition, to make the main tendency in our life that of Buddhahood.

Buddhahood then becomes the life state that we move into more often than any other.

Now let us look at the world of animality.

Animality is the world that Nichiren Daishonin described as the world of stupidity or ignorance.

It is an instinctive world, an animal world where people act and react without any thought or preparation or planning. Instinctively in the moment.

Neither reason nor conscience works in the world of animality, in this world, you only make impulsive and instinctive actions.

The nature of animals is to threaten the weak and bow to the strong.

In the world of animality, the tendency is to bow before someone you feel is superior to you or it is perhaps to bully and dominate someone who you feel is weaker than you.

This is a very, very common tendency in human life.

This is the world of animality, an instinctive world, it is the world of the struggle to survive, the struggle for the species survival or to save the species.

Instinctively animals react in a certain way and so do human beings.

There is a line from Nichiren Daishonin's writings which says.

"Fish out of their instinct for survival shun a ponds shallow places and dig holes to hide themselves yet tricked by bait they take the hook."

This is the world of animality, because they wanted to survive but their hunger makes them forget about everything.

Having dug their hole and hidden themselves they come out and take the hook and get caught.

Many things in human lives arise from the world of animality.

It is a fact that from the world of animality and hunger together come such matters as environmental degradation, global warming and the current climate crisis, also the fight for survival can sometimes lead to war.

The world of animality is a blind world of instinct in which humanity could quite easily destroy itself.

Again this world has its positive side, and it is also an essential part of life as are all the other worlds.

The instinctive action to preserve yourself and those you love and the actions that you take are very important.

For example, if a baby falls into a fire, the mother without a moment's thought will grab it and save it.

This is animality at work, an instinctive desire to save that baby's life that arises in that mother's heart.

This is the good side of this world, the instinctive action to preserve the species.

Changing Poison into Medicine

From this world there have grown many amazing discoveries for the production of food and medicines to cure illness which never existed before.
We are aware that food is becoming short as humanity reproduces in ever larger numbers and as the world population increases, humanity in its determination to make sure the species survives is moving into all sorts of differing fields and innovative areas to find fresh sources of food and nutrition.
This is partly the instinct of survival, but it also contains the world of hunger where humanity turns away from that pure animal instinct to survive and towards the desire for profit in the process and we are, as a species, now experiencing all the negative consequences that unfold due to this uncontrolled desire in ever more disastrous ways.
This is becoming more and more apparent in the world around us today to the point of an unprecedented environmental catastrophe in the form of the current climate crisis.
Now let us look at the world of anger.
Anger is not the world of frustrated, seething, tormenting anger of the world of hell.
Anger is the world of domination.
The world in which a person desires to dominate everyone and everything in their environment and it is very much the world of the selfish ego.
Other people's feelings are ignored for the sake of personal profit or personal power.
People in this world can be ruthless in their criticism and their actions.
Anger is the dominance of the selfish ego.
It renders people deaf to all other people and drives them to a feverish pursuit of personal profit and egocentric goals.
The self in the world of anger is thus intensely egoistic.
T'ien T'ai, The Great Chinese Buddhist Master (538-597. A.D.), who is also known as The Buddha of The Middle Day, who was born about one thousand years after Shakyamuni Buddha's death, wrote.

"He who is in the world of anger motivated by the warped desire to win everything, despises others and tries to justify and value himself above all else.
He is like a hawk sweeping the sky in search of prey, he may have superficial benevolence, righteousness, propriety, wisdom and sincerity and seems to have some kind of moral sense, but his heart remains in anger."

People in the world of anger are quite often very difficult to discern, because outwardly they seem to be moral and to behave correctly, but inwardly their desire is to dominate and control.

This is also the world of self-consciousness, such people are very self-conscious.

They often see their own lives rather poorly.

They lack confidence and therefore they build this protective barrier around themselves or a high wall from which they take pot shots at everyone else around them.

War arises from this world of anger and arrogance.

The positive side of it is passion.

Anger when it is positive can be called passion.

A passion for justice, or for fair play or for good treatment for old people, or for poor people, or for social justice.

A passion to see the world's resources fairly shared amongst developing countries and so on.

Let us now look at the world of tranquillity.

The world of tranquillity is as its name suggests, a very peaceful and calm world.

It is also known in Buddhism as the world of humanity.

That may sound strange as so few of us humans ever seem to be in the world of tranquillity in these days modern times.

It is called that because it is the point of balance in human life between the lower worlds which can be so negative and destructive and the higher worlds which can be so positive.

It is a world that is stagnant.

Basically it is a neutral world in which nothing particular happens.

A world maybe where you relax and do not think of anything in particular and switch on the radio or play some of your favourite music and do nothing really productive in that time.

Nevertheless, it is important to life, sometimes we must relax and be tranquil.

The problem is that it is very, very difficult to stay in that world.

You want to be tranquil at the end of a hard day's work and then just as your settling down and relaxing the telephone rings and your brother is on the line pouring out all his problems into your ear.

There are so many ways that tranquillity can be spoiled, a million different ways.

How often do we really achieve tranquillity in the lives we live today, very, very rarely can we sustain it.

From the point of view of Nichiren Shoshu Buddhism you need great wisdom to sustain tranquillity for as long as it is valuable for you.

Changing Poison into Medicine

When you have achieved it only your wisdom in handling your life and controlling your environment will enable you to stay there for as long as it is good for you.

Tranquillity also has its bad side, its negative side, which is that it is stagnant.

The world of tranquillity produces nothing of value except rest and peace for yourself, which is certainly valuable but so far as the world is concerned it is creating nothing.

Therefore if you are always seeking tranquillity it is probable that you are trying to escape from your life.

The positive side which has already been explained is that some tranquillity is necessary for our personal wellbeing.

Last of all in the six lower worlds is rapture or heaven.

Rapture is the world where you achieve your desires and as you do so you feel so thrilled, you feel heady, light, your steps are bouncy, you feel full of the joy of life, and because of that I am afraid you do not look where you are going.

Rapture is a dangerous world, it is beautiful, it is wonderful, but it only lasts for a very short time.

It is the world in which you are so rapturous that you do not notice the manhole cover that has been left open in front of you and you can fall in and end up in the world of hell again in a moment. Unfortunately there are many things can pull you from rapture or heaven straight into hell state once more.

This concludes the six lower worlds and leaves us now to go on to the four higher worlds and these are the worlds where we have to make an effort to experience them.

The first one is very simple and straightforward.

Learning, the world in which you make effort to master a particular craft or subject to gain knowledge to elevate your life through learning.

In the very early days of Buddhism, when Shakyamuni Buddha taught that each world was separate, he would try through his teachings to elevate someone from a lower world into the world of learning, through encouragement, to improve their way of life. This was Shakyamuni Buddha's intention in the early days of his teaching.

After Learning comes Realisation.

Realisation or absorption is also called the world of partial enlightenment.

The world of realisation is the world where the human mind totally concentrates on some particular and partial aspect of life. Artists will do this.

A great artist in order to create a great painting will concentrate their whole life, their whole mind and their whole energy, into that area of life which they wish to depict.

This is the world of absorption.

In concentrating your mind in this way, enlightenment definitely comes to a particular aspect of life.

To that aspect of life on which the mind is concentrated through this intense effort and thought.

This is why it also called the world of partial enlightenment but also it can be a very narrow world.

Both Learning and Realisation have their negative side, which is that it can be so narrow and so blinkered.

Many great artists have led desperately unhappy lives and how much of that was due to the fact that they were so absorbed in their art and creativity that they ignored and neglected everything else around them, this is the world of realisation or absorption.

It can also be an arrogant world.

It is very easy to move from the two worlds of learning and realisation into anger because they can both become very egotistical and very self centred.

Nothing should interrupt, or argue with, or suggest other, or different, to a person in the world of absorption.

This is the negative side of this world, which is being totally absorbed in the self.

Now let us look at the world of Bodhisattva where you desire above everything else to help others.

This world comes naturally in the form of, for example, dedicated nurses, dedicated G.P.'s and doctors and other people doing great work in helping in natural disasters and so on.

This is the world of Bodhisattva.

The problem with the world of bodhisattva is that it is extremely difficult to sustain.

When your strength in the state of bodhisattva is beginning to weaken it becomes the world of self-sacrifice or martyrdom.

The negative side of the world of bodhisattva is that a pure completely noble intention can in the end become an area for your ego to get to work in the form of self-sacrifice.

"I am doing this great work for others, I am superior to those others, but I am doing it all for them," for the poor, for those debilitated in one way or another.

This can wear thin and turn into egoism.

This is the terrible danger of bodhisattva in its normal state.

Fortunately the world of Buddha or Buddhahood, the highest

world of all, reveals itself as action in life in and through the world of bodhisattva.

Nichiren Shoshu Buddhism says that you can only sustain bodhisattva actions through a lifetime or over a long period through activating your inherent Buddha state.

Then actions in the bodhisattva state will be pure and entirely noble in quality and self-sacrifice will never enter into it.

If you are to live in the world of bodhisattva and take actions as a bodhisattva, you must attain the ascendency of the Buddha state in your life in order to do so.

Finally let us look at the world of Buddha the highest state of all is of course extremely difficult to describe.

We already know one aspect of its qualities which is in the world of bodhisattva.

Buddhahood is a state of life where you are awakened and enlightened to everything about life.

To the workings of life, to the law of cause and effect, to the mechanics of life, which are not just theories but are living things which you totally understand and live.

Because there are no corners that are dark in life, therefore there is no fear.

We fear the unknown, therefore if you become enlightened to life there are no areas of unknown and fear leaves us.

This is one of the great freedoms of The Buddha or the Buddha state or Buddhahood.

There is absolutely no fear.

Secondly there are no limitations and because you understand how life works.

You challenge things that would otherwise never be challenged, because everyone else says and thinks it is impossible, this would not necessarily be impossible to a Buddha.

The Buddha understands the workings of life and knows in fact that there are no limitations to what humanity can achieve, provided you use the power of life in order to do so.

Buddha is the state of life that is wholly positive.

It is the state of existence where you use all the other nine worlds positively, to their highest and full potential.

This is the important point that we have been coming to all through this chapter.

Each of the other nine worlds has a positive side.

The positive side of each world is essential and so is the negative side of those other worlds, as they can be used as a driving force in life.

In the world of Buddha or Buddhahood, even though the world of anger may be working in your life, and as each world has the

other nine in it, that anger will turn one hundred and eighty degrees and appear in a positive form or force in your life.
Everything in life is working positively in the Buddha state or the world of Buddhahood.
Every other world that passes through it is turned from negative to positive.
Buddha or Buddhahood is a state of absolute freedom.
Freedom from fear, freedom from any limitations of any sort, through total enlightenment to the meaning and workings of life and the great benefit that can be attained from it.
I hope that through this chapter that you now have some idea about the purpose and goal of Buddhist practice.
It has only one purpose and that is to make the main tendency of your life Buddha, rather than that of hunger, anger, animality, learning or even absorption.
This is the primary and ultimate purpose of the practice.
Buddha is not a superhuman or a god.
It is a human being revealing her, his or their absolute full potential, using their life to the absolute fullest in every single direction and in every way to create absolute freedom and happiness for themselves, for others in society, and even in the environment of our Planet Earth itself.

The True Object of Worship.

Dai Gohonzon.

Changing Poison into Medicine

The invocation of Nam Myoho Renge Kyo, which is the fundamental practice of Nichiren Shoshu Buddhism, is also known as The First Great Secret Law.
Secret, in that it was known only to The Buddha's until it was revealed to everybody by Nichiren Daishonin when he declared Nam Myoho Renge Kyo on the 28th April 1253.
In this chapter of the book we are going to explain the Second Great Secret Law of The Three Great Secret Laws, which are the foundation of faith in Nichiren Shoshu Buddhism.
This second Great Secret Law is known as Dai Gohonzon.
The Third Great Secret Law is known in Japanese by the word Kaidan, meaning sanctuary.
The High Sanctuary in which the object of devotion The Dai Gohonzon is enshrined is The Hoando at The Head Temple, Taiseki ji at Mount Fuji in Japan.
These Three Great Secret Laws, as they are known, make up the One Great Law of The Lotus, Nam Myoho Renge Kyo.
The Three Great Secret Laws have a complete cohesion, you chant Nam Myoho Renge Kyo, The Invocation, to the true object of devotion, The Gohonzon, in The Sanctuary which is where you have enshrined The Gohonzon in your own home.
Gohonzon is available to all of us.
It is available to anyone who wants to practice Nichiren Shoshu Buddhism, providing they are willing to make the commitment of protecting and practicing to The Gohonzon throughout their life, then they may receive one.
Your own bed-sitter or your own sitting room, or wherever, becomes the Kaidan or High Sanctuary as far as your own Gohonzon is concerned.
This is the centre point of your devotion and is known as 'The Buddha Land' and because of your devotion 'The Buddha Land' spreads out further and further outwards from that sanctuary.
In the early days of Nichiren Daishonin's teaching, after he declared Nam Myoho Renge Kyo in 1253, people practiced without The Gohonzon.
The reason for this was that they were at the very beginning of their understanding of this faith.
Today we may practice for three months, six months, or nine months or however long it takes for us to make up our minds to commit ourselves to Buddhism and receiving The Gohonzon is like the fruit of that commitment.
Today also we have more support available to us, to help us to understand Nichiren Shoshu Buddhism, which were not available to people in those days.

Changing Poison into Medicine

We have books and magazines and there are other members with years of practice we can talk to.
There are now various Temples around the globe, and we also now have the internet, and so on.
The Dharma or Teachings can be made available far more easily now than in the thirteenth century, and as Shakyamuni predicted in The Lotus Sutra, in this age people more and more have the intellectual capacity to see the need for Nam Myoho Renge Kyo and to place it in its right context in this universe in which we exist.
After a time Nichiren Daishonin then began to give a few Gohonzon, objects of worship or devotion, to certain of his followers who were advancing the best in faith.
Those who would be able to appreciate the need to have a Gohonzon, in order to help them with their practice and with the advance of the reformation of their lives which the practice involves.
These Gohonzons were developed more and more, still comparatively few in number, until finally in 1279 on the 12th of October, Nichiren Daishonin inscribed what is known as The Dai Gohonzon, The Supreme Gohonzon, though this was a gradual progression and the inscription of The Dai Gohonzon by Nichiren Daishonin was the culmination of his purpose in life or advent in this world.
This was the ultimate realization of his mission in life.

Through the inscription of The Dai Gohonzon, from which all other Gohonzon are transcribed by each consecutive High Priests of Nichiren Shoshu, he was able to perpetuate this Buddhism into the future after he died.

The Gohonzon is in fact a piece of parchment or paper, or it can be made of wood, and it is the central object of our practice and can hang with ease in any room and is therefore easily available to everybody.

Those that are made of parchment are nowadays in this modern age, printed.

When they make The Gohonzon from wood, this is a process which is always kept quite secret, and this is the process where they take the inscription and transfer it from the original parchment onto a piece of camphor wood as this wood is the most resistant to attacks from insects.

With a Gohonzon of such a nature, one that it is going to be used by a great many people, such as in a Temple, they will make the wood block immediately after the parchment has been inscribed.

That is then kept until the parchment Gohonzon wears out, which it naturally does in the end, and it is then replaced by the wooden one.

These are just a few facts for those of you have not encountered or know much about what The Gohonzon is.

Let us now explain why The Gohonzon is necessary.

Why is it that an object of devotion is important to this practice and indeed as Nichiren Daishonin explained, what is its importance for a human being?

The word Gohonzon is Japanese, and the character Go is an honorific title and Honzon means object of devotion, so Gohonzon means the honourable object of devotion.

Japanese people make it even more polite because they say Gohonzon sama, which means 'Mister' The Honourable Object of Devotion.

Nichiren Daishonin in one of his most important writings called The Gohonzon, Kanjin No Honzon Sho, which means the object of devotion for observing the mind, or life.

That actually sums up what the purpose of The Gohonzon is.

It is the object of devotion by means of which you can observe your life and all its workings.

It was Nichiren Daishonin's wisdom which brought him to the point where he realised that a human being needs an object of devotion and if you do not give a human being an object of devotion, they will make one up for themselves.

Changing Poison into Medicine

We can see this tendency in many instances, we see it in christianity.

In the history of the christian church it was one of the great commandments that no graven image would be made of god, but human beings down the centuries could not resist making some sort of image.

They made an image of Mary, Jesus's mother, or of the cross, or of christ actually on the cross.

There was a need or a desire to concentrate their life on something and this is a natural human instinct which Nichiren Daishonin well understood.

Shakyamuni Buddha, who was the first recorded Buddha in the history of this world also said do not worship me, worship The Dharma or Law.

Nevertheless down through the ages from his time, human beings could not resist this desire to make something concrete to concentrate their minds on.

All over the Far East you will find many statues of The Buddha, lying down, resting, meditating, laughing, all sorts of different positions and images.

Some are made of gold, some of turquoise, some studded with precious jewels, another made of marble and so on.

There is this innate desire in a human being to have an object of devotion.

Most religions in one way or another have concluded that an object of devotion is necessary.

In primitive religions, tribal religions, this is very obvious as they made totem poles and strange statues in wood and stone.

It is a human beings need and if humans do not find one through the wisdom of someone else, they will make one up.

If you look now at this materialistic age, which began around three hundred years ago as humans became disillusioned to a great extent to the religions of the day of our contemporary times, they have turned their attention to other forms of objects of devotion.

It may be money, it may be sport, it may be their partner, it may be their work, it may be a pet dog, but one way or another they always have struggled to concentrate their lives on something.

The trouble with these objects of devotion in this very materialistic age is that they are the most impermanent.

If you make your life partner your object of devotion and you adore them unceasingly, for a year or two years, you never know quite what is going to happen next.

They may meet someone else, they may become sick, they may have an accident, so many things can happen to make that object of devotion shake, crumble and disappear.

People behave in amazing ways with their chosen objects of devotion.

There was an article in a newspaper about a businessman whose passion was golf, and he had been playing golf in Brazil and his golf ball, after the tee off, went into the bushes and when he went to find it he couldn't find it anywhere.

He realised from some giggling that a small boy had taken it and as he walked towards him the boy ran away, so this man pulled out a gun and shot him.

That is utterly insane and almost in a terrible way laughable, but the fact is that man's object of devotion was his game of golf, his life was totally taken up by it.

Maybe you know people whose lives are totally taken up in some way with a sport.

They think about it in every moment of their lives, they think about it all week, if possible they try to make their business appointments around games of golf.

It can take precedent over their families and totally absorbs their life until something changes, maybe they get too old for it, and maybe for some reason known only to themselves their passion turns from golf to a girlfriend, or a new car, or whatever.

This is innate in human life, humans needs an object of devotion, and can go to an extreme extent to invent one and then is quite absorbed by that devotion until something changes.

Nichiren Daishonin recognised this and in inscribing The Dai Gohonzon his determination was to give people an object of devotion that was absolute, unchanging and constant, that could become the prime point of any human being's life, which would never change, would always be there, always constant.

Constant in its meaning and constant in its appearance, something which if you devote your life to it will never let you down, will never get sick.

Something that you could never get tired of because the depth of the meaning of it is so complete and all embracing.

This is what he set out to do when he inscribed this piece of parchment called The Gohonzon.

The way you react to an object of devotion depends on its form and if it is made by humans it depends on the state of life of the person who makes it or creates it.

Take a painting by an artist, if an artist is angry when they paint, if they are a person who is seething with frustrated anger perhaps at the state of the world, they will produce a picture that makes

65

us either angry or frightened, that is presuming they are a great artist.

If a sculptor is hammering out something from stone, what they produce will reflect their state of life.

If they are in a state of rapture as they create it the work will convey that mood or state of life.

If they are in an unbelievable state of tranquillity, the same thing will happen.

Their work of art or what they create will reflect the state of life that they are in exactly.

This is The Ten Worlds at work, which are conveyed through that person's creativity.

Even a statue of The Buddha if it is created in gold could reflect the world of hunger, the world of desiring things.

A statue of The Buddha reclining could reflect tranquillity.

Likewise if you look at a picture or at a statue of christ on the cross, it will probably reflect guilt.

This will depend upon the state of life of the person who makes that object.

Nichiren Daishonin's purpose, his prime purpose was to produce an object of devotion which reflected his Buddhahood or enlightenment, his state of Buddhahood which he had achieved so that anyone looking at it would find that it would gradually bring out the Buddha state in them.

This is the purpose of The Gohonzon to bring the Buddha state into the foremost position in our lives through devoting ourselves or practicing too or looking at The Gohonzon which Nichiren Daishonin has himself inscribed.

When he inscribed The Gohonzon he said.

"I have inscribed my life in sumi ink, so believe in this Gohonzon with your whole heart."

I am inscribing my life so that you can believe with your whole heart.

He inscribed in the Buddha state itself which is his life so that we can draw that same state out of our own lives.

How can a piece of paper do such a thing, after all it is a piece of paper covered with a lot of Chinese characters, how can it possibly draw anything out of me?

The fact is that pieces of paper can draw incredible things out of us can they not?

We have already mentioned a picture by an artist can draw anger or rapture or whatever mood you can think of out of people.

66

A fifty pound note brings something out of us, it is still a piece of paper.

If we get a letter from our partner and it contains the marvellous romantic and exciting language that we hoped for, it draws out a fantastic rapture from us.

But if they say it is over and they are finishing with us, ending the relationship, it can put us straight into hell.

A piece of paper can be incredibly powerful, it reflects the life state of the person who creates it.

Nichiren Daishonin when he inscribed The Gohonzon was in the Buddha state and therefore it reflects the Buddha state to anyone who devotes themselves to it.

Each High Priest of Nichiren Shoshu down through the ages has inherited not only that right but that ability to inscribe a Gohonzon in the Buddha state so that it draws the Buddha state out of us.

How do I know that the High Priest was in the Buddha state when he did it?

The answer is that you get the actual proof, The Gohonzon never fails.

From the very moment you start to practice to The Gohonzon you begin to see the change in your life.

In order to decide on how he was going to produce this object of devotion, Nichiren Daishonin spent many years studying all the Buddhist teachings that were in Japan at that time.

In the process of doing that he realised totally in his life that The Lotus Sutra was supreme just as Shakyamuni himself had taught in The Lotus Sutra at that time.

Nichiren Daishonin took The Gohonzon out of the manuscript of The Lotus Sutra and in that way he was able to substantiate the flow of Buddhism down through the ages from Shakyamuni to himself.

In The Lotus Sutra there is a chapter in which an extraordinary ceremony is described known as 'The Ceremony in The Air' and in this ceremony an incredible and great treasure tower appears.

This treasure tower, as it is called, was vast and it was encrusted with precious jewels and gems, and it was the most beautiful object you can imagine.

After sometime as this ceremony developed it was seen that there was a Buddha sitting in the centre of this great treasure tower.

This Buddha's name is Taho in Japanese, and Prabhutaratna in Sanskrit and he is a legendary Buddha, a Buddha whose name represents one of the great principles of Buddhism.

After a while Shakyamuni joined him and sat beside him within the treasure tower and finally four great Bodhisattvas appeared and presented themselves to these two Buddha's sitting side by side in this magnificent treasure tower and furthermore countless other Bodhisattvas rose up out the earth and assembled in a great crowd or mass around the treasure tower.

This was a figurative means that Shakyamuni used in order to explain the flow of Buddhism into the future.

Shakyamuni Buddha in that treasure tower represented wisdom, the subjective wisdom that exists in every one of us, the wisdom that arises from the Buddha state.

Taho Buddha represents the good fortune that people can draw into their lives from outside them through the qualities of wisdom and compassion from the Buddha state and those four great Bodhisattvas that presented themselves in front of the treasure tower, represent the most wonderful qualities which each human being innately has in their life.

The people who arose out of the earth are you and I or 'The Bodhisattvas of The Earth' and their followers who inherit Buddhism and chant Nam Myoho Renge Kyo, if you choose and decide to do so.

The meaning of this story is that Shakyamuni and Taho, the two Buddhas who were both sitting in that treasure tower represent all the greatness of the Buddha state which exists in every human being.

The wisdom on the one side, and the ability to draw good fortune to your life through elevating the Buddha state in you, were joined by the four great Bodhisattvas who were the leaders of all the Bodhisattvas of the Earth and their followers and in the process of the ceremony the heritage of The Dharma or Law was transferred to the greatest of those leaders whose name was Jogyo.

Bodhisattva Jogyo the leader of The Bodhisattvas of the Earth inherited The Dharma, which the treasure tower represented.

The Dharma of Nam Myoho Renge Kyo and it was the task of all those Bodhisattvas and their followers greater in number, the sutra says, than all the sands of ten thousand, ten million, Ganges rivers, were the people in due course of time in the age of Mappo, which is the age that began around 900 A.D.

They inherit The Dharma, passing it on to each other, one by one.

This is the historical background to the design of The Gohonzon. It lives in the whole history and flow of Buddhism.

On the Gohonzon to the left and right of Nam Myoho Renge Kyo down the centre, at the top, are the characters representing Taho and Shakyamuni Buddhas.

There on the left is all the wisdom of the Buddha state represented through that character for Shakyamuni and on the right, through the Chinese character for Taho, is all the good fortune of the universe which can be drawn from outside you into your life.

All around those characters and all around Nam Myoho Renge Kyo down the centre are many, many, many other Chinese characters.

These are the characters that show The Ten Worlds, or the ten basic at states of life, from hell at its worst, to Buddhahood at its greatest.

Also all the forces of the universe.

The forces that affect our lives either adversely or advantageously depending upon whether we are following a positive and wise course in life or not.

The Sun is a great force of the universe, a great creator, the Sun is on the Gohonzon.

The Moon and stars and many other forces that are not so easy to describe.

Like the force that stops you on the edge of the pavement and prevents you from going further and a motorcycle passes you at eighty miles an hour and misses you by an inch.

All these many and varied forces that work in order to protect our lives, provided that we are moving in a positive direction towards Buddhahood are depicted on The Gohonzon.

There to are those four great Bodhisattvas, which represent life force and purity, justice and compassion, the qualities that are so great in human life which we all possess, are written across the top of The Gohonzon.

The other characters not only include light, brightness but also darkness in the form of Devadatta, the cousin of Shakyamuni Buddha who tried to kill him on several occasions and constantly frustrated Shakyamuni's plans, he is also included on The Gohonzon.

A female demon called Kishimojin who had ten daughters and a very devouring nature, until she promised to work with The Dharma and not against it, is also there.

Devadatta lives in every one of us as every one of us has that devilish instinct inside of us.

If we did not have it how could there be wars.

Kishimojin also lives in us.

Kishimojin who rather than see her babies starve, fed them with other people's children.

We all have such an instinct in us even though it is not in charge of us, it is there.

Sometimes it can appear, that strongly possessive jealous nature.

Changing Poison into Medicine

This Gohonzon is the most incredible thing, every aspect of life, every shade and colour of it is represented by those Chinese characters and a Chinese character in itself is a whole story.
This is why they are probably the most economical method of writing and conveying ideas that has ever existed in the history of the world.
Each Chinese ideogram conveys so much that people could write a book on each one of them.
The Gohonzon as Nichiren Daishonin said, described his life.
His life as a human being.
His life of which he was perfectly well aware, contained good and bad, darkness and light, shadows and brightness.
He wanted to give an object of devotion to which everyone could relate, whether that, at the moment they got down in front of it were in the world of hell, or anger, or rapture.
He did not want to produce an object of devotion that someone would only find themselves bowing in shame to, in guilt and misery, asking for forgiveness.
He wanted to produce an object of devotion which even though you might feel miserable and ashamed, you could practice to and realise that you are nothing unusual, that the devilish states and worlds of existence that exist in yourself also exist in your neighbours and in everyone else around you and the most important of all, in The Buddha, who is also a human being.
Then taking his brush and his sumi ink, he inscribed down the centre of it all, in great bold characters, Nam Myoho Renge Kyo, Nichiren.
Nam Myoho Renge Kyo being the expression of the Buddha state in words or characters, all the incredible qualities of that state, contained in the single phrase, Nam Myoho Renge Kyo and to emphasise the point, he put Nichiren at the base of it.
Nichiren the human being, but Nichiren who was also enlightened.
This is a very difficult thing to take in, especially in a comparatively short time like reading this book.
Having described The Gohonzon itself, even only briefly, lets now explain to you how it works.
In Nichiren Shoshu Buddhism there are three practices.
One is to perform the ceremony of Gongyo and Shodai, which is to recite The Lotus Sutra and chant Nam Myoho Renge Kyo in front of The Gohonzon and the second practice is to teach others about this Buddhism and the third practice is to study.
Study, not in the sense of academic study, but to read the writings of Nichiren Daishonin as taught and explained by the learned

Priesthood or Sangha in order to understand the full spirit and meaning.

Through a combination of these three practices you can begin to understand more and more what Nichiren Daishonin's life was like.

You begin to understand his qualities, his courage, the breadth, and depth and width and height of his wisdom, his incredible compassion even for his enemies who were hounding him throughout his life, and many other characteristics.

Through this study, and the picture you get of Nichiren Daishonin, the characters on The Gohonzon more and more begin to live in your life.

When you first look at The Gohonzon, you think, "Oh yes, it is rather beautiful, it's a paper with all these beautiful Chinese characters on" but as you go on practicing to it, day after day, month after month, year after year, decade after decade, so each of those characters begin to live in your life.

Devadatta, the wicked cousin of Shakyamuni, you begin to relate to him in your life.

You begin to understand what purity really means because you see it living in Nichiren Daishonin's life and actions and when you begin to teach others about Nichiren Shoshu Buddhism and through that you are compelled to get involved with another person's life, you feel their sufferings, you share them with them, and get to know what their lives are made up of.

You also learn a great deal about your own life, and you can relate those experiences to the teachings of Nichiren Daishonin which were all in the end, aimed to help us to overcome these sufferings.

The more you look at The Gohonzon and the more you concentrate your mind on it, the more it begins to live.

At the same time you are also becoming more and more perceptive about yourself.

This is inevitable because as you look at The Gohonzon you are seeing all the qualities of life.

Especially of the life in the Buddha state and it is a perfectly natural thing that you will compare that with the state of life that you are in at the moment you are looking at The Gohonzon. The state of life you are in day by day.

Inevitably you begin to see the gaps and differences between what is represented there on The Gohonzon and what is the actuality of your life today, tomorrow or the next day.

The more you understand The Gohonzon the more you admire the qualities which are contained on and in it.

Changing Poison into Medicine

Perfectly naturally you will desire to develop those same qualities in your own life and thus close the gaps and differences between your state of life now and the state of life in the Buddha state which is on The Gohonzon.

This is an extraordinary thing, and it is extremely difficult to understand but the fact is that it works.

Not one of us who practices would go on practicing unless we constantly got actual proof that it works.

You may say, "hold on a moment, I am chanting Nam Myoho Renge Kyo without The Gohonzon, and I am seeing the benefits," and that is perfectly right and reasonable.

You might also say, "therefore why must I have The Gohonzon, if I am getting the benefits of chanting, isn't that good enough?"

The answer to that is yes you do need The Gohonzon, not because I am saying so but because The Buddha in all his wisdom said we need The Gohonzon.

Although it is true through propelling your prayers, your determinations, and your desires out from your life and also back into your life, through chanting Nam Myoho Renge Kyo, and through that activation of your Buddha state combined with your prayers, the Buddha state in your environment will reflect itself and therefore benefits will begin to come to you.

You cannot make full use of those benefits unless you practice to The Gohonzon.

The reason for that is that you cannot change your negative karma without The Gohonzon.

Nichiren Daishonin inscribed The Gohonzon, and he called it in Japanese, 'Kanjin no Honzon' or The Object of Devotion for Observing the Mind.

It is only through seeing the gaps and differences between your state of life now and what you know more and more what The Gohonzon represents that you can discover your unhappy or negative karma.

Some unhappy karma is very easy to see, you can see the surface of it.

You may say that my unhappy karma is debt, I am always in debt, no matter how much I spend, however much I earn, the bank account is always red, this is my karma.

I have lived for twenty or thirty years, and it has always been the same.

And you are right of course, but why are you always in debt? That is only the surface, what is the deep reason for being in debt?

This is what you have to discover if you are going to change it. You have to get to the root cause of it.

Changing Poison into Medicine

You can moan and say, "I have been married three times and they have always failed," and that is true and that is a miserable state of affairs, but what is the cause deep in your life for getting married and divorcing three times?

What is the cause for being in debt?

What is the deep cause for being sick or ill so much?

What is the deep cause for having an addiction disorder?

What is the deep cause for always being so angry that you upset everybody wherever you go?

What is the deep cause for finding it so difficult to come outwards and relate to people?

The surface is easy, but how do you get to the root of it?

The sad thing is that people are always just putting a plaster on the problem and not addressing the deeper causes.

The purpose of this practice is to get to the root of it, to the root cause and you can only understand that by getting at the depths of your life and revealing what it is deep down there which is causing these surface problems to occur over and over and over again.

Kanjin no Honzon, The True Object of Devotion for Observing The Mind (Life).

On the Gohonzon is life in the Buddha state and by observing your own life you will see the differences between the two.

The more you go on with your practice, once you know your enemy, that is what unhappy karma lies within your life, then you can set about overcoming that enemy and changing your life. Buddhism is so rounded that it gives you a practice which provides you with the strength to do just that.

The Gohonzon that I hope you are beginning to understand is vital to your practice to change your karma so that you can reap to the full the good fortune of the benefits that come into your life.

Otherwise those benefits will be wasted.

If you do an incredible amount of chanting and you receive great benefits and you gain a great happiness, that is no good if you are going to die tomorrow.

You have to change that negative aspect of your karma and live the whole of your natural lifespan in order to make full use of those benefits.

Nam Myoho Renge Kyo is the law of the universe, the creative force that produces all the marvellous, myriad things you can see around you, it is the very nature of that law to require fullness of life.

Life has a purpose from beginning to end and the purpose of that law is to create beautiful, wonderful things which will live a whole lifespan, which is the correct lifespan in the rhythm of the universe in which to achieve the purpose of that particular phenomenon. That includes a human being, why should we be so arrogant as to think it does not.

We have a natural lifespan which we should live and not only live it but live it to the full, then every single one of us can achieve our true purpose in life and reach our full potential.

If we have our life shortened through accident or illness or even loneliness or sadness, we are failing to fulfil our purpose in some way, it is chopped off and the world becomes an unhappier place because of it.

The Gohonzon has two main functions.

One of its functions is to enable you to observe your mind or life like a mirror and the other function of The Gohonzon is to act as the link not only between the physical you that is chanting those words, Nam Myoho Renge Kyo, and the unseen you that exists in your life but also to act as the link between your life and its unseen state and the unseen state in life all around you.

In other words, you physically chant Nam Myoho Renge Kyo to The Gohonzon and you spiritually determine to take a great deal of action to change yourself and your circumstances.

This reflects deep within your life and through the practice, which activates the Buddha state, that then reflects itself up and out into your environment.

It is very easy to see that an angry person reflects their state of their life to everybody that they come into contact with during the day.

An angry person can make a whole office or a whole school room miserable, even frightened.

It is not so obvious that the person in the Buddha state can do the same thing, reflecting the Buddha state in everybody.

This is very difficult to see because it reveals itself in many ways that are difficult to perceive and understand.

It reveals itself in some sort of a radiance or in some sort of a wisdom in something that person says.

In some sort of a kindness or an ability to listen or whatever, but in one way or another that Buddha state and all its qualities will reflect itself into everything in the environment.

That is the second function of The Gohonzon.

The first to show you yourself so that you can change your negative unhappy karma and the second to act as the prime point, the focal point, of your highest quality of life which in turn reflects itself into all of life that exists around you.

Changing Poison into Medicine

When Nichiren Daishonin was talking about the practice he said words to the effect that the moment that you sit in front of The Gohonzon and chant Nam Myoho Renge Kyo, you are in the Buddha state.

It may be very difficult to see it or feel it or realise this.

You may feel irritable sometimes when you sit down in front of The Gohonzon.

It may be the last thing on earth you want to do, to chant Nam Myoho Renge Kyo, but the fact is you could not even get yourself down, kneeling or sitting in front of The Gohonzon and chanting Nam Myoho Renge Kyo unless you were in the Buddha state.

The Ten Worlds, the ten basic states of life, each contain the other nine basic states.

If Buddha was here, and hell was there, and there was nothing joining those two then Buddha would be superhuman, but Buddha contains hell and hell contains Buddha.

Buddha is a human being.

Therefore sometimes after you have done Gongyo & Shodai you do not feel like you are in the Buddha state, but gradually you realise through the practice, that what Nichiren Daishonin said is true.

You discover that you are getting glimpses of wisdom you never thought you possessed, of compassion you never believed you could release in certain circumstances and courage that certainly was not there before.

These are the great qualities of the Buddha state.

You are in the Buddha state when you practice and this is why the benefits come, reflecting back from your environment.

Nichiren Daishonin said in the famous Gosho, On Attaining Buddhahood.

"It is the same with a Buddha and a common mortal, while deluded one is called a common mortal, but once enlightened one is called a Buddha.

Even a tarnished mirror will shine like a jewel if it is polished.

A mind which is presently clouded by illusions, originating from the innate darkness of life, is like a tarnished mirror, but once it is polished, it will become clear, reflecting the enlightenment of the immutable truth, arouse deep faith and polish your mirror night and day.

How should you polish it?

Only by chanting Nam Myoho Renge Kyo."

Changing Poison into Medicine

Our practice to The Gohonzon is polishing that mirror, this is the most wonderful way of explaining it, far better than any words that have been used thus far.

Through polishing that mirror through your practice, day in and day out, you reveal the jewel which is in everybody's life, yet they know it not, and that is the Buddha state or Buddhahood.

This is the purpose of The Gohonzon to act as a mirror and of course most importantly of all, the purpose of The Gohonzon that Nichiren Daishonin inscribed, is to reveal The Gohonzon that exists within you, within your own life itself.

In Nichiren Shoshu Buddhism there is the teaching of The Four Powers (Jap. Shi-riki) that explain these functions, these are.

The power of The Buddha.

The power of The Law.

The power of faith.

The power of practice.

They are known as the four powers of 'The Mystic Law.'

The interaction of these four Laws or Dharma's enables you to have your prayers answered and to attain Buddhahood.

The power of The Buddha (Nichiren Daishonin) is The Buddha's compassion in saving all living beings or all people.

The power of The Law or Dharma indicates the boundless capacity of The Mystic Law (embodied in Dai Gohonzon) to lead all people to enlightenment or Buddhahood.

The power of faith is to believe in The Dai Gohonzon, the true object of devotion that embodies the two powers of The Buddha and The Dharma.

The power of practice is to Chant Nam Myoho Renge Kyo and recite The Lotus Sutra (Gongyo & Shodai) and to teach others to do the same.

To the extent that you bring forth your power of faith and practice, you can manifest the power of The Buddha and The Law within your life.

What Nichiren Daishonin inscribed has no power in your life until you 'activate' the power that actually exists within you, within your life.

It is not a magic charm, it is not something from outer space. It is something incredibly precious, an unbelievable treasure, the fruits of all the wisdom of all The Buddhas, which in its amazing way enables you to draw forth the Buddha state in your life through your own effort.

To be able to inscribe a Gohonzon you have be a Buddha.

If those Chinese characters revealed anger, or impatience, greed, that would also reflect in us.

In that sense The Gohonzon has power but actually it is drawing the power out of your own life.

In many Gosho, Nichiren Daishonin spoke very strictly about this point.

If you believe the Gohonzon is anywhere outside of yourself he said, you are not practicing this Buddhism.

This is quite a difficult concept to understand but gradually your mind will adjust to it as you practice and furthermore you begin to see the results.

You know that it really is drawing something, of a quality previously unimaginable, out of your own life.

The Gohonzon becomes in this way the prime point of your life, every morning and every evening and sometimes more if you wish too.

You feel more and more of a desire to come back to that prime point, to that absolute, constant, unchanging prime point.

The only thing in this incredible world we live in, which is totally constant, totally unchanging, however long you look at it, even for a whole lifetime.

You bring yourself back to that prime point, furthermore this practice can and must be developed onto a social scale.

In Nichiren Shoshu Temples there are Gohonzons enshrined, and we are able to go there to visit if we are fortunate enough to live in a country with enough Nichiren Shoshu Buddhists to maintain one.

If not, we gather in our homes to chant together either way the prime point of our efforts is to chant together to The Gohonzon for the peace and happiness of ourselves and our country.

We have Temples in Paris and Madrid for the peace of all of Europe, which are the prime points for all of us European members and we can visit if we are able.

Also The Priest from Myosho Ji Temple in Madrid comes to visit us here in the UK so we can meet and chant together at a prime point with The Temple Gohonzon that he brings along.

We also have the opportunity to travel to Japan to the Head Temple at Taiseki Ji where we can worship Dai Gohonzon.

This represents the prime point of our human effort for the future peace and happiness of the whole world.

The prime point of unity of all humanity, the unchanging constant reality of life because what else is Nichiren Shoshu Buddhism teaching but the unbelievable treasure that is life itself, the inherent dignity of life.

The dignity of life that is represented by and on The Gohonzon.
Life with all its amazing workings.

Changing Poison into Medicine

Finally, to conclude, let us now introduce the Buddhist Dharma or principle of the Three Truths, represented by the Chinese characters of:
Ku, (The truth of non-substantiality/unseen)
Ke, (The truth of temporary existence/seen) and
Chu, (The Middle Way/ Myoho Renge Kyo)

These principles very clearly bring out the vital importance The Gohonzon plays not only in our own lives but also in the lives of the human family as a whole.
If you look at this world at the moment you see an incredible amount of progress which is unbelievably haphazard and chaotic.
Everywhere you look amazing new technology is being invented, we have Space Travel, The Internet, Smart Phones, Artificial Intelligence, Quantum Computing, Gene Editing and Modification, incredible technological advancements are being made all around us and it is so haphazard and so fast that it is really beginning to frighten more and more people.
We wonder if we are really in control of all this and when we think of nuclear missiles, biochemical weapons, and all the rest of the paraphernalia of nuclear and biological warfare technology, it makes us shiver even more.
We think of the one person who can press a button and start it all, suppose they goes insane, a mad person and we could not stop them.
Then there is the climate crisis and the global warming and climate change due to our species effect on the environment and the impending social and environmental chaos that it will bring.
This is also frightening to everybody.
There is not anyone now who does not at times think about these points, they may hide their heads and eyes from it, but most people recognise the great risks and problems facing humanity at this time.
This haphazard and dynamic and often dangerous progress and change is arising out of the spirit of humanity.
That is Ke, the first of the three truths that represents the physical aspect or truth that you see manifested in all these technological advances and on the other hand you have humanities natural desire to want to harmonise with each other and the environment.
No one really wants war and environmental devastation.
They may get swept away by emotion and get involved in war in no time at all, but they do not really want it.

In their hearts people want peace and harmony.
In their hearts they want to be able to get on with their daily lives, conducting their business and bringing up their children in their family and whatever else, in peace and harmony.
This is the real desire of human beings.
Even the most blood thirsty revolutionary, even the worst terrorist, even the most maniacal extremists that exist in the world have some sort of great high ideal that they say they are working for even though they maybe undermining that ideal in the way they do it.
Everyone desires peace and harmony.
This desire from deep in your life is the second of the three truths or Ku, the unseen part of the world or the spiritual aspect or the unseen part of life.
Here we have these two extraordinary phenomenon.
On the one side a world going mad with technological and scientific advances with absolutely no cohesion at all, with the risk of war and violence and also the environmental destruction that these advances bring, manifesting in the current climate crisis and on the other side you have humanities innate desire for harmony and peace.
Humankind has always desired harmony, although it has never been able to achieve it, not once in the whole of human history in a lasting and deep way.
Why is this?
What is missing?
How can you have these two extremes co existing side by side?
In this way arising out of a society or civilization created by human beings who are clever, unbelievably clever, you only have to look at the technological advances to see that, so how can it be that they can be so crazy?
This is what The Buddha of course observed in the world although he did not see the world as it is now, but he knew what was coming.
Shakyamuni Buddha three thousand years ago said this age of Mappo, which will begin two thousand years after my death, will be an age of chaos and disasters and there will be no harmony and a great deal of suffering and unhappiness.
Shakyamuni Buddha like all The Buddhas understood the workings of the law of cause and effect, he also knew the potential in each human life for destruction.
We have this situation happening today and something is missing. That thing that is in fact the link between all things unseen or spiritual and all things seen or physical is the law of life and the universe itself which is Nam Myoho Renge Kyo.

Changing Poison into Medicine

If you look at nature you do not see this chaos and destruction going on.
You see amazing things occurring in nature, fantastic natural advances, in the way each myriad form of life grows.
What is more amazing than that?
Incredibly enough this unbelievable myriad of life forms, of natural occurrences, works in complete balance and harmony with the whole of our natural world.
It is only humanity, with our own free will, our own ability to think and judge who is not working in that way.
This is because humanity does not understand that there is a link between those two aspects of life, Ku and Ke.
Ku the spiritual or the unseen part of life and Ke, life's physical manifestations in all the myriad phenomena we see around us.
That linking point which exists, and you can prove exists in nature, is the third of The Three Truths of existence, that expressed as Chu.
Chu is The Middle Way or Nam Myoho Renge Kyo.
Chu is the Buddha state.
The Buddha state that is vitally progressive, dynamic and yet at the same time is totally harmonious.
Chu is represented by The Dai Gohonzon of Nam Myoho Renge Kyo which Nichiren Daishonin inscribed.
Therefore if you bring your life back to the prime point of Chu, regularly, throughout your life, day in, day out, then you will always come to the path of The Middle Way.
The path of balance, the path that is in no sense a compromise.
The path which is a path of dynamic advance with total natural balance and harmony.
This is what Chu is.
This is what The Dai Gohonzon of Nam Myoho Renge Kyo represents.
This is what exists in every single human life, yet sadly we cannot see it and do not yet understand it.
This is what The Buddha of this age, Nichiren Daishonin, through his wisdom, compassion and courage, worked to reveal by inscribing Dai Gohonzon for the enlightenment of all living beings and that of course includes us and all of humanity living here on our one and only Planet Earth.

The Recitation of The Lotus Sutra or Gongyo.

Changing Poison into Medicine

I hope through this section of the book, those of you who have started to learn Gongyo, or those of you who have never done Gongyo, will get some idea of the purpose of our doing what sounds like something that is very difficult indeed, but actually once you have got into the rhythm of it, becomes a joy.
Learning Gongyo is rather like learning to ride a bicycle, to begin with you teeter about and find it very difficult, but suddenly everything seems to click into place if you really persevere.
If you are struggling to learn Gongyo right now, or if you are looking at The Liturgy Book and thinking "how am I ever going to learn it," or you're thinking, "I don't think I can ever do this practice of Buddhism, if I have got to learn a thing like that."
What I can promise you is that what has happened to everyone else is that you really do reach a point after about two months of doing it slowly and steadily when suddenly something just seems to click in your life, and you find yourself in rhythm.
It is exactly like learning to ride a bicycle.
Gongyo is an incredibly powerful form of prayer.
Let us look at what Nichiren Daishonin said about practice to The Gohonzon in.

Reply to Lady Nichinyo.

"Never seek this Gohonzon outside yourself.
This Gohonzon exists within the mortal flesh of us ordinary people who embrace The Lotus Sutra and chant Nam Myoho Renge Kyo.
To be endowed with The Ten Worlds, means that all The Ten Worlds without exception are contained within the one world of Buddhahood, only with faith can one enter Buddhahood".

Faith in Nichiren Shoshu Buddhism is action.
Action to practice exactly as The Buddha taught and the practice of Gongyo is exactly what The Buddha taught us to do.
If we do Gongyo day in and day out, we will find that with the other two practices of teaching others and study, we will in this lifetime attain enlightenment or Buddhahood.
The very practice of Gongyo is to gradually open the door to your Buddha state, your Buddha nature.
When Nichiren Daishonin stated.

"Never seek this Gohonzon outside yourself.
This Gohonzon exists within the flesh of us ordinary people who embrace The Lotus Sutra and chant Nam Myoho Renge Kyo".

Changing Poison into Medicine

He means that when you practice to The Gohonzon, what you are in fact doing is entering it, or fusing your life with it.

You come to realise that your life is The Gohonzon and that The Dai Gohonzon that was inscribed by Nichiren Daishonin is a mirror of your life itself.

The purpose of this practice called Gongyo is to enter The Gohonzon.

Over months and years of doing it, you gradually open the doors of your life and realise that you also, just as The Buddha promised, possess the Buddha state, the highest state of human life.

In achieving this state, we have to purify our life and put it in balance and rhythm.

Looking at it from a shallower point of view, the purpose of our daily Gongyo is to put our life in perfect balance and rhythm.

Practicing Gongyo is like digging a pipeline down through your life into its depths where the Buddha nature lies.

When you are learning Gongyo, struggling with it every day and giving up your precious time in order to learn it, you are digging that pipeline down through all the layers of your life until finally you hit the Buddha nature.

Once you do that it is then necessary to keep the pipeline open and that is what the daily practice is all about.

To purify your life everyday so that the pipeline to Buddhahood is pure and clean and the great qualities of Buddhahood which are compassion, wisdom, life force and courage, can actually flow freely and cleanly through your life.

Having done the practice of Gongyo, you then carry out the fundamental practice of Nichiren Shoshu Buddhism, which is to chant The Daimoku, Nam Myoho Renge Kyo over and over again, which is called the practice of Shodai.

By the time you are chanting Shodai, after completing Gongyo, your life is perfectly in balance and purified and therefore your great prayers as you chant, will propel themselves outwards and inwards with the maximum effect.

The Gyo of Gongyo means practice and the Gon of Gongyo means assiduous or eager or endeavouring strongly, striving hard, all those things can be meant by the character that is pronounced Gon.

Gongyo is assiduous practice, or practice involving strong endeavour or eager and enthusiastic practice.

Gongyo means 'Let's Go!'

Gongyo and its formula is entirely based on the law of cause and effect.

Changing Poison into Medicine

Through the great effort to do this assiduous practice and your
determination to do it well, you make an incredibly pure cause
which will bring an incredibly pure effect or benefit into your life.
Cause and effect are exactly related to each other.
You do something great and something great will occur and
return to you.
You do something destructive and something destructive will
return to you.
Gongyo is the very purest cause you can make.
You give up your time, maybe you have to get up an hour earlier
in the morning to do it, that takes effort, but it brings incredible
rewards.
Nothing is free in this life; we have to work for everything.
If you are going to win a race or play a sport well or be an expert
in any particular field of science or the arts, you have to work at it.
If you want to attain the highest state of human life and be
happy then you will have to work for it and that work is the
practice of Gongyo and chanting Shodai or Nam Myoho Renge
Kyo.
How did this all begin?
How was this practice of Gongyo conjured up in the wisdom of
The Buddha?
It started with Nichiren Daishonin himself.
Nichiren Daishonin said that we should first of all read, recite and
chant, two chapters of The Lotus Sutra, which were the key
chapters in which the meaning of the whole of the sutra was
contained.
They are the second chapter, called The Hoben Chapter and the
sixteenth chapter called The Juryo chapter, part of which, and
only a part of which, we recite in Gongyo.
These are the key words of The Lotus Sutra.
Nichiren Daishonin said that if you recite the Hoben and Juryo
chapters it is as if you are reciting all twenty eight chapters of The
Lotus Sutra because the meaning is all contained in those two
core chapters.
Since The Lotus Sutra embraces all the other sutras that have ever
been taught by Shakyamuni in his Buddhism, all eighty eight
thousand of them, to recite the Hoben and Juryo chapters of The
Lotus Sutra is to recite all the sutras of all the Buddhas.
To recite those two chapters is embracing in your life all the
teachings of all the Buddhas since time began.
Nichiren Daishonin also said that the basic practice is chanting
Nam Myoho Renge Kyo over and over again, to your hearts
content.

Changing Poison into Medicine

With these two guidelines from Nichiren Daishonin at some time during the thirteenth or fourteenth century, no one exactly knows the actual date, The High Priest of Nichiren Shoshu decided to establish a firm practice of Gongyo which the Priests at the Head Temple would carry out daily.

This involved moving in procession from Temple to Temple within the precincts of The Head Temple itself, reciting the various prayers of Gongyo.

Each of those prayers was carried out at a different Temple.

After they had completed one prayer, they would move to the next Temple to complete the next one and each Temple had some significant relationship with the prayer itself, this is how Gongyo began.

Gongyo consists of three sections.

In the first section you chant or recite the two chapters of The Sutra and in the second section you make silent prayer, and in the third section you chant Shodai, that is to chant the Daimoku, or title of The Lotus Sutra, Nam Myoho Renge Kyo continuously.

In the morning there are five different prayers and then chanting and then conclude and in the evening, three prayers, and then chanting and then conclude.

There are three distinct parts of the practice, reciting The Sutra, saying the silent prayers, and then chanting Shodai or Nam Myoho Renge Kyo.

The purpose of this practice is to purify your life, but what is it your actually purifying?

The answer to that is that you are overcoming in the process of the practice the negativity that exists in your life.

This negativity exists inherently in every single one of us and the practice is transforming that negativity into a force for positive growth.

Changing poison into medicine.

You are overcoming in that process, desires that are shallow and selfish and broadening and widening your life into desires that create good in both your own life and in other people's lives.

You can really feel this when you do Gongyo, this process of purification, and somehow the world always does look brighter when you have completed Gongyo.

Everything is purified and all that negativity, that destructive quality which causes us so much trouble in life, is cleared in the process of Gongyo and this is why we do it twice a day.

You do Gongyo in the morning when you get up.

Through the night your life has become very muddled.

Changing Poison into Medicine

During sleep you dream, maybe you have nightmares, whatever happens, your life is always a bit of a muddle when you wake up in the morning.
Sometimes you can have the most negative of thoughts when you are making your ablutions or making your first cup of tea or coffee.
After that muddle that has occurred whilst you sleep, you need to purify your life again and get it into balance.
We can really feel off balance when we get out of bed and get up in the morning, so the purpose of Gongyo is to immediately put your life back into balance once again.
In the evening we have come back home maybe from a day's work, maybe there have been many problems, difficulties and obstacles, people getting angry and irritated.
The rush and the pressure all around you in daily life.
We need to put our life into balance again in order to spend an enjoyable and constructive evening and go to sleep happily.
Evening Gongyo means evening, not good night Gongyo.
It should be done in the evening while you are still reasonably fresh.
If you perform it just before you go to bed, then you are droopy and tired, all you really feel like is getting into your bed and going to sleep.
It is an evening practice conducted depending on people's lifestyle, which is normally done anywhere between 4.00pm and 8.00 or 9.00pm in the evening.
What is this pipeline that I am digging down into my life?
What is this process?
What am I digging this pipeline down through?
Nichiren Shoshu Buddhism teaches that we have nine distinct levels of consciousness, which you have to go through, in order to reach the ninth, which is the state or consciousness of the Buddha nature.
The first five are very simple, your ordinary senses of hearing, seeing, tasting, smelling and touch.
The sixth consciousness is your thinking mind, any psychiatrist will agree with this so far.
The seventh consciousness is the first layer of your sub conscious.
That is the area of your desires, in other words, your ego.
Nichiren Shoshu Buddhism teaches the importance of desire.
Some religions try to deny desire, but desire is an inevitable part of life, and it is an important part of life because it is a driving force, therefore Nichiren Shoshu Buddhism follows the principle of transforming earthly desires into enlightenment.

Through your great effort to fulfil your desires you chant Nam Myoho Renge Kyo, which in turn is so strong a force that inevitably it brings you into the Buddha state.

Even if your desires are wrongly directed in a way that could harm you or others, they will be turned, through the process of chanting, into a positive direction.

Those desires arise out of the seventh consciousness, and below that lies the eighth consciousness, which is a vast area.

Often it has been said that the sub consciousness and the conscious areas of life are like the tip of an iceberg compared to the huge area under the water.

The sub conscious is enormous, in fact it is universal.

The eighth consciousness or the subconscious is called in western psychology the collective unconscious and is the area which all your experiences of all your whole eternal life are stored.

If at one time the entity which is you went through the stage of swimming in the sea and then developing little legs and crawling up onto the mud and eventually evolving some sort of body that could withstand life on land, all those memories are there.

The memory of your babyhood, the memory of when you were in your mother's womb, everything is stored in that amazing area of the eighth consciousness so you can understand therefore that this is the area where your karma or destiny is stored.

All the effects of all the causes that you have ever made in your eternal life are contained in the huge ocean of the eighth consciousness.

This is very much a shared consciousness.

It is the shared consciousness of the entire human race and all the other myriad forms of life, all of which is contained in this vast, fathomless area of the universal mind.

It is no wonder our dreams are such a muddle.

We are drawing in our dreams on that eighth consciousness on the memories and things that have happened to us in the remotest past as well as in the near past.

Then finally deep below that lies the ninth consciousness, which is the original, pure universal consciousness.

The consciousness, which is shared with everything in the whole universe, the Buddha consciousness or Buddha nature.

The universe that exists in us, in our oneness with the universe.

The great universe itself is the ninth consciousness that is called in Japanese, Amala Shiki, the fundamental pure sense or the purifying source of all life.

The pure essence of life shared by every living thing or Myoho Renge Kyo, the greater self, whereas the seventh consciousness, the area of the ego, is the lesser self.

Changing Poison into Medicine

Unless we understand and tap into this ninth consciousness, human life is inevitably at the mercy of the eight and seventh consciousnesses.

Those who understand psychology and are experts in that field, are fully aware of the seventh and eighth consciousnesses and the way it effects our lives but up to the present day they are not aware of the ninth.

The purpose of practicing Nichiren Shoshu Buddhism is to plumb the depths of your life to the ninth consciousness.

All that radiates from that fundamental level of being will then filter through the seventh and eight consciousnesses, purifying it on the way, which will lead you to carry out thoughts, words and deeds which are wholly positive and harmonious.

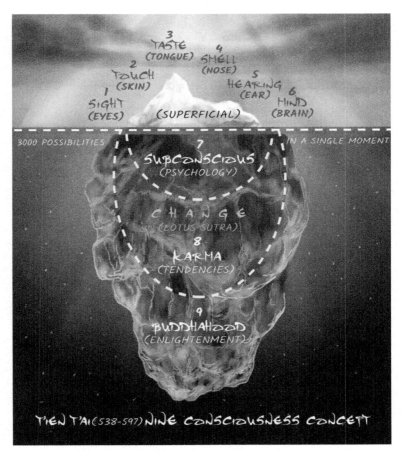

Changing Poison into Medicine

In a very theoretical way that again is what is happening when you perform Gongyo.

Quite often you will find that when you begin to do Gongyo you may feel uncomfortable, you may start to fidget.

Maybe you scratch your head or go to look at your smart phone, you may even feel irritable and angry or whatever.

That is because at that point your pushing your way down through the senses.

From the first to the fifth, to the sixth and then through the seventh and eighth consciousness and after a while your concentration seems to improve.

You seem to be really totally absorbed in Gongyo.

Then your Buddha state is revealed in Gongyo and continues to be revealed throughout your chanting of Shodai or Nam Myoho Renge Kyo.

When you get up and go outside and find you have to queue for twenty minutes for the bus you may rapidly find yourself leaving the Buddha state and going into some other state of life.

But the fact is the more you practice the more that will not happen and the longer you will stay in the Buddha state throughout the day and your actions will reveal that too.

Gongyo is a daily battle with the negative and destructive forces that are absolutely inherent in every single human life.

It is a battle against the lower worlds and a great struggle to turn everything in your life from negative to a positive experience.

For this reason you can understand that Gongyo must not be too easy, neither of course, must it be too difficult because we all have normal daily lives to lead.

Gongyo must be difficult enough to cause us to make effort because unless we make effort, we are not going to defeat that negative force which is so strong in our lives.

And yet it has got to be easy enough for us to fit into our daily programme.

It is an amazing practice in this sense because you can fit it into your daily life, if you really have a mind to do so.

When I first started to practice this Buddhism, I did not think it was possible for me to do Gongyo.

Not because I believed that I could not do it, but because I thought I was such a busy person.

I thought I couldn't possibly find the time in my schedule to do Gongyo twice a day and chant Shodai as well.

Then someone who had practiced a long time said to me,

Changing Poison into Medicine

"I do understand your feelings but please remember that the practice of Gongyo and Shodai activates your wisdom, so you will find you are using your time more wisely."

This has really proved to be true.
When I managed to fit in Gongyo and Shodai it seemed to me that sometimes I did twice as much in the day as I had done previously as I did not waste any time and I used every minute wisely the more and more that I practiced.
Gongyo for those of you who feel "have I really got to do this every day?"
Gongyo is meant to be difficult if it was not difficult it would be useless.
Gongyo is the great effort needed to change your life tendencies from negative to positive.
To change poison into medicine.
The more you get used to doing it, the more you get to see what you need to change before you even start Gongyo.
As you begin you get up and get ready to start it and your aware of yourself "wow I feel really irritable this morning" or "I feel so lethargic today, right so by the end of this Gongyo I have to change," that is the attitude, and it will change.
Reciting the Sutra is not prayer it is an exercise.
We are taught to recite it rhythmically, to pronounce each syllable correctly and clearly and to be firm and vigorous as we do it.
This is the exercise by which you begin to purify your life.
If you slur it or recite it in a slovenly way, or if you are not alert, then of course the effect will be that much less.
The Lotus Sutra has the deepest meaning, and it is very important that it should have a deep meaning otherwise you would get fed up with it after doing it for a couple of years but the very fact that it takes you many, many, many, years to fully understand every line of those chapters of The Lotus Sutra, means that you can never become bored with what you are saying.
It is also significant that what you are saying is in fact the very essence and core of the whole of The Buddhist Canon or teachings.
It has an immense meaning, and you can always keep your interest in it by trying to understand more and more what the words mean but in fact if you do not even understand what any of the words mean it still has an effect.
Gongyo is an exercise, an exercise of practising Gongyo, rhythmically and clearly.

Changing Poison into Medicine

This reciting of The Sutra leading up towards your silent prayers and your chanting of Nam Myoho Renge Kyo or Shodai is purifying your life more and more every day.
Gongyo is like the run up before you actually leap over the high jump.
You have to run and make more and more effort, you can then achieve your victory by going over the top of the jump.
In the words of the Juryo chapter the sixteenth chapter that we recite its says:

"Isshin yokken butsu, Fuji shaku shinmyo."

Those words mean:

"In my great desire to see The Buddha appear in my life, I do not begrudge it in the least".

This is really the spirit of Gongyo.
It is your desire to advance and open up and develop the highest state of your life, so you do not begrudge the time it takes to do Gongyo, and you put your utmost into it.
The Hoben chapter, which is the first chapter you recite, is really the theory of the mechanics of life and of the existence of the state of Buddha in it and in every human life.
The Juryo chapter is Shakyamuni Buddha's own experience of Buddhahood and the eternity of life.
The fact that we recite the Hoben chapter is expressing our praise of The Buddha's wisdom and of our expectation of revealing the same wisdom in ourselves.
Reciting the Juryo chapter is again praise for all that we have learnt through The Buddha's experience, first through Shakyamuni's experience and then above all else Nichiren Daishonin's experience and our expectation of being able to experience the same enlightenment as him.
Reciting The Lotus Sutra, although it is an exercise, is also praise.
We are praising the wisdom of The Buddha's in teaching life to us.
Through reciting the Lotus Sutra we honour, we praise, and we express our gratitude.
Gongyo is really a ceremony of gratitude.
Gratitude is an area of life which if you have not got a key to it, causes you to miss an immense part of the joy and happiness in this world.
Gratitude opens the door of a huge area of your life that you have never realised before.

Changing Poison into Medicine

Gongyo is very much a ceremony of gratitude for life itself and especially for your own life.
The Lotus Sutra is really an incredible teaching.
It is set on a stage which is far beyond the confines of this world or our particular environment here on Planet Earth.
It is set on a universal stage as it talks in terms of the universe itself.
It expresses things in terms of aeons and light years and the eternity of life and the boundlessness of the universe.
It is not concerned with time or space.
The more you perform Gongyo the more you feel that connection with the great vast universe.
You feel less and less confined by time and space as we know it.
You feel the ability of your life and its achievements to expand far beyond your earlier imagination.
Since this is concerned with the rhythm of life itself, it is very dynamic.
This rhythm or energy or life force, which makes the tides ebb and flow, and the seasons change, and the Earth move around the Sun and causes the winds to blow, is an incredibly dynamic force.
The rhythm of life is in itself vigorous and vibrant, therefore your recitation of The Lotus Sutra should also be vigorous and vibrant.
It is not supposed to be recited in a slurred, slow and funeral like pace, it should be at the speed of a galloping horse.
It takes time to get to that sort of rhythm and it will come to you when you have been practicing for a while.
This does not take so long, just a matter of a few months.
The practice of Gongyo is to revitalise your life force for the day, every day.
In Nichiren Shoshu Buddhism there is the teaching of The Three Acts of Body, Mouth and Heart.
Gongyo is the act of the body that you place in front of The Gohonzon and start to practice, through this you are giving your body to the practice.
The act of the mouth is of course the words that come out from it, do those words really ring out firmly?
If you are giving your mouth to The Buddha, they should be firm and strong and vibrant.
It does not mean they should be shouted, and it does not mean they should be whispered.
They should be firm and clear, and as you chant to The Gohonzon, the vibrations of your voice should travel out to The Gohonzon, so that they return back to you and then go out into the universe.
A firm, clear, steady voice, this is the act of giving your mouth.

The act of giving your heart.

This of course is the most important of all and this is where gratitude comes in once again.

The very effort of performing Gongyo is expressing your gratitude, expressing your faith in what The Buddha taught because you are actually carrying out what he said you should do.

This gratitude, this desire to do it no matter what, even if you are feeling lousy when you get up, that is really the act of giving your heart.

In that giving you should clear your mind of any slander or hatred or any ill feelings about anybody, and in the process of reciting The Lotus Sutra you will find an amazing way that will make that happen.

The Silent Prayers in Japanese are Go Kannen Mon.

Go is the honorific prefix as in Gohonzon or the honourable.

Mon means passage or a sentence, and Kannen means concentration of the mind or meditation with a purpose of attaining enlightenment.

The purpose of The Silent Prayers of Gongyo is to concentrate your whole life on whatever that particular silent prayer is about. This is not just reading.

Of course you do read the silent prayers to refresh your mind on the words and their meaning and even if you can recite the whole of Gongyo without the liturgy book, you should still read the silent prayers, because it is very difficult to concentrate without taking in each word.

It is not just reading, it is living what you read with your whole life.

In Nichiren Shoshu Buddhism, the silent prayers are a daily refreshment, first of your gratitude for being alive and for the benefits which the practice is bringing you and then your determination to clear your life of your unhappy, negative karma and in the process, make other people in your environment happy.

The recitation of The Lotus Sutra is an exercise to put your life in rhythm and balance so that when you come to do the silent prayers your life is purified and that they have the greatest possible effect.

That is to bring up and refresh your whole determination to carve out a better life for yourself and others in the future.

The First Silent Prayer of Gongyo is to the Shoten Zenjin or the forces of the universe.

There are a myriad forces that are at work in the universe which can either work with us, protecting us, or ignoring us, depending upon how positive or negative our life state is.

Changing Poison into Medicine

The purpose of the first silent prayer is to refresh your gratitude for the protection you have received up to the present and for the determination to practice strongly again in order to continue that protection in the future and in the process feed and strengthen those forces that are created by the very rhythm of life in order to produce a happy and harmonious world.

Through our efforts to be in rhythm, we are feeding these forces, and if we do not feed them they can leave us and leave our environment.

This is the purpose of the first silent prayer, for those forces to work through other people in our environment to help us, those forces of the universe working within another person to support us.

There are many different forms of this, all of which are forces outside of and beyond this planet which exist in the universe itself, which have a direct effect on our life here.

The Second Silent Prayer in Gongyo concerns gratitude to the Dai Gohonzon which it explains in its many virtues and is an expression of gratitude for the power of the Dai Gohonzon working in your life bringing benefits to yourself and others.

These virtues may be difficult to understand in the beginning of your practice but the more you study and the more you practice and get experience of the workings of the Dai Gohonzon and Nam Myoho Renge Kyo in your life, the more you will understand each one.

The Third Silent Prayer of Gongyo is again concerned with gratitude and is a series of thankyou's to all the people who have brought you to Dai Gohonzon and have brought you Nam Myoho Renge Kyo and have opened your eyes to the law of life or the ultimate truth.

Starting with Nichiren Daishonin and going on from there to Nikko Shonin who succeeded him and to Nichimoku Shonin and all the High Priests of Nichiren Shoshu who over centuries have protected The Great Pure Law and its teachings down through time until the present day.

The Fourth Silent Prayer is for determination to work for your own enlightenment and to overcome your negative, unhappy karma and to elevate your life state so you can create and contribute to a more peaceful world and rid yourself of the destructive elements within your life which could otherwise cause unhappiness and chaos.

It is also for the whole movement for world peace or Kosen Rufu, so we can teach others and they can then also teach others thus expanding the revolution within people's lives and this is when we also say our personal prayers.

Changing Poison into Medicine

The Fifth and Final Silent Prayer in Gongyo is when we remember our ancestors and the people who have died who have had some particular connection to us.
This is very important.
We send concentrated prayer and Shodai to those who are deceased, especially family who have a very close life link to us and through that we keep the life link between us and them and we purify that link every time we send prayer and Shodai to them. This helps to project them on through the state of death to their new life.
Those are the silent prayers of Gongyo explained briefly and each one has tremendous meaning and then finally after doing those five prayers in the morning or three of them in the evening you start to chant Shodai.
So why five prayers in the morning and three in the evening?
The answer to that is The First Silent Prayer is for the protective forces in the universe or the Buddhist Shoten Zenjin should be at the dawn of the day.
Some of us do not always get up at the dawn of the day, but that is the reason behind it.
We face east as the sun rises and as the forces of the universe begin to work through another day, we should put our life into rhythm with those forces.
In the evening we have already been through the day and done morning Gongyo, so our practice does not have to be quite so assiduous in the evening.
We have already mentioned The Three Acts of Body, Mouth and Heart and of course these apply to chanting Nam Myoho Renge Kyo during Gongyo.
It should be firm, clear and resonant to be really effective and Kyo is sound or vibration.
A firm voice does not need enormous volume but should be very firm and concise and should hit The Gohonzon and come back to you, so you connect directly to The Gohonzon.
So as you chant Nam Myoho Renge Kyo and to pray to see the Buddha in your life, to become a happier person and say prayers for yourself and others, maybe for the peace of the world, for others to grow in faith and for others to meet the Dai Gohonzon.
In that process your prayers will bring you everything you need for your happiness and enlightenment.
Being human we cannot help but sometimes concentrate our minds and prayer on our own personal difficulties and this is quite reasonable to do so but it should not absorb your whole mind.
You can become to absorbed with your own particular problem or difficulty but like all things if you become obsessed or absorbed

by them, it will become magnified in your mind and it will seem impossible to overcome.

If you are really practicing as The Buddha taught, that is to say practice for yourself and practice for others then your problem whatever it may be will take its right shape and size in your mind and you will find it remarkably easy to overcome.

This is an important point.

We practice in Japanese Jigyo and Keta, which translates as practice for oneself and practice for others.

If you neglect others and become absorbed with yourself you will get a form of indigestion, or stagnation because your problem will become vast in your mind whereas in fact it is not vast in relation to the power of Dai Gohonzon.

This is a very important point.

You must chant to your hearts content.

It is chanting until you feel like you have chanted enough. It is a feeling in your own life, have I chanted enough, honestly?

Yes, I have, OK that is enough, or no I haven't so I will chant more, perhaps another five or ten minutes.

There are times when one Daimoku is enough and yet there are times when ten thousand is not enough.

It depends on so many things.

Your state of life when you begin to chant, the hugeness of your problem, the depth of the negative karma you want to change, so many different factors, each one of us is different.

As a general rule or guideline on average you need to chant about three thousand Daimoku a day, that is a steady flow everyday of about forty five minutes to an hour of Shodai.

That is the ideal and if you can keep that going consistently, year in, year out, that's much better than doing a sporadic practice.

Nichiren Daishonin said practice should be like flowing water, so that steady rhythm of practice is the most important thing of all and there is no rule about how much Shodai we should chant.

We should chant to our hearts content.

Listen to your wisdom, chant until you feel joy.

If you stop in the middle and are still worried and anxious about your life, then that would be ineffective, so chant until you feel better, until you feel joy rising up from the depths of your life, the very core and heart of your being.

So chanting Nam Myoho Renge Kyo is the final triumphant act of an amazing ceremony which the more you do it the more you feel its significance in your life.

Changing Poison into Medicine

Nichiren Daishonin said.

"When you bow to the mirror, the image in the mirror bows back to you".

The mirror he is referring to is The Gohonzon.
The mirror which reflects your Buddha state.
The Buddha state in your life will be working with you through the mirror of the Buddha state inscribed on The Gohonzon.
This practice of Gongyo affects you, yourself and activates the Buddha state and allows your wisdom and compassion to flow.
At the same time through the character Kyo it flows out into your environment and affects the Buddha state in every single thing in your entire environment and beyond into the whole universe.
At first it is difficult to believe but the more and more you do it, you will prove it to yourself.
Our attitude in Gongyo should be strong, vigorous, and upright.
We have to make effort from the moment we begin.
Our whole life state will reflect the way we do Gongyo.
If you miss Gongyo one morning, do not feel guilty, do a better one tomorrow morning.
If you find yourself getting into the habit of missing Gongyo, then I recommend you get into the habit of doing it wherever you can at some point during the day.
Above all do not feel guilty about it.
If you missed it, there is nothing you can do about it, you cannot bring that time back, so take it in your stride and determine to do a better one the next day.
Nichiren Daishonin wrote in a Gosho called "Honin Myo Sho"

"The common mortal themself is The Buddha when they devote their lives to Nam Myoho Renge Kyo by chanting with strong faith they attain enlightenment or Buddhahood in this world without discarding their life as a common mortal."

The purpose of the practice of Gongyo as instructed or taught by the Buddha of this age Nichiren Daishonin, is to achieve Buddhahood exactly as he said in this Gosho, without discarding our life as a common mortal.

Rissho Ankoku Ron.

Changing Poison into Medicine

Rissho Ankoku Ron is usually translated as:

'On Securing The Peace of The Land Through The Propagation of True Buddhism.'

This is one of the most important writings of Nichiren Daishonin and is known as his will and testament.
Nikko Shonin who inherited all of Nichiren Daishonin's teachings and became the second High Priest of Nichiren Shoshu, said that Nichiren Daishonin's teachings began with Rissho Ankoku Ron and ended with Rissho Ankoku Ron.
The more you study this writing and follow it, the more you understand this.
Rissho Ankoku Ron is totally relevant to the existential crisis and problems that are happening in our world today.
It was written about the problems and ills of the smaller world of Japan in medieval times in the thirteenth century.
Today it is now totally applicable globally to the whole of Planet Earth.
It concerns the solutions to the problems that threaten our existence today and cause people throughout the world immense suffering, such as wars, violence, vandalism, famines, the destruction of the natural environment, global warming and the current climate crisis, also global pandemics, such as we are currently experiencing with the Covid 19 pandemic, all caused through greed, ignorance and the spiritual pollution and corruption of human beings and of life itself.
Nichiren Shoshu Buddhism views this as the fruits of 'The Three Poisons' of anger, greed and stupidity or ignorance, which arise from the fundamental darkness inherent in life and which fill the world in this current age.
When you observe the world now, war and violence is rife.
There is a continuing threat of war and proxy wars between the superpowers of China and America and their political machinations on the planet.
Huge sums of money are being spent by all the major governments of the world in preparation for nothing else but war.
Yet at least one third of the world has insufficient food to eat to sustain a proper active life.
And even now the nuclear race continues with development of new types of nuclear weapons, called tactical nuclear weapons, adding to the already vast stockpiles that the nuclear nations hold onto in fear, the United Kingdom being one of those nations.
And now in the 21st century that threat of war has now gone beyond the planet and has even reached into space.

Changing Poison into Medicine

This is one of the greatest threats that could be imagined to our continued existence and sometimes feels that it is completely out of control.
Adding to this situation there is another existential threat to humanity in the form of environmental degradation and the effects of globalization in the form of rampant consumerism and materialism which has led to the consequence of global warming and the current climate crisis.
This is the terrible and frightening position that humanity faces at this moment in history and the evolution of our species.
If we leave this up to the leaders or politicians we seem destined to be passive bystanders and voyeurs of our own imminent self destruction.
Our task as Nichiren Shoshu Buddhists is to build and establish an overwhelming force for peace and harmony and this force has to be strong and powerful enough to hold the balance in the world.
It has to be powerful enough to stop human beings from going even more insane and doing even more and more, ignorant, absurd, and ultimately self destructive things.

Rissho Ankoku Ron could easily be translated as:

'On Securing the Peace of The World through The Propagation of True Buddhism.'

It is the foundation of all our activities as Nichiren Shoshu Buddhists as we strive through self transformation to create a peaceful and harmonious planet.
We should understand this writing and do our utmost to engrave the teachings in this remarkable thesis of The Original Buddha of Time Without Beginning, Nichiren Daishonin, in the very depths of our lives at the heart and core of our being.
This writing becomes over time, more and more relevant to the precarious situation humanity now finds itself in in this Anthropocene age that we have been born into today.
This year 2021 is the 800th anniversary of the appearance on our planet of Nichiren Daishonin and is of great significance as we move into the next phase of Kosen Rufu or the widespread propagation of Nichiren Shoshu Buddhism throughout the entire world, so it encompasses the entire Planet.
We have to move forward basing our actions on Rissho Ankoku Ron.
Why did Nichiren Daishonin write this important treatise?

Changing Poison into Medicine

Nichiren Daishonin declared his teaching of Nam Myoho Renge Kyo on the 28th April 1253 and it was only three years later, in between 1256 and 1261, that the worst series of natural disasters that had ever been known in all of Japanese history occurred. 1256 itself was an especially terrible year.

It was the culmination of a succession of natural disasters, which began not long after the great period of history in Japan called The Heian Period, a period of great peace and prosperity and culture.

A period based, in fact, on the theoretical understandings of The Lotus Sutra when the Tien Tai (Jap: Tendai) School of Buddhism rose to prominence in Japan.

After that period ended, Buddhism became fragmented in Japan and these terrible disasters began to occur.

Epidemics of huge extent, earthquakes, huge powerful storms and typhoons, droughts and fires, and intense cold spells during winter.

The people, through this, were in absolute desperation and agony and death was literally everywhere.

It is beyond our imagination really, living as we do in a so called prosperous western society.

Before Nichiren Daishonin declared Nam Myoho Renge Kyo in 1253, he had spent fourteen years studying all the various Buddhist sutras that were available in all the various schools and temples in Japan in his day.

His purpose was to discover why was it that if Buddhism was the true teaching, why were the people of Japan suffering so intensely.

This was his period of preparation but when Nichiren Daishonin saw these disasters coming to a head in 1256 he determined he must take concrete action to save the people from their sufferings and felt he must remonstrate with the government and the religious authorities and try to enlighten them to his teachings.

To make them understand the only teaching with the power to save Japan and to rectify the dreadful situation of The Nation at that time was Nam Myoho Renge Kyo.

In that age it was a feudal society, and the sovereign of the nation was not the people as it is now in western democracies. The sovereign was The Emperor and in that time in Japan The Emperor was only a puppet and Japan was ruled by a Samurai government (The Kamakura Shogunate) who controlled the people very strictly.

Nichiren Daishonin knew that he must go directly to The Samurai rulers and try to convince them.

Changing Poison into Medicine

This courageous man all on his own at the time, with very few followers, who had this incredible determination in his life to challenge the ruling powers of that time in Japan which happened to be one of the most violent and ruthless military dictatorships in the history of humankind, the newly created Japanese Shogunate of The Samurai.

First of all, before he took this brave and courageous course of action and confrontation, he wanted to get his references absolutely right in stating his case to the government in order to show it was in the direct, correct and orthodox line of Buddhism that the people should chant Nam Myoho Renge Kyo.

He set off in 1258 to a Temple called Jisso Ji, which is not too far from where The Head Temple of Nichiren Shoshu is today.

Here he spent two years preparing and framing his case and making sure it was correctly annotated to all the Buddhist Scriptures.

During this period of his life, while he was there, he met Nikko Shonin who was a young acolyte who became his disciple and stayed with him from that time onwards throughout all his lifelong persecutions.

Then he returned to the relatively new seat of government, which was in Kamakura and on the 16th July 1260 he submitted his great thesis Rissho Ankoku Ron to the government represented by the most powerful man in Japan at that time who was called Hojo Tokiyori.

Hojo Tokiyori was actually a retired regent but behind the scenes was the ultimate power.

At that time Nichiren Daishonin was only 39 years old, and seven years had now passed since he first declared Nam Myoho Renge Kyo.

Nichiren Daishonin knew that if his great exhortation failed he would inevitably suffer intense persecution and oppression.

He had no doubt about that whatsoever, but he felt he must do everything in his life to try to make the government see sense and through that to help the people to see sense.

This effort on his part rose out of his great compassion and so he challenged the entire establishment of the nation of Japan.

Just a month after he had presented the thesis to Hojo Tokiyori the first attack on his life occurred.

He lived in a small cottage in the outskirts of Kamakura in a place called Matsugbagayatsu and the cottage was attacked by followers of the Nembutsu or The Pure Land sect, who had been provoked by the authorities to do so.

They tried to kill him and burn his cottage down to the ground, but fortunately he escaped.

Changing Poison into Medicine

This was the sign that Hojo Tokiyori had ignored his warning.
By the 12th May of the next year he was already in exile.
His first exile was on the Izu Peninsula, but two years later Hojo
Tokiyori died and eight years later Nichiren Daishonin's prediction
in Rissho Ankoku Ron that inevitably. if things continued as they
were, Japan would suffer from a foreign invasion actually took
place when The Mongols sent their first delegation to Japan from
Kublai Khan, demanding Japan's subjugation to their rule.
Japan refused this but it threw the nation into a great panic and
six years later The Mongols attacked Kyushu Island.
All Nichiren Daishonin's persecutions, culminating in the attempt
to behead him on Tatsunokuchi beach and the subsequent exile
to that grim place Sado Island had begun from when he wrote
and presented the Rissho Ankoku Ron.
Why should this writing have such a great effect?
Nichiren Daishonin had already declared The Three Great Secret
Laws of Nichiren Shoshu Buddhism and Rissho Ankoku Ron was
really the description of the action from understanding and
practicing those Three Great Secret Laws.
The action that would take place within the individual self, within
society, and in the land itself, which are known as 'The Three
Realms of Existence' in Buddhism.
Rissho Ankoku Ron is the reason or the basis of why Kosen Rufu is
essential for the happiness and wellbeing of all people
everywhere.
Although he submitted it to Hojo Tokiyori, in fact behind Hojo
Tokiyori there are all the leaders down through history.
He was addressing everybody who is ignorant of the true
meaning of life and especially to the leaders and those who
follow them.
This is why Rissho Ankoku Ron will never become out of date.
It is as valid today as it was yesterday and will be as valid
tomorrow until Kosen Rufu is achieved and maintained.
It is as valid for Mr Joe Biden and Mr Boris Johnson as it will be for
their successors, as it was for Hojo Tokiyori.
The whole purpose of our efforts in unity together is to carry these
teachings forward and to make them known to as many people
as possible.
We must make sure that this heritage is transmitted to our children
and on to our children's children until Kosen Rufu is achieved.
The purpose is to save the world from destruction.
It is not in the true nature of things that this world should destroy
itself.
This world has a purpose in the universe as a whole and it is the
very task of 'The Bodhisattvas of The Earth' and their followers to

make sure that this world is not destroyed through disseminating or spreading the ultimate truth of life.

The writing of this thesis, since it gives the argument or the basis of debate on this subject, was a monumental cause to make.

It had, of course, a monumental effect.

All the negative forces of life tried in every way possible to stop this movement from beginning and especially this negative force was felt in Nichiren Daishonin's own life.

It manifested itself in the intense persecutions which he had to suffer from the beginning of his struggle to the very end.

In another famous Gosho, called Letter to The Brothers, Nichiren Daishonin wrote.

"If you propagate it, (Dai Gohonzon) devils will arise without fail. Where it not for these, there would be no way of knowing that this is the true teaching."

Anything that is immensely positive and progressive encounters natural opposition from the opposing negative force.

Nichiren Daishonin's teaching of Dai Gohonzon and Nam Myoho Renge Kyo has met with such opposition throughout the last 800 years, until this very day.

There are also other important points in this famous thesis which caused it to have such a great effect.

Firstly, Rissho Ankoku Ron is one of the proofs of Nichiren Daishonin's enlightenment.

His predictions that he made in this great work all came true through his understanding of Buddhism and the law of cause and effect.

Traditionally, especially in those times in medieval Japan, a Buddha's predictions coming true was proof that he was a Great (Dai) Shonin (Sage) or a Buddha.

In his turn Nichiren Daishonin had proved the predictions of Shakyamuni Buddha.

Secondly, it is the prime teaching on which all further remonstrations and debates and arguments have been based on from that time onwards.

It contains everything that is necessary to help people to understand the validity of the true teaching.

Thirdly, it was a very important public declaration of the validity and necessity of Nam Myoho Renge Kyo.

This writing or Gosho was not addressed to his followers.

It was addressed to society, represented by Hojo Tokiyori, the retired regent.

In that sense, it differs from all other Gosho.

It was written in classical Chinese in the formal way of the day and addressed to the government and through that the people. Rissho Ankoku Ron was a work of action not theory.

It is the thesis of a great Buddha, addressed to society for society's benefit.

Nichiren Daishonin develops this thesis through question and answer, and the whole of this Gosho is based on this dialogue. He sets the scene for it by a role play.

The questions are asked by a traveller who has called at the home of somebody to spend the night there as a guest, and during the course of the evening they get into a serious discussion about the state of Japan.

The host who answers the questions is Nichiren Daishonin.

In this way he is asking Hojo Tokiyori, the Regent, to stop for a moment on his journey of life and pause and think and face what was going on before he continues any further.

The traveller is a Nembutsu believer and at the time this was the fastest growing school of Buddhism in Japan.

Nembutsu or The Jodo School of Buddhism teaches a doctrine of pure escapism.

A doctrine which claimed that a person who practiced it would go to a paradise or a pure land after death.

It was saying that there is nothing you can do about the state of things as they are now and the state of your life as it is now, except to be good and chant what we tell you to chant and then you will go to the pure land after death.

Truly this school was pure opium for the people, and it spread very quickly.

Nichiren Daishonin was addressing this Gosho not only to Hojo Tokiyori but also all ignorant and misguided people who were suffering so much as a result.

He wished to prove through this Gosho that a religion is only true when it improves the lives of and gives happiness to the people, in the midst of this ordinary mundane world, in the midst of daily life and daily affairs.

There are a total of ten questions asked by the traveller.

These roughly cover three different subjects.

First of all they cover the state of Japan which we could also say now in this age, is the state of our world at this time in history.

Secondly, questions about the reasons for this situation.

Thirdly, questions which brought out the solution to the problem and how it can be transmitted into the future.

Nichiren Daishonin was following his usual sequence of preparation, revelation and transmission.

Changing Poison into Medicine

There are ten questions, but Nichiren Daishonin only gives nine answers.
The tenth question required no answer because the guest by that time had become enlightened to the truth and knew the answer himself and was determining to carry it out.
The title Rissho Ankoku Ron is important as it is in all teachings of The Buddha because the title contains the essence of everything that is in that teaching.
This title is translated as,

'On Securing the Peace of The Land Through The Propagation of True Buddhism.'
This is a slightly narrow interpretation as the actual translation of each word it would be more precise to call it:

'Thesis on Securing Peace in The Land through Establishing the Ultimate Truth.'

If we examine the title more deeply then you can see why that interpretation is more meaningful.
Chinese characters carry within them the capacity to go immensely deep in their meaning.
They can contain so many shades of meaning, an enormous amount in a very small space.
Even in the west we try to give things good titles.
The word England of course conjures up everything you know about England.
This title Rissho Ankoku Ron contains an enormous amount.
Taking the last character of all, 'Ron.'
This character means thesis, but it is a thesis concerning actuality or reality or present day conditions.
This word Ron is much more than a thesis.
It is a very important thesis, a great Buddha's thesis, addressed to society for society's benefit.
A thing of the utmost importance.
Then the words Rissho and Ankoku.
Rissho is a shortening of two characters, Ritsu and Sho, Ritsu-sho, shortened to Rissho, meaning establishing the ultimate truth and Ankoku, meaning securing peace in the land or the country or the world, or the entire Planet.
The land has no boundaries.
It could mean your hometown, or your own house, or the whole of England or the whole world.

Changing Poison into Medicine

In using this word Rissho, Nichiren Daishonin was conveying instantly something that was very important which we cannot really understand without a knowledge of the Japanese and Chinese language but learned people of those days would be concerned about it immediately.

In saying Rissho, 'establishing the ultimate truth,' he was firmly saying from the outset that the ultimate truth is not yet established, that is point number one.

Immediately to anyone who was a leader of the land this would be a shaking point from the very beginning.

It was something that would shock them.

Nichiren Daishonin is incorporating what is known as, 'The Five Fold Comparisons,' which lead to the establishment that Nam Myoho Renge Kyo is the highest most profound and the ultimate of all Buddhist Dharma or teachings.

There are five stages.

Firstly that Buddhism is more profound than other philosophies or religions.

Secondly that Mahayana Buddhism is more profound than Hinayana or Theravada Buddhism.

Thirdly that The Lotus Sutra is more profound than the pre Lotus Sutra teachings.

Fourth is that the essential teachings in The Lotus Sutra, that is chapters 15-28 are more profound than the theoretical teachings in chapters 1-14.

Fifth and finally that Nichiren Daishonin's Buddhism of Nam Myoho Renge Kyo, 'The Buddhism of the True Cause' or 'The Sowing' is therefore a deeper and a higher teaching than the Buddhism of Shakyamuni or of 'The Harvest'.

This word Rissho incorporates all that profound knowledge.

It also includes The Three Great Secret Laws.

The Three Great Secret Laws are:

1) Honmon no Daimoku: The Essential or True Invocation. (Nam Myoho Renge Kyo)

2) Honmon no Honzon: The Essential or True Object of Worship. (Dai Gohonzon)

3) Honmon no Kaidan: The Essential or True Sanctuary. (Head Temple at Taiseki-ji)

Let us first take 'Honmon no Honzon,' The Essential Object of Worship.

Sho of Rissho, means the ultimate truth.

Changing Poison into Medicine

The ultimate truth is Myo of Myoho Renge Kyo.
The Ultimate Truth or the unseen law which is called Myoho Renge Kyo is expressed and embodied in The Dai Gohonzon.
Rissho means to establish the Dai Gohonzon in the time of Mappo.
Secondly there is 'Honmon no Daimoku,' The Essential or True Invocation.
Chanting the Daimoku is faith and practice.
The motivation for us to chant is faith and the result of our chanting is to take action.
By having faith in the ultimate truth, which is Sho in Rissho, this leads to us taking action, which is based on the ultimate truth, which is establishing.
Action is the action to establish The Ultimate Truth.
By chanting Nam Myoho Renge Kyo we are establishing The Ultimate Truth in the land or the world.
First of all we establish this in our own lives and gradually as we teach others, out into society as a whole.
We are establishing the correct action and the correct way of being.
This is Sho, the ultimate truth and the action of establishing that ultimate truth.
Tien Tai said,
"That by understanding The Mystic Law, true action will follow."
This is Rissho.
Thirdly, 'Honmon no Kaidan' or The Essential Sanctuary.
Ritsu of Rissho means establishing or establishing in one place or land or world or Planet.
So Rissho means establishing The Ultimate Truth in one place and it also means 'The Sanctuary.'
The Sanctuary can be a formal one such as your Butsudan or Buddhist altar at home or The Hoando where The Dai Gohonzon is enshrined at The Head Temple, Taiseki Ji.
It can also be the land, your town, or wherever people are gathering to practice to The Gohonzon or gradually over time with the spreading of these teachings, the whole world, or the entire Planet, thus creating The Buddha's Land.
Rissho contains The Three Great Secret Laws.
In that one word or two characters, meaning that by establishing the ultimate truth and the correct practice in your life, it can change the lives of everybody.
This is what Rissho Ankoku Ron is all about.
That one person can change a whole country or indeed the whole world or even the entire Planet.

Changing Poison into Medicine

Nichiren Daishonin said in the Gosho, The True Entity of Life.

"Only I Nichiren first chanted Nam Myoho Renge Kyo, but then, two, three, and a hundred followed, chanting and teaching others.
Likewise, propagation will unfold in this way in the future, doesn't this signify emerging from the earth, at the time of Kosen Rufu the entire Japanese nation will chant Nam Myoho Renge Kyo as surely as an arrow aimed at the earth cannot miss its target."

Rissho Ankoku Ron really is the foundation for all our efforts to teach others and spread these remarkable teachings and that it is applicable not just to Japan but to the whole world, all of Planet Earth as it is today.

Let us begin with the first question in The Rissho Ankoku Ron, asked by the traveller representing the retired regent Hojo Tokiyori to the host which represents Nichiren Daishonin.

Question One.

"Once there was a traveller, who staying as a guest at the house of another, spoke these words in sorrow.

Beginning in recent years and continuing until today, we find unusual happenings in the heavens, strange occurrences on earth, famine and pestilence all filling every corner of the empire and spreading throughout the land.

Oxen and horses lie dead in the streets and the bones of the dead crowd the highways.

Over half the population have already been carried away by death and there is not a person who does not grieve for some member of their family.

During this time there have been some who putting all their faith in the 'sharp sword' of The Buddha Amida, intone this name of the lord of the Western Paradise.

Others believing that The Buddha Yakushi will 'heal all ills,' and recite the sutra that describes him as The Tathagata of the Eastern Region.

Some, putting their trust in the passage of The Lotus Sutra that says, 'Illness shall vanish at once, and he will find perpetual youth and eternal life' pay homage to the wonderful words of that sutra.

Others citing the passage in the Ninno Sutra that reads, 'The seven difficulties vanish, the seven blessings at once appear,' conduct ceremonies at which a hundred preachers expound the teachings of the Shingon sect and conduct rituals by filling five jars with water, and others who devote themselves entirely to the Zen type meditation and perceive the emptiness of all phenomena as clearly as the moon.

Some write out the names of the seven guardian spirits and paste them on a thousand gates, others paint pictures of the five mighty bodhisattvas and hang them over ten thousand thresholds, and still others pray to the gods of heaven and the deities of earth in ceremonies conducted at the four corners of the capital and on the four boundaries of the nation.

Others taking pity on the plight of the common people, make certain that government on the national and local levels is carried out in a benevolent manner.

But despite all these efforts, they merely exhaust themselves in vain.

Famine and disease rage more fiercely than ever, beggars are everywhere in sight, and scenes of death fill our eyes.

Cadavers pile up in mounds like observation platforms, dead bodies lie side by side like planks on a bridge.

If we look about, we see that the sun and moon continue to move in their accustomed orbits, and the five planets follow the proper course.
The Three Treasures of Buddhism continue to exist, and the period of five hundred reigns, during which the Bodhisattva Hachiman vowed to protect the nation, has not yet expired.
Then why is it that the world has already fallen into decline and that the laws of the state have come to an end?
What mistake has been made, what error has been committed?"

This first question sets out fairly briefly but very dramatically the intense sufferings of the people of that time.
It shows how both the people, and their leaders were groping about wildly in ignorance and darkness trying to find a solution, but they failed, nothing was effective.
Their prayers, their rituals, their ceremonies carried out according to all the religious beliefs in Japan of that time were to no avail and disasters continued to occur one after another.
The setting is medieval Japan, but a similar situation could be found in many other parts of the world from time to time ever since those days in the thirteenth century to the present day with the present Covid 19 global pandemic raging at this time as this book is written.
This is the age of Mappo.
Just as The Buddha Shakyamuni predicted nearly three thousand years ago so exactly in the sutras.
The Buddhas prediction has come true in the sense that this is Mappo, and we are referring to the whole world as it is to be found today, in 'The West' as well as in 'The East' and today as well as eight hundred years ago.
The question at the end is so clear.
A question that is in the hearts of thousands perhaps millions of people today.
A question which many people hide from feeling baffled and apathetic by the situation they see all around them.
Why is it that the world has already fallen into decline when we are doing our best, but the laws of the state have come to an end.
They have no value in the situation facing humanity today.
What mistake is causing this?
What error has brought this about?
This question sets the stage for the whole of this Gosho and leads to Nichiren Daishonin explaining in the greatest depths the reason for this situation and how it can be solved.

The scenes that the traveller describes are absolutely accurate and in no way exaggerated, there are plenty of contemporary accounts written at the time which are excellent.

A book called 'The Children of Hachiman,' captures Japan very well at that time and it is well worth reading for an insight into Japan during that era.

Here in Europe The Black Death, the great plague that swept across Europe in the fourteenth and again in the fifteenth century ocurred, when thousands and thousands died, and the bodies were literally piled up in a similar way to the description in this Gosho.

People died so fast, there was no time to give them normal burials.

Places like Blackheath and other open spaces in London, that are still not built on, were the mass burial grounds in the time of the plague.

Not only was pestilence afflicting the people of Japan at that time but there were also storms and typhoons, droughts, fires and tremendous earthquakes that destroyed up to a half or more of the countries buildings in the towns and cities.

Inevitably there was great social upheaval.

Historically it was a time of great social upheaval because the old order of The Emperor had lost power and the Samurai had taken control of the land.

There was a great deal of fear and anxiety amongst many Japanese people towards this new military government and what they might do next.

The priests of many of the Buddhist sects were treated like gods and were also totally authoritarian in their rule.

They were supported and bolstered by the natural superstitions of the people of those days.

The temples of many of the sects were immensely rich which is very similar to the medieval monasteries here in the United Kingdom.

Their income was derived from their land and property and above all things, far above their faith, they wished to defend these material benefits.

The absurd situation arose where the temples organised armies of monks.

These were warrior monks whose job it was to protect the estates and lands of each temple.

The temple authorities would intrigue with the government, with whoever they thought would be the ruling power to make sure they stayed in their favour.

This chaos resulting from both social upheaval and natural disasters meant that there was no organised work or labour.
There was poverty everywhere.
People could only live by stealing and most of them were starving.
Their houses had collapsed through fire or flood and even at times there were outbreaks of cannibalism.
The people had totally lost the will to live and escapist religions were playing on the fears and superstitions of the people in order to give them something to hide their heads in.
When Nichiren Daishonin answers this question he relates all these terrible happenings to the teaching or Dharma known in Buddhism as 'The Three Calamities and Seven Disasters.'
These were taught by Shakyamuni Buddha in a sutra called The Yakushi Sutra and in many other sutras.
These are the calamities and disasters that would inevitably arise in the end when people were following and believing in the wrong, incorrect, erroneous and distorted Buddhist teachings.
The Three Calamities are war, inflation and huge widespread epidemics.
The Seven Disasters are foreign invasion, pestilence, civil war, unseasonable storms, unseasonable droughts, changes in the heavens and solar eclipses.
These are 'The Three Calamities and Seven Disasters' that are revealed in the Buddhist sutras.
Nichiren Daishonin's writing of Rissho Ankoku Ron was in order for people to understand this and to change their beliefs and thinking and through that their behaviour.
He castigated the priests for condoning violence by forming armies of warrior monks and he pointed out that the teachings of Shakyamuni, just as Shakyamuni had said himself, would not be effective in the time or age of Mappo.
Looking now at the rest of the world we can see how Shakyamuni's predictions about this age of Mappo do not apply only to Japan or only to the Far East or Asia, but they truly apply to the whole world, and it is amazing to think that Shakyamuni predicted this so accurately such a long, long, long time ago.
The thirteenth to the fifteenth centuries were really a turning point in human history and a turning point most importantly in its religious history.
Religion is fundamental to humanity.
It reflects everything and creates everything in society in that sense.

Changing Poison into Medicine

Unless religion can give proof of its power in everyday life it cannot be the true religion, and this was what Nichiren Daishonin was constantly pointing out.
Not only in Shakyamuni's Buddhism but also in the other great religions of 'The Middle East' and 'The West.'
This period was one when the prevalent world religions became formalised and ritualised and authoritarian.
They became gradually, from this point on, separated from the people because of this authoritarianism and also the fact that the people had to approach the ultimate object of devotion through the priest in order to gain benefit.
Shakyamuni had predicted this for the age of Zoho, in his teaching of the three ages of Shobo, Zoho and Mappo.
Shobo started from the time he entered nirvana and lasted for two, five hundred year periods.
Zoho began with the third five hundred year period after his death and Mappo began in the fifth of the five hundred year periods after his death.
He said that his teaching of The Pure Dharma that he had taught would lose its impact or ability to help the people because of this ritualisation and ceremonialism and at that time, right through to the time when Nichiren Daishonin wrote this Gosho, the temples had become places purely and simply of rituals where the people could no longer take part in the daily practice of Buddhism.
In The West too, a little later in the twelfth century onwards, the great cathedrals were being built and religious dogma was taking a strong place in religion.
Rituals and a system of rule was being established both in christianity and to some extent also in islam.
Religion was losing its hold on the people.
It was only in the very beginning of this transition in The West, but it was definitely happening slowly.
There was also great conflict in The West within religions as well as in Japan.
It was about that time that there was 'The Hundred Year War' which was entirely a religious war.
It had of course political overtones and by the fifteenth century King Henry the Eighth was plotting to reject the pope and Rome and establish his own church and during that period also such reformers as Luther and Calvin were at work.
War particularly was rife and these wars, most of the time, had a religious reason to them.
The Crusades continued on and off for two hundred years.
There was immense bloodshed in The Crusades, The Hundred Year War and many other wars.

115

War was beginning to become a habit.

It was becoming to be engrained deeply in the karma of nations and the cause and effect of this culminated in the two world wars of the Twentieth Century in 1914/18 and 1939/45 when twenty or even, some say, thirty million lives were lost.

In The Far East at that time the Mongolians were ravaging the whole of Asia under Kublai Kahn the grandson of Genghis Kahn causing a great deal of slaughter and brutality.

Islam was beginning to expand its movement after the crusades into Europe itself and at this time pestilence effected Europe horribly.

Enormous numbers of people died from 'The Black Death,' a third of the population of Europe was said to have died at that time. These figures are unbelievable and difficult to visualise.

At the same time in Europe from the thirteenth to the fifteenth centuries there was very icy weather.

The Baltic was frozen from coast to coast.

The Thames was frozen over on a number of occasions.

The harvests were very poor and there was a great deal of poverty and a lack of sustenance as a result.

In England like many other countries in Europe and the world, various power groups were just beginning to form.

These would lead in England, in the end, to 'The Civil War' and the beheading of King Charles the First and the end of 'The Divine Right of Kings.'

At the same time as all these horrors were happening, transport and communications were improving.

The world was being discovered.

From Marco Polo to Columbus, Francis Drake and Magellan.

Through these improvements in communications the great religions of the world were beginning to become aware of each other in a way that they had not really done before.

Between the thirteenth and fifteenth centuries the existing order that had been established for thousands of years was beginning to show signs of decline and collapse.

We can now see that looking back but it would have been very difficult for anyone to see at that time and out of this muddy and bloody swamp, just as Shakyamuni predicted, The Great White Lotus appeared in the form of Nichiren Daishonin and Nam Myoho Renge Kyo.

Today still of course 'The Three Calamities and The Seven Disasters' are very much at work in the form of the current global pandemic of Covid-19 and the impending climate crisis with the unfolding environmental disaster in the form of global warming and climate change.

Despite the horrors of the two world wars when so many millions and millions of people were killed there are still wars and threat of wars all over the planet with the still continuing threat of nuclear annihilation.

It is all a form of insanity.

Pestilence still appears and in The West we also have the epidemic of mental illnesses and the addictions and deaths from suicide that arise from people self medicating because of it.

Although medicine has become so advanced, and the traditional forms of sickness have begun to decline they have been replaced by other forms of sickness especially various mental health conditions.

Earthquakes still occur regularly across the world and incredibly strong storms and hurricanes created by global warming ravage various countries.

Droughts still occur in the equatorial regions in ever more numbers and also in the United States and Australasia and the conflagrations that accompany them occur ever more frequently even in the artic region of Siberia.

Two thirds of the world experience some sort of poverty and malnutrition.

Even today the changes in the heavens continue to occur.

The atmosphere is becoming more and more polluted with carbon emissions from the continued burning of various fossil fuels.

In certain cities around the globe, you cannot see a clear sun during the day nor the moon at night.

On top of this you have the mass destruction of the planet's lungs or tropical rain forests for industrial farming and mining and the ocean floors are being destroyed by industrial fishing in ever more gargantuan and rapid ways.

What will happen in the next twenty years if humanity goes on with its technological advancements in ever more ingenious ways of uncontrolled consumption and destruction of the planets limited resources based on utter ignorance, stupidity and greed?

We really are today asking the very same question in our hearts are we not?

What mistake is causing this?

What error has brought this about?

Often we complain about our politicians and our leaders.

We say there is no longer such a thing as a great leader in the world anymore.

Everyone is bemoaning their fate but in actuality it is not the fault of the leaders as they are just as ignorant as everyone else.

The fault is through the wrong teachings and the wrong philosophies and the fact that the ultimate truth has not yet been

established in this world and our leaders are as powerless and impotent as everyone else.
Nichiren Daishonin makes that clear in this short extract.

"The Rulers, taking pity on the plight of the common people, make certain that government on the national and local levels is carried out in a benevolent manner.
But despite all these efforts, they merely exhaust themselves in vain."

Rissho Ankoku Ron was written and submitted to The Japanese Shogunate to try to shake the people out of their apathy, out of the traditional ruts that they had got into.
To shake them out of their superstitious beliefs and to try to make them see the truth and of course it is our task as Nichiren Shoshu Buddhists to continue with this task from this moment on and on into the future.
All the religious rituals that are described in this first question were being carried out with the utmost sincerity by the people, but they were all totally useless.
Today you could say the same.
There are great religions, but they seem powerless to prevent the world sliding towards destruction and indeed they seem powerless even in certain cases to hold the people.
The last paragraph of this question is important from this point of view.

"If we look about, we see that the sun and moon continue to move in their accustomed orbits, and the five planets follow the proper course.
The Three Treasures of Buddhism continue to exist, and the period of a hundred reigns, during which the Bodhisattva Hachiman vowed to protect the nation, has not yet expired.
Then why is it that the world has already fallen into decline and that the laws of the state have come to an end?
What mistake has been made?
What error has been committed?"

Nichiren Daishonin is saying that if you look at things from a broader point of view everything seems to be the same. The seasons come and go, the Moon is still there, the Sun is still there, the stars are still there, and he says The Three Treasures of Buddhism continue to exist.

He means that the established schools of Japan are there as they were previously, just as we can say that christianity and islam and judaism and hinduism are all here today.
The Earth has not suddenly tilted by forty degrees.
We are still on the same axis, still revolving in the same way, yet these disasters and sufferings are still happening everywhere.
He is saying that neither these religions or as we could say today, science nor technology, are proving that they can cure the situation in which the world finds itself in today.
Neither for that matter can politics or economics or social sciences.
On their own they are powerless.
They can only attack the evil on the surface, but they cannot get to the root cause of it.
You have to discover the root cause of the sickness.
Many diseases are being cured by immunisation, but others still appear in their place.
People of good will are trying their very utmost but they are failing, and this is most apparent when we look at the world stage.
We cannot overcome 'The Three Calamities and The Seven Disasters' by technology or science alone because these 'Three Calamities and Seven Disasters' arise from life itself, from the hearts of human beings and therefore the only way to overcome them is through changing the hearts of human beings and to purify life from its distortion and corruption.
The relationship between social chaos and natural disasters is very plain to see if you really make a study of it and in history you find it is most apparent.
All life is connected.
Buddhism teaches the great principle of Esho Funi, the inseparability of humanity and its environment and that environment includes, in old fashioned terms, the heavens and the earth.
If humanity's heart is shaking so everything else in humanity's environment, including the climate will be shaking as well.
We are so ignorant and stupid these days that we do not connect them.
Although now due to the climate crisis some people are just beginning to awaken to this fact, but even they make the mistake of believing that a change in the political structures of society will cure this.
Aboriginal peoples still understand this totally.
In the Gosho On Attaining Buddhahood, Nichiren Daishonin writes.

"If the minds of the people are impure, their land is also impure but if their minds are pure, so is their land.
There are not two lands pure or impure in themselves, the difference lies solely in the good or evil of our minds."

The problem is this duality in humankind.
Even though those who will say that they are yearning for peace, will go out and kill for the sake of their country or whatever other mistaken ideal they believe in.
Our future depends on the number of people who can open their eyes to the ultimate truth of life and the universe.
Who is going to open their eyes to the ultimate truth except the followers of Nichiren Daishonin basing their actions on this Gosho.
This is our task as Nichiren Shoshu Buddhists.
This is what Nichiren Daishonin was hoping that without fail we will achieve, and we must do it.
Let us now look at the first answer to the first question that was put forth in this remarkable, totally unique and historic treatise.
The Host then spoke,
"I have been brooding alone upon this matter, indignant yet unable to speak, but now that you have come, we can lament together.
Let us discuss the question at length.
When a man leaves family life and enters The Buddhist Way it is because he hopes through the teachings of The Dharma to attain Buddhahood, but these days attempts to move The Gods fail to have any effect and appeals to the power of The Buddha's produce no results.
When I look carefully at the state of the world today I see stupid people who give way to doubts because of their naivety.
Therefore they look up at the heavens and mouth their resentment or gaze down at the earth and sink deep into anxiety.
I have pondered the matters carefully with what limited resources I possess and have searched rather widely in the scriptures for an answer.
The people of today all turn their backs upon what is right, to a man they all give their allegiance to evil.
That is the reason why The Benevolent Deities have abandoned The Nation and gone away, why Sages leave their places and do not return and in their stead come devils and demons, disasters and calamities, that arise one after another.
I cannot help but speak of the matter, I cannot help being filled with fear."

Changing Poison into Medicine

This is quite a short answer, yet it is one of the most important parts of this whole Gosho.

It explains in very simple terms, simple words, almost too simple it may seem, the cause of all this suffering and unhappiness and furthermore the cause of 'The Three Calamities and Seven Disasters' which were occurring at that time in Japan, and which are occurring at this very time in the world all around us on Planet Earth.

The most important sentence in that answer is.

"The people of today all turn their backs on what is right, to a man they all give their allegiance to evil, that is the reason why all The Benevolent Deities have abandoned The Nation and gone away and why Sages leave their places and do not return and in their stead come devils and demons, disasters and calamities arise one after another."

The whole of the answer is in that one sentence.

Nichiren Daishonin is developing an argument, the first being what is the purpose of life?

What is the sort of life that we should be leading?

And secondly if life is for happiness then what is happiness? What is true happiness?

And the third point is that it is inferior or incorrect and erroneous teachings which are the enemy of happiness in this world.

Therefore we must seek the highest of all teachings and go on seeking until we find it, find the ultimate truth of life and the universe.

Many of you who are reading this book have such a seeking mind.

For some reason or other you were dissatisfied with the state of affairs of your own life or of this world and you set out to seek something.

Maybe you did not do it consciously maybe it was quite sub consciously, but because of that motivation in your life you found Sun Lotus Recovery and through participating in it you found The Dai Gohonzon.

Firstly I want to explain to you Nichiren Daishonin's views which are very briefly set out in that one short answer by means of relating it to The Ten Worlds Teaching.

And secondly relating it to our life and our happiness by relating it to this theory and also to the concept of benefit.

And thirdly to the protection of what we call The Buddhist Gods, the Shoten Zenjin, or as we call them in colloquial language, to the protective forces of The Universe.

"The people of today turn their backs on what is right,"

From the title of this Gosho, Rissho Ankoku Ron, we know that what they are turning their backs on is the ultimate truth of life or from the perspective of Buddhism they are turning their backs on The Law or The Dharma or in Nichiren Shoshu Buddhism on Nam Myoho Renge Kyo and The Dai Gohonzon.
This question of turning your back in the terms Nichiren Daishonin has written here is not said in any way as a derogatory remark about the people of that day.
In many other places in this Gosho and other Gosho he points out that the people are deceived by incorrect, erroneous, or inferior teachings.
This does not even mean to say that the people who are teaching these inferior teachings are doing it deliberately or purposefully.
It is a matter of ignorance.
The World is in innate darkness.
Our eyes, he said in another Gosho, are in innate darkness, a state of ignorance as to the ultimate truth about life.
In the Buddhist explanation about 'The Three Calamities and The Seven Disasters' these are natural disasters which will occur when people are not in rhythm and harmony with the universe and leading a buoyant and happy life.
The first of those causes of 'The Three Calamities and The Seven Disasters' is turning your back on or slandering, however ignorantly, The Law or The Dharma.
The true natural law of the universe.
And the second cause of these calamities and disasters is that the people are out of rhythm because they turn their backs on the truth.
However ignorant it may be they will be out of rhythm with The Law of Nam Myoho Renge Kyo.
These disasters and calamities occur because life is not in rhythm with universal life.
This causes chaos and confusion, not only in the hearts and minds of the people and in a country but also in all the elements.
This is according to the fundamental Buddhist principle of Esho Funi, the inseparability of life and its environment.
The environment reflects the state of the people and the people's lives.
If the state of the people's lives is negative the environment will react negatively.

If the state of the people's lives is positive then the environment will react positively.
And the third cause of the 'Three Calamities and Seven Disasters' is because of that negative state, what are known in the oldest terms as demons and devils, will then take the place of the Benevolent Deities.
Because the people are out of rhythm then the environment will react in a way which seems to the people devilish because it is not in harmony with their lives.
All the great teachings of Buddhism are in this one answer.
Let us now start to deal with this answer in more detail.

"When a man leaves family life, and enters the Buddhist Way, it is because he hopes through the teachings of The Dharma to attain Buddhahood."

Leaving family life applies to the old Buddhism of Shakyamuni's days.
Shakyamuni himself left his family and the palace and the luxurious circumstances of his very privileged life and set out to wander in the forests in order to find the ultimate truth of life.
This was the ancient way of those who sought enlightenment in India in those times.
We do not do that anymore and anyway it would be very difficult nowadays to find a place where you could escape to.
This in modern terms means that you look beyond your garden fence.
You look beyond the walls of your own house.
You look beyond what your neighbours say, what the people in your workplace say and you try hard to open your eyes to something greater.
To life in a broader perspective, a new dimension and discover the true purpose that lies in the depths of life.
Something that is beyond daily work and the family.
Beyond the mundane everyday existence of our lives.
At the end of the sentence Nichiren Daishonin says:

"He hopes through the teachings of The Dharma to attain Buddhahood."

That was a very startling declaration at that time in Japan.
It is difficult for us to understand now that someone saying,
"He hopes through the teachings of The Dharma to attain Buddhahood,"

123

should cause such a stir but Buddhism by then had become so distorted that Buddhism or Buddhahood was the preserve of the priests and the elite.

The idea of any person being able to attain Buddhahood had totally been lost, even though Shakyamuni had referred to it two thousand years before in The Lotus Sutra.

Here was Nichiren Daishonin saying that everyone can attain Buddhahood.

In other words all the people are equal to the priests or to the elite of Japan and that they all had the potential to attain Buddhahood.

In a Medieval society that was an earth shattering statement.

It was that sort of remark that brought and caused persecutions to rain down on him.

In another Gosho Nichiren Daishonin really castigates the priests who wore the priestly robes but did not practice the teachings.

Faith is not having a shaven head.

Faith is devoting yourself to the practice and struggling to overcome your negative karma and attain enlightenment in this lifetime.

These words were dynamite at that particular time.

It is no wonder that he suffered so much after saying these statements and he of course expected this.

Even today this sort of teaching when understood is a shock to certain societies in this world.

Nichiren Daishonin's Buddhism cannot be practiced freely and openly in certain countries of the world.

Those who understand even a little of it realise that the aim of this practice is for ordinary people like you and I to attain Buddhahood which means great wisdom and life force.

Inevitably that would threaten a fascist oriented government.

Even to this day such teachings can cause alarm and can shake the foundations of a government or authority in certain parts of the world.

This is the world we live in.

We practice Nichiren Shoshu Buddhism to attain Buddhahood or enlightenment, nothing more, nothing less.

Just as everyone has practiced Buddhism for this purpose in the past and that requires courage, conviction and commitment.

You have to have these three qualities to attain Buddhahood and you put The Gohonzon first in everything in your life.

So what is Buddhahood?

I am not sure I can answer that very well myself, but why is it that we should struggle for enlightenment?

Changing Poison into Medicine

We certainly know that enlightenment means that in some sort of way that you find true happiness and of course that is the ultimate meaning of it, indestructible happiness.

Buddhahood is to understand the workings of life so well and so intensely that there are no dark areas anymore and when there are no dark areas there is no fear.

Fear or anxiety is one of the things that people suffer from so dreadfully.

Many of us have fears but we only have fears because of dark areas that we cannot see into and do not understand.

The Buddha's understand everything and have no fear and because they have no fear they understand their purpose and they know they can fulfil it.

They know that they can turn the impossible into possible.

They are not bounded by fear because of this too, they know that life is eternal and free.

Fear breeds doubt, fear breeds guilt, without fear therefore you are free of doubt and guilt and life has no boundaries.

It is this freedom and the achievement as a result of it that brings indestructible happiness which nobody could possibly take away from you.

There are many concepts of happiness.

All philosophies ever since people we able to speak and write have been concerned with human happiness.

Socrates and Plato felt that happiness could be obtained by having a social order and true democracy.

Capitalism and Socialism could say that they believe that happiness come from making the majority happy.

If the majority are happy and prosperous then they will make those who are not happy and prosperous, happy and prosperous.

Communism thinks that happiness will come from a society in which all material needs are centrally supplied and controlled by the state and through this satisfaction of material needs there is a freedom from the restrictions of competition and class.

Nichiren Shoshu Buddhism on the other hand is totally different.

Nichiren Shoshu Buddhism's teaching is nothing to do with relative happiness, that is happiness compared with this or happiness compared with that.

Nichiren Shoshu Buddhism goes to the depths and seeks happiness in the very depths of your life on the theory that if you are happy in the very depths of your being you will be happy in every other possible aspect of your life.

Buddhist happiness does not rely on anything external.

It does not matter what may be happening around you as you know you can overcome it.

Buddhist happiness is not influenced by external conditions or by time or space.

It is a universal happiness and that is very true because it comes from realizing that each individual person is in fact a universe in themselves.

If you look at this from the point of view of The Ten Worlds Teaching it is quite interesting.

We all know that we cannot escape from The Ten Worlds.

Our lives are revolving through them all the time so if we cannot escape from them obviously if they are an inherent part of human existence and we must make the best of them.

This is what Buddhism sets out to do.

We can turn even The Six Lower Worlds or The Three Evil Paths, that is hell, hunger and animality, even with these we can turn the poison into medicine, suffering into happiness and wellbeing.

If there was no hell, how could we ever know heaven.

Without hell we would not understand what happiness is.

Without hunger and desire we would have no driving force to establish a better life or a better world.

Without animality that instinctive world there would be no instinctive love of a child for a mother.

Without anger there could be no passion for peace and justice.

Without tranquillity how could you know the joy of action?

Without rapture our desires would have no driving force.

Without the effect of learning there could be no progress.

Without realization there could be no culture.

Without the world of Boddhisattva there could be no expression of The Buddha Nature in daily life and the joy of helping others.

Through embracing Buddhism and practicing it, we can turn every one of The Ten Worlds, even hell, hunger, animality and anger, that can be so dismal and so incredibly destructive into happiness in this world.

Buddhism is saying do not deny The Ten Worlds.

Do not deny that you have the six lower worlds and that you have the three evil paths because even they are a vital part of life.

This is a very different teaching to what all the other religions have taught.

In Buddhism there is the concept of benefit.

In Buddhism our whole practice is based on benefit, however much we might like to hide from this fact, this is in fact what Buddhist practice is based on.

We can and do turn poison into medicine and this is benefit, we can turn misfortune into fortune, we can change punishment or retribution into something good for us.

Changing Poison into Medicine

Some people really object to this, many people will say this sounds like a very selfish religion.

There are people in the world who think that to practice self-denial is the only way to be good and righteous and saintly.

This has arisen form the history and tradition of christian martyrdom and is deeply entrenched in the life of the United Kingdom and all of The West.

The truth is, as Nichiren Shoshu Buddhism explains, that it is natural to seek benefit.

This is a natural human tendency.

If a teaching denies benefit in this life it is distorting human life itself and a human life that is distorted not only cannot be happy, but it can also be downright dangerous.

Because people are brought up, however remotely, through these traditions and customs to believe that there is something nasty about benefit, then this world will continue to be riddled with guilt and recrimination.

Hospitals will not cease to be fill of mentally ill people and the addictions that occur due to people self medicating these illnesses.

The suicides that result from this thinking will continue until this has changed.

It is through this teaching of self-denial or decrying benefit that deep in their lives, however they may have been brought up, people feel that they should not be doing things for their own benefit and that they do not deserve it.

The result of this in The West is that lives are over strained and repressed.

To deny benefit is a most dangerous philosophy to follow.

The reason why so many philosophies and religions have practiced self-denial and denied benefit in this daily life is because they did not understand how to control desire.

Desire is so strong, and we all know that it can lead us into awful troubles and unhappiness and as a recovering addict I know this only too well.

It was the lack of finding a way to control desire adequately that caused religions to say that the only thing to do is to supress it.

The Lotus Sutra teaches in The Ten Worlds Teaching that desires are a function of life.

You cannot supress them.

If you try to they will come bouncing out like a burst spring and if you do supress it you are tampering with life itself and distorting it.

Why not get yourself into the Buddha state and you will find that your desires are still working as strongly as ever but instead of being for your own destruction or other people's unhappiness, they will be for progress and enlightenment for yourself and others.

Buddhism says here is the practice that will give you the power to enable you to sustain it by using your desires for yourself and others greatest happiness.

This is the very heart of Nichiren Shoshu Buddhism, the great principle of 'Bonno Soku Bodai' or 'Earthly Desires are Enlightenment' or transforming your earthly desires into enlightenment.

Changing poison into medicine.

It is inscribed on The Gohonzon and is at the very heart of everything.

Desires are vitally important, it is through the satisfaction of our desires that we originally in the first year or two of our practice get actual proof of the power of The Gohonzon and then as we practice more and more, as the Buddha state takes a greater and more important position in your life, so our desires quite naturally become more discerning.

Instead of desires based on hunger or greed of any sort they become desires based at a higher level.

This is a natural process as the Buddha state, the highest state of life takes the ascendence.

This is an amazing thing no other philosophy or practice could ever believe that such a thing was possible.

The fact remains that correct Buddhist practice does this and this is its unique greatness.

Some intellectuals say that true happiness can only be found in the spiritual world, but can you live like a saint?

Such statements are really haughty and hypocritical.

All the Buddha's have taught the realistic philosophy of benefit.

From Shakyamuni down to this day and we should not hesitate to expound it even though we may get attacked by people who say, "this is very selfish," or "I do not like the sound of this."

We should firmly defend it because in fact not to practice for benefit is indefensible.

In the Gosho, Happiness in This World, Nichiren Daishonin said.

"The Sutra says, the people there in my land are happy and at ease, happy and at ease, means that joy derived from The Dharma."

These are benefits and in this quote from The Lotus Sutra, he further says that.

"You are obviously included amongst the people who are happy and at ease, and there in my land indicates the entire world."

That is to say nowhere else but in this life.
There is no greater happiness than having faith in The Lotus Sutra and Nam Myoho Renge Kyo.
It promises peace and security in this life and good circumstances in the next.
This is the joy and benefit of practice.

"When I look carefully at the state of the world today, I see stupid people who give way to doubts because of their naivety.
Therefore, they look up at the heavens and mouth their resentment or gaze down at the earth and sink deep into anxiety.
I have pondered the matters carefully, with what limited resources I possess and have searched rather widely in the scriptures for an answer."

This a very graphic description.
We have done this ourselves I am sure.
Looking up to the heavens and mouthing resentments and gazing down at the earth and sinking deeply into anxiety.
I have done both on many occasions.
I hope that we are doing it less and less, but we see people everywhere doing this,
"Oh my god, I cannot stand this," looking up at the heavens in resentment or looking down at the ground.
"I have no idea what I am going to do about it!"
The words are so graphic and everywhere we go we see it and that is because it is an unhappy world.
People feel helpless, hopeless and useless which is worse than anything, and have no power to change it.
We have to teach others about Nam Myoho Renge Kyo.
We must do Shakubuku and tell others about the power of The Gohonzon so that we don't have to look up to the heavens in resentment not knowing what to do about it or shake our heads and stare at the ground in hell.
We know we can pull ourselves out of it through the power of the practice, so how can we go on denying this to other people.
Of course people will reject it and people will not want to listen but there will always be some who want to listen whose lives are really ready and waiting to hear this teaching.

Changing Poison into Medicine

"The people of today all turn their backs on what is right, to a man they all give their allegiance to evil, that is the reason why all the benevolent deities have abandoned The Nation and gone away, why sages leave their places and do not return and in their stead come devils and demons, disasters and calamities that arise one after another".

Nichiren Daishonin's conviction was absolutely complete. He says in one of his most important writings, Kaimoku Sho or The Opening of The Eyes.

"Thus over a period of countless lifetimes, men are deceived more often than there are sands in the Ganges, until they abandon their faith in The Lotus Sutra, and descend to the teachings of the provisional Mahayana Sutra's, abandon these and descend to the teachings of the Hinayana Sutra's and eventually abandon even these and descend to the teachings and scriptures of the non Buddhist doctrines.
I understand all too well how in the end men have come in this way to fall into the evil states of existence.
I Nichiren am the only person in all Japan who understands this. Whether tempted by good, or threatened by evil, if one casts aside The Lotus Sutra, he destines himself for hell.
Here I will make a great vow, though I might be offered the rulership of Japan, if I will only abandon The Lotus Sutra, accept the teachings of the Kamuryrujo sutra, and look forward to rebirth in the western land, though I might be told that my father and mother will have their throats cut if I do not recite the Nembutsu, whatever persecutions I might encounter, so long as men of wisdom do not prove my teachings to be false, then I will never accept the practices of the other sects.
All other troubles are no more to me than dust before the wind.
I will be the pillar of Japan, I will be the eyes of Japan, I will be the great ship of Japan, this is my vow, and I will never forsake it".

These are very moving words and emphasise his absolute conviction that what he believed was right, that he really was enlightened to the law of life itself and so long as people were ignorant of that law and therefore out of rhythm with universal life these sufferings would continue.
Buddhism sees to the depths of human life and human activity. What Nichiren Daishonin and all The Buddha's have seen and taught is that your daily life and activities are just a manifestation of what we are believing or thinking in the depths of our being.

Every action, every word, every thought is related to that.
If someone speaks to you, you relate it to what you believe in, to what you stand on, to what you believe life is all about.
Whatever belief or philosophy we have as a human being, this colours everything that we do.
Every thought, every word and every small action, as well as the big ones.
Therefore what we believe in is of the utmost importance.
If someone says something against what we believe, we feel irritated or angry and upset in some way deep in our lives even though we may not show it or try hard not to.
Nevertheless we radiate that feeling of anger and it affects everything around us.
Everything is coloured by the way in which we relay things that we hear and see to our own personal beliefs or world view.
This is why Nichiren Daishonin when writing these Gosho's was saying you must listen, please listen, to what I am saying.
If what we believe in is distorted and wrong then without even realising it our actions will reflect that in every way into our environment and the environment will react accordingly.
We do Gongyo and Shodai everyday so that we renew our understanding and our pure belief towards Buddhism so that we radiate and reflect everything based on that ultimate truth.
At the beginning of the first quote from The Opening of The Eyes, Nichiren Daishonin said:

"Thus over a period of countless lifetimes, men are deceived by these wrong teachings"

This is not a conscious thing necessarily, sometimes it is, but mostly ignorance breeds ignorance.
This is why Nichiren Daishonin was so strong in refuting these other teachings that he was surrounded by at that time in Japan.
It was no good compromising.
He had prepared patient and careful arguments and debate in order to prove the truth of what he was teaching.
There was no compromise, there could be no compromise.
It is these wrong or incorrect fundamental thoughts which are colouring life in the world today and creating the situation that we see now.
The proof of the pudding is in the eating.
Buddhism is very clear that all the higher religions have and had an important part to play in the development of this world but now we have reached the age of Mappo when people have the intellectual capacity to understand The Lotus Sutra.

131

Therefore Shakyamuni said three thousand years ago that this is the age when to find true happiness they must understand 'The True Dharma.'

Taking first of all the religion we know best, christianity and its history.

In medieval times the church had absolute power, related to and closely tied to the political power of the day.

In many instances people argue and scholars discuss how theology was bent in order to be the servant of the power of the church and if anyone disagreed they were persecuted by such things as 'The Inquisition' and so on.

To give you one example there are people who will argue that the worship of the mother Mary in christianity is to encourage apathy, softness and weakness.

To lay your head on the mother of Jesus' bosom when you are in trouble.

This does not breed a strong sense of fighting spirit.

Then in another time in history the church condemned Galileo for saying that the world was round and not at the centre of creation.

There have been many instances where to break the grip of the church, people have revolted and sadly many, many people have been killed, such as the massacre of St Bartholomew's Day when so many people, thousands and thousands of them were killed at that time.

We know of the persecutions of the protestants by Queen Mary. The burnings at the stake and after she had gone, the persecutions of the catholics, when the same thing happened.

'The Thirty Years War' was between protestants and catholics brought with it disease and appalling suffering and slaughter.

Even up to the eighteenth century was a time when the church was supressing medical and scientific discoveries for their own ends and right into the Twenty First century we still see to this day violence in Northern Ireland between catholic and protestant and the struggle that the catholic and other churches are having with birth control, LGBTQ+ rights, and child sexual abuse and so on.

However fundamentally good and righteous an original teaching may have been, and no one can deny that what Jesus Christ taught was good and righteous, if it is not complete, if there are gaps in its philosophy then the devils or universal negative functions will enter and cause a thousand years of fighting and war.

Today the church's influence has greatly declined, but in The West and in each one of our individual lives, the christian moral teachings are very deeply engrained.

I am not saying they are all wrong, far from it, but these feelings are very deep in our lives.

Even to this day, in Italy in certain areas a person cannot get a job without getting a recommendation from his parish priest.

This a great way for the church to maintain control over people.

In Ireland to, in rural areas such things continue.

Jesus Christ himself taught love and goodness and humanism but it never has produced a peaceful world.

We have to face that fact.

It is an idealistic religion which certainly has produced good, but it has also produced an immense amount of harm.

Let us look at Communism.

This is a religion without a god, based on materialism and we all know that under Stalin, tens of thousands of people were slaughtered.

The Party became as absolute as The Tzars were back in their day and basing itself on materialism it seems that anyone who was opposed to the regime could be disposed of in a materialistic way.

It denies the dignity of individual life and freedom has disappeared.

We all know about Nazism, it is another form of religion.

Worship of ancestors is what nazism was partly based on, worship of the nation or the race.

Six to seven million jewish people were killed by the nazi's based on that philosophy and up to eleven million in slave labour camps suffered and were slaughtered during that time.

This was the most enormous tragedy in human history but at the root of this there was religion.

If it had not been for the traditional concept of christianity towards the jewish people going back over centuries, such an evil era could never have begun.

The pope of that time was criticized because he never expressed any opposition to the horrors of nazism.

An inferior, incorrect or incomplete philosophy like nazism is designed to breed passion.

The people believed in nazism, and it coloured all their actions.

If you turn to Asia, India and Pakistan at the time of independence, there was incredible slaughter.

The official figure is about five hundred thousand killed but the unofficial estimate is more like two to three million hindu's and muslim's slaughtered at the time of partition.

133

This was without a doubt based on religion and very much on the exclusive rigid caste system of the hindu's.

Southeast Asia, where hinayana Buddhism is practiced in Vietnam, Cambodia, Myanmar and so on.

They have a history of being downtrodden, throughout their history they have always been conquered or at war with one people after another or oppressed by their own totalitarian militarist governments.

Hinayana Buddhism supresses human desire, it is passive and breeds apathy.

Hinayana Buddhism was taught by Shakyamuni Buddha to overcome the effects of Brahmanism which was very much concerned with minute by minute transient pleasures.

This was the reason why for several years he taught hinayana teachings at the beginning of this period of his teaching and travels.

If false teachings are engrained in people's lives then they will colour all their actions and therefore it pervades all society.

This creates immutable karma which exists in the lives of people and races and nations to this day.

Through believing something we create an incredible power, a force of thought, speech and action which spreads from ourselves outwards into our environment and then reflects back.

Last of all Japan.

Before world war two the military government of Japan determined to force all other religions including Buddhism and christianity to accept certain tenets of Shintoism into their own religion.

Distorting their teachings in order to include Shintoism and especially the aspect of emperor worship which they wanted to use to develop militant nationalism.

The people believed this at the time.

They believed that they would win the war and that Japan had incredible power centred around the divinity of the emperor and these beliefs coloured all their actions.

Nichiren Daishonin said that inferior teachings are the sake (rice wine) of the ignorant which is rather similar to Karl Marx when he said religion is the opium of the masses.

Wherever you see hell in the world the root of the trouble is religion and philosophy or the wrong, erroneous, incorrect, incomplete thinking or teachings.

Whatever our previous beliefs or practices, the life philosophy or religion we previously believed in before we found Nichiren Shoshu Buddhism and Dai Gohonzon, we should not cling to these from the point of view of sentimentality.

Changing Poison into Medicine

We should look at history and realise that the root cause of all the troubles in this world are those teachings.
This is not to say that they did not serve a purpose in their time.
We have to remember that this age is Mappo when The True Dharma can be understood by the people.
In the Gosho, 'On The Embankments of Faith,' Nichiren Daishonin said.

"Chang an wrote that if you befriend another person but lack the mercy to correct them, you are in fact his enemy."

There is no need for human beings to be deceived anymore but of course it means that we and our fellow Nichiren Shoshu Buddhists in many countries of the world must get to work.
We have to tell people otherwise how can they know?
Let us have conviction in the greatness of this teaching of the ultimate truth or Dharma of Life.
Nichiren Daishonin said,

"I will never give up unless someone proves these teachings to be false".

We should have this spirit and spread the teachings whenever we can as there is no other way that the evil in this world will be eradicated, that I firmly believe.
In the passage that we are looking at Nichiren Daishonin says,

"That is the reason why the Benevolent Deities have abandoned the nation and gone away".

This refers to the Buddhist Deities so let us look at this concept of Gods or Deities.
The God of all creation is one sort of God.
Buddhism's view of the God of all creation is that this was something which human beings had to conjure up in their minds in order to justify the fact that there was some sort of a rhythm and pattern to life.
That there was something that seemed to be in control.
The very fact that everyone's view of God is probably different is proof of this.
It is something in the imagination, though to some people it may seem different.
To a child it may be an old man, to others it is a distant incredible Mr Who, everyone has a different concept of it.

Changing Poison into Medicine

As time is going on there is now a trend in christianity to call god or refer to god in a way which might indicate some sort of force or energy behind the universe.
Nichiren Shoshu Buddhism then goes on to find very exactly what this force or energy is and how it functions, which christianity is unable to do.
This is of course Nam Myoho Renge Kyo and all the amazing teachings that explain the mechanics of how this universal force of life actually works.
The second type of god is the god of the ancestors which we have talked about in relation to the nazi's.
And the third type of god is the Shoten Zenjin, the Buddhist Gods or forces of the universe.
These forces react to the state of life which it is in.
If you are in a negative state then those forces of the universe will react or interact negatively to you.
If your life state is in a very positive and vigorous state then the forces of the universe will react accordingly.
The Sun as a simple example can protect you if you are positive and wise.
If you set out on a dessert expedition and use your good sense and plan thoroughly and prepare for it and move vigorously forward but if you dilly dally and get lost and are foolish enough to set off without water, then the Sun will destroy you.
This is the way all the forces of the universe act and react.
In the Gosho On Practicing The Buddha's Teaching Nichiren Daishonin said.

"When our prayers for Buddhahood are answered and we dwell in the land of eternal enlightenment where we will experience the boundless joy of The Dharma, what pity we will feel for those suffering incessantly in the depths of hell".

The land of eternal enlightenment is not a distant paradise or heaven it is here, in this life, in this world.
When each individual is practicing in such a way where their life is resilient and always moving energetically and positively forward, the more that do that, the more society as a whole will have the protection of the Buddhist Deities.
If this fades due to incorrect teachings in their lives, the Buddhist Deities will disappear and demons and devils, as this Gosho says, will take their place.
This is why social disasters occur and why natural disasters occur, the two are totally linked.

Changing Poison into Medicine

Every phenomena, the movement of the Planets and the Sun and the Moon and the rain, the wind, all other animals, other human beings and every form of life is there for nothing else but to promote and protect harmony and happiness.
This universe is not supposed to be in disharmony.
Our life and the life of everything around us is to protect the happiness of every other living thing and it is sublimely beautiful and pure.
These are the workings of life itself or Myoho Renge Kyo.
This is the reality of the universe as Nichiren Shoshu Buddhism sees it.
Everything is interdependent.
If we understand this and get to the very depths of our lives through the practice of Nam Myoho Renge Kyo then we shall move in rhythm.
The more we teach others, they will also move in rhythm and so once more the Benevolent Deities, the protective forces of the universe, as this Gosho says will reappear in this world.
In all the corners where they have left it and the devils and demons (slanderous teachings in the hearts of the people) that are causing so much suffering and sadness, unhappiness and tragedy will gradually disappear.
This is what we are working for, this is Kosen Rufu.
Let us now look at the second question asked by the guest to the host in this famous treatise.

#

Question Two.

Changing Poison into Medicine

The guest said,
"These disasters that befall The Empire, these calamities of The Nation, I am not the only one pained by them, the whole populace is weighed down with sorrow.
Now I have been privileged to enter your home and listen to these enlightened words of yours.
You speak of The Gods and of Sages taking leave and of disasters and calamities arising side by side.
Upon what Sutra's do you base your views?
Could you describe for me the passages of proof?"

The most important sentence here is "I am not the only one pained by them, the whole populace is weighed down with sorrow."
This question is divided into four parts.
In the first part it shows the need to respect the dignity of life in government and politics.
In the second part we will explore the power of Jihi, in Japanese, that is to say Buddhist mercy or compassion and the comparison of this concept with the western concept of love.
Thirdly, we will consider the reform of society and the individuals in society through an understanding of the eternity of life, which in turn gives us an understanding of our place and the place of our planet Earth in the entire universe.
And the fourth part concerns our inseparability with our environment.
The great and fundamental Buddhist principle of Esho Funi, or the inseparability of life and its environment.
This last point is fundamental to the first three.

"I am not the only one pained by them, the whole populace is weighed down with sorrow."

Ideally this would be the spirit and the feelings of the leaders of the world today.
There is not one country in this world today where the people are not suffering in one way or another and the world is so close and interconnected now in this age of Mappo.
This age of globalization when the sufferings of one country spill over and cause sufferings in other countries.
If we all, and especially the leaders, felt pained by these sufferings truly in our hearts, what a difference it might make to this world.
Are our leaders really pained?
When looking at countries like Syria, Libya, Yemen, Palestine and Iraq and Afghanistan, Myanmar and countless other places

throughout the world we see that the problem is that the sufferings are so continual, so constant and so varied in their nature.

They have become so continual and ongoing that we have become totally numbed or desensitized by them.

Even in our own country there is tremendous inequality, rising poverty with food banks appearing everywhere throughout the country.

Homelessness and people working so hard for a low minimum wage that they can never earn enough to cope with spiralling childcare and housing costs.

The statistics for people suffering from a mental illness is climbing and the numbers of people with substance misuse and addiction disorders as a result of this is also on the increase.

We have one of the highest divorce rates in the world which shatters and fragments families, and countless other sufferings even in this land which still fortunately for us is free and reasonably safe to walk in.

People get conditioned to passively accept this situation in the world, and this of course includes politicians and leaders and governments.

We take all this as somehow inevitable.

It is true that Buddhism teaches that suffering is a part of life but not suffering that goes on and on and on and gets worse and worse and worse for the whole of your life.

Sufferings are meant to be overcome.

This is what Nichiren Shoshu Buddhism teaches.

The situation in the world today is that these sufferings go on and on and they are never cured, and they continue to get worse and worse in the process.

The true aim of politics should be that everyone should enjoy life to the full, in circumstances of their own choice.

It seems almost impossible to imagine.

Yet it is not impossible if we can achieve a harmonious balance with each other and our environment in this world.

This is what the concept of Kosen Rufu truly means.

If we look back over the history of politics and the history of government, there has been an incredible succession of examples of cruelty, egoism, greed and selfishness and this has gone on throughout history until today.

This is due to a total lack of any sense of humanity.

If we go back further in history we can see that this was the reason for such things as the rise of the caste system in India and the feudal system in many countries of the world along with ruthless colonization and most and worst of all war.

Always in the end it is people, the ordinary people who must sacrifice themselves, sometimes with their lives, sometimes with their happiness and wellbeing.

Human history has been a succession of wars.

The scars of war carved into human life are never healed.

The scars of war are how it effects human beings in their minds.

The emptiness, the grief, the anger, the absurdity of life, the cynicism.

"What does it matter what anybody does."

"What did it matter to follow the principles we follow in society."

"What is the use of religion, god is a myth, either god is a myth or someone incredibly cruel."

War leaves humans in a spiritual or philosophical vacuum, and this destroys human minds, these are the scars of war.

In The Lotus Sutra, Shakyamuni says,

"People say, I came into the world to save the people, but on the contrary, it was the people themselves who called me."

People are crying out in their hearts.

You were probably crying out, which was why you found The Gohonzon.

It is because of this crying of the hearts of the people all over the world that Nichiren Daishonin appeared in thirteenth century Japan.

It is why the Dai Gohonzon of Nichiren Shoshu Buddhism has now travelled from Japan to many, many countries in this world.

Unless we really fight now, unless we feel the pain, as this question says, and make this the driving force behind our efforts to teach others about The Gohonzon and Nichiren Shoshu Buddhism, war and all the other horrors of life will go on and on and on, over and over and over again just the same as our karma has repeated itself in our lives.

From this world, war will go out into space.

All the films that are about this are just more war propaganda, preparing the next generation for even more war.

Just as it has always been.

How can we stop it?

It is an immense task and the only way we can stop it is by establishing the ultimate truth in as many hearts as possible, so that people look beyond their eyebrows and beyond the end of their noses and really start to look at the world from a new dimension.

Changing Poison into Medicine

There are around one million people at this time on the planet who have faith in The Dai Gohonzon of Nichiren Shoshu Buddhism, this will increase with all our efforts as each year passes.

Mahatma Gandhi totally changed India without firing a single shot through nonviolence.

The means by which we will change things will not be those means but it will be through our individual and communal influence.

It is through people seeing the wisdom and compassion of what we do and what we say that others will follow.

We will then start to exert a positive, enlightened influence not only in our own countries but also because of our joint efforts, throughout the whole world, all over our blue Panet Earth.

Numbers are not necessarily the answer, in some countries they are but quality is far more important than quantity, especially here in the West, in Europe and the United States of America.

Strong practitioners with a strong practice.

Practitioners who will never give in no matter what they encounter.

Nichiren Shoshu Buddhists who are wise, sensible and intelligent, with wisdom, good sense and intelligence which cannot be denied by anybody.

Nichiren Shoshu Buddhists who have completely turned their lives around through the practice and you know who you are reading this.

This is far more important than enormous numbers in a country of our nature.

Though this would not apply to a country such as China.

We can do this, and we must do this.

If we can achieve this by 2050 so that our influence is being felt in every field of society in this country, then definitely huge numbers will follow us after that point is reached.

We will do it because Nam Myoho Renge Kyo, which we practice, naturally draws up into our lives wisdom, compassion and courage and through this we will more and more feel the pain and suffering of the people of the world.

This is Jihi, Buddhist compassion.

Ji means nourish, Hi means sorrow, this means to take away sorrow or suffering and replace it with joy and happiness or nourishment, to nourish so that sorrow is replaced with happiness and wellbeing.

Nourish means an act that enables something to grow healthy and strong until it is able to stand alone.

This is what Jihi means.

Changing Poison into Medicine

You could expand its meaning to mean to take away suffering and replace with eternal happiness or lasting wellbeing.
Furthermore Jihi does not mean nourishing to your own self-sacrifice or detriment.
Jihi means benefit for all concerned, for the nourisher as well as the nourished, not nourishment which is followed by the exhaustion of the giver.
In the last prayer of Gongyo we say.

"May the impartial benefits of Myoho Renge Kyo spread equally to the farthest reaches of the universe, so that I, together with all other existence, may attain the tranquil state of enlightened life."

This is the quality of Buddhist compassion, founded on chanting Nam Myoho Renge Kyo to The Gohonzon.
What is the difference of this concept of Jihi and love?
It is not an emotion, it is not some ideal, Jihi is not in any sense like that.
Jihi is a reality, love is emotional, and it can be sentimental or even romantic, it is always changing.
This is like the waves on the surface of the sea, but Jihi is a fundamental deep current of Buddhist compassion which lies in everyone's life which can be activated by practicing with The Gohonzon of Nichiren Shoshu Buddhism.
Jihi is the ultimate deep state of human life itself.
A natural state and is the product of enlightenment or Buddhahood the highest and best state of human life.
Jihi goes beyond those who you are closely connected to, Jihi embraces everybody and everything.
It is not flattering or easing or giving temporary joy like giving someone a meal, it is to give happiness and wellbeing permanently.
This is what you are all trying to do as you teach others about Nichiren Shoshu Buddhism and Nam Myoho Renge Kyo.
It is this quality of Jihi which should be at the base of all social activities including politics and government and leadership.
Then we would have wise politics, wise government, wise social welfare, wise international relations and foreign policy and a wise environmental policy.
In the Gosho called On Reprimanding Hachiman, Nichiren Daishonin says.

"Nichiren's sufferings are the sufferings of the entire Nation."

Changing Poison into Medicine

This should be the spirit in which we approach our own personal environment.

Ideally it should be the spirit of the leaders of our country and the leaders of the whole world.

We can do it because this amazing quality of Jihi is already flowing in your life and a million others.

Let us determine to let it flow outwards beyond, not just our minds and hearts, but into real action in our own environment, in this real world called Planet Earth.

At the end of the question, the traveller or guest asked Nichiren Daishonin or the host, for proof in the Sutras to support the opinion that he stated.

These opinions were summarised in one sentence.

"The people of today all turn their backs upon what is right, to a man they all give their allegiance to evil, that is the reason why the benevolent deities have abandoned the nation and gone away, why sages leave their places and do not return and in their stead come devils and demons, disasters and calamities, that arise one after another."

Like most other people at that stage in their dialogue, the traveller could not understand this.

It was not in the least bit realistic to him, it seemed too simple to him.

Probably in this day and age it seems old fashioned to us.

Either way, whether simple or old fashioned it had the effect that he could not take this in and it is no wonder that when we talk about this to people we are discussing Buddhism with, that they cannot believe it either, it is all too simple, too old fashioned.

In another Gosho called, 'Thus I Heard,' Nichiren Daishonin talks about this.

"Therefore, when I expounded it people refused to believe it, thinking that it must be a false teaching, this is perfectly understandable, for example if a lowly soldier had announced that he seduced the beautiful court lady Wang Chao Chun no one would have believed it, similarly people cannot believe that a priest of such lowly birth could expound Nam Myoho Renge Kyo, the heart of The Lotus Sutra, which even Tien Tai and Dengyo who rank as highly as ministers and court nobles did not propagate."

It seems too simple; it seems old fashioned but in fact it is unbelievably deep.

Changing Poison into Medicine

Nichiren Daishonin's answer to the problems of the world is based on the Buddha's view of society in its relationship with the entire universe.

Inevitably when we first talk to someone about Buddhism, they cannot understand the power of The Gohonzon.

How could they, nor could we when we were first introduced.

Inevitably they tend to argue on a shallow even emotional level.

We must not get angry, and we must not get upset, it is natural that people find it difficult to accept this easily.

That is why the guest asked Nichiren Daishonin for proof, in his case as he was living in a Buddhist land so, he naturally asked for documentary or historical proof.

Through all this gradually the guest understood, just like we hope the people we talk to will also understand Nichiren Shoshu Buddhism.

We have talked about governments and leaders and politics.

Let us now have a look at social life, at society itself.

The ultimate truth if it is the ultimate truth must affect every aspect of life, family life, our social life, the life of the whole country and the whole world.

This occurs when people start to practice and gain actual proof in their own lives.

The reformation of our lives begins through activating our life force, wisdom, compassion and courage and ridding ourselves of the three poisons of greed, anger and ignorance through chanting Nam Myoho Renge Kyo to The Gohonzon.

This is called changing our personal bespoke poison into medicine.

Fundamental to this process is a growing understanding that life is actually eternal, you cannot destroy consciousness or life whilst the physical self, must like all physical things, disintegrate and decay in the end.

Through understanding that life is eternal, the three poisons gradually disappear from your life.

Let us look at Greed.

We realise, once we know that life is eternal, that we are going to leave everything behind anyway, so what is the point of being greedy and grabbing at the expense of others.

This is a natural adjustment as we come to understand the eternity of life.

Then Anger.

Why should we be competitive and ruthless and destructive when more and more we find ourselves wanting happiness for ourselves and everybody else.

Changing Poison into Medicine

This is the power of The Gohonzon working in our lives and this will naturally lead to these realisations.
And finally Fear.
Fear caused by the third poison that is ignorance or stupidity, the fear of death disappears when you really understand that life is eternal, therefore you fear nothing else.
These are the three poisons which will disperse once eternal life becomes a realistic living thing in your own mind and lived experience.
Through the process of changing poison into medicine and ridding ourselves of the three poisons we can change our negative or unhappy karma and boundless wisdom and compassion can begin to flow absolutely freely more and more from within our life as we go through this steady progress of self reformation.
In relation to the universe, the eternity of life and our understanding of it is particularly important.
Nichiren Shoshu Buddhism explains that the universe is an eternally living thing, a living body, a living organism of boundless size.
It is supported by a myriad of other independent, yet interdependent organisms and we are just one of them.
Every other living entity, every other living thing is an organism each with its own environment and each of those environments over lapping and supporting each other.
This is the Buddhist view of the universe in a nutshell.
It is the great life force of Nam Myoho Renge Kyo that keeps it vibrantly living and progressing and developing positively.
This happens more and more if that life force is undeterred by the effect of destruction and negativity.
Life force generates many other forces that are at work in the universe.
An obvious one is gravity and modern science is beginning to understand all about that.
Sound and light waves are another force in the universe that are at work, the pull of the moon on the tides is another example of the force of the universe at work.
The Sun's nourishment to ourselves and to plants, these are all universal forces at work.
On top of these very obvious ones there are a myriad others much more subtle, much less obvious that are at work in and around us twenty four hours a day.
These are what we call in Buddhism the Shoten Zenjin or in its old fashioned name The Buddhist Gods.

Changing Poison into Medicine

By striving to follow a positive enlightened force of life these forces will protect us because their very nature is aiming towards creation and progress.
Whenever you do Gongyo the Buddhist Gods are lined up either side of you and as you bow to The Gohonzon, they bow with you.
We feed the forces of the universe with our positive enlightened life force generated through Buddhist practice, through our Gongyo and Shodai.
Then they will work with us, for us, rather than working against us or disappearing all together if we are in a negative or destructive ignorant state of life.
This is what it means in this Gosho when it says that the Sages and the Buddhist Gods leave the country.
If people are ignorant and negative then the forces of creation, positive enlightened growth and progress will leave because they have nothing to work on, nothing to relate to, nothing to be in rhythm with.
This is how and why the change in a single individual life can change their karma, the karma of their country and the karma of the whole planet.
One person working in rhythm with these universal forces can change everything in their environment and then further and further out into the environment in general just as the Buddha Nichiren Daishonin has showed us by his own example.
At the end of this Gosho, Rissho Ankoku Ron the guest says, and by that time he has been Shakubuku'd, and he is answering his own question with the following lines.

"Therefore you must quickly reform the tenets that you hold in your heart and embrace the one true vehicle, the single good doctrine of The Lotus Sutra, if you do so then the threefold world would all become The Buddha Land and how could a Buddha Land ever decline.
The regions in the ten directions will all become treasure realms and how could a treasure realm ever suffer harm.
If you live in a country that knows no decline or diminution, in a land that suffers no harm or disruption, then your body will find rest and security and your mind will be calm and untroubled.
You must believe my words, heed what I say."

In another Gosho called 'On Practicing The Buddha's Teachings.' Nichiren Daishonin says,

Changing Poison into Medicine

"In that time because all people chant Nam Myoho Renge Kyo together, the wind will not beleaguer the branches or bows, nor will the rain fall hard enough to break a clod.
The world will become as it was in the ages of Fu Hsi and Shen Nung in ancient China.
Disasters will be driven from the land and the people will be rid of misfortune, they will also learn the art of living long, fulfilling lives.
Realise that the time will come when the truth will be revealed that both The Person and The Law are unageing and eternal.
There cannot be the slightest doubt about the sutra's solemn promise of a peaceful life in this world."

This is the whole purpose of what we practice and what we teach, the whole purpose of Nichiren Shoshu Buddhism.
Of course there will be rainstorms, of course there will be rough seas but because of the natural wisdom and compassion flowing in the lives of the people they will be able to overcome any such natural events.
Despite science and technology humanity needs the ultimate truth in order to be able to understand the world correctly and live in it harmoniously and happily.
Our progress is chaotic at the moment and so we must go out and teach others about this amazing practice of Nichiren Shoshu Buddhism.
All this is based on the Buddhist principle of Esho Funi.
This principle covers our relationship with each other and with everything else around us including the entire universe.
It concerns our relationship with those forces of the universe that we mentioned earlier.
The word Esho is a combination of two words, Eho and Shoho.
Eho means dependant on, and Ho means reward, dependant on something else for reward, this is Eho.
Shoho, sho of shoho means entity, ho again means reward.
The entity in itself is rewarding so shoho the entity has its ability to gain reward or good fortune built into it or inherently.
Shoho is us, the entity.
Eho that thing which is dependent on something else for reward is our environment, Eho.
Shoho and Eho are different entities us and our environment, yet they are absolutely inseparable.
Every action on my part effects my environment just as these words I am writing now will affect all of those who are in their environments reading these words.
Funi of Esho Funi means two but not two, two things which are inseparable.

Esho Funi therefore means the inseparability of a living entity and its environment.

Nichiren Daishonin said Shoho is like our body and Eho is like the shadow.

When the body moves the shadow moves and when the body is stationary the shadow is stationary.

The body being us and the shadow being our environment.

When we bow to The Gohonzon according to this principle of Esho Funi our environment bows as well, when we are angry our environment will be equally upset and when we are in the state of Buddha our environment will join us in the Buddha state as well.

We can prove this for ourselves in our daily lives and it is through the workings of this principle that we gain benefit.

We find that as we practice our environment does begin to work with us.

This benefit is caused by that, by the environment bending towards us rather than against us or away from us.

The environment also has a great effect on the entity or person and science is fully aware of this.

In medicine there is greater and greater understanding of the effect of the environment on us.

Such things that were unknown quantities, that before were laughed at, such as thunder causing headaches, snow or impending snow causing a feeling of unease, an east wind causing tension and dryness, these things were not recognised by medical science in its early days.

Scientists are beginning to know about how life began through the action and reaction of simple elements working upon each other.

In sociology today we are beginning to understand the awful effect of tower blocks and deprivation has on the minds of people, the environment's effect on the person.

The great relationship between the entity and the environment is very clear to us and to science, so far as the environment's effect on us is concerned.

The other way around is the thing that has not been so clear but is unfortunately becoming clearer and clearer due to our negative effect on the environment causing climate change, global warming, environmental destruction and the current global climate crisis that we are in the midst of.

The environment can easily sway us, but can it give us happiness? Of course the answer is no because the environment is always changing, what may be here today can disappear tomorrow.

Changing Poison into Medicine

What matters is that we are strong in the centre of our environment basing our life on the highest condition of life Buddhahood or Buddha Nature, then everything in that environment will be affected in just the same way as the environment can affect us, the same forces, the same linkage is there.

Philosophy or religions concern is with the inner realm.

How can we achieve that highest and best life state and thus make sure that our environment acts in the highest state as well? This is what the practice of Nichiren Shoshu Buddhism is all about. This is the key to happiness.

If we reveal the Buddha state in our own life the environment will reflect the Buddha state by the unchanging, inescapable law of Esho Funi.

If you take a house, its atmosphere depends on the people living there, a house can feel joyful when you go into it, or it can feel spooky and creepy.

This is not the house itself, this is the reflection of the lives of the people who are living there through the law of cause and effect and its relationship with the principle of Esho Funi.

We get no more or no less than what we deserve.

Let us hope we can feel more and more that this universe that we are a part of is an incredible, vibrating world of life with its countless, myriad entities, each an organism in itself and each with an environment and all those environments overlapping one another, creating one limitless entity of life.

We can then understand that what I do now and say now affects not just me or you but the whole universe.

If we live a life filled with the three poisons, then the three poisons will be rampant in our environment.

If we live a life where we make an effort to elevate our state of life to its highest or Buddhahood, then that is what the environment will reflect, that perfect awakened and enlightened state of being.

It is so simple yet so incredibly vast and profound.

This is why people find it so difficult to understand and believe it, yet it is so natural and that is why it is so simple.

In the end the only way is for people to try it and get the proof. Nichiren Daishonin on the beach at Tatsunokuchi proved our relationship with the universe when he was saved from being beheaded, when the sword was actually above his head, through the phenomena of this incredible, brilliant meteorite shooting across the sky lighting everything up as brilliantly as day so that the samurai fled in fear and their horses broke loose in the chaos.

He proved through his strong prayer which he carried out just before he got to the execution site, that life is totally interconnected with the universe and everything in it.

Scientists know that meteorites, comets and stars have an effect on the earth but what they do not know is why such phenomena occur at a particular time, it was at a particular time that the brilliant meteor shot across the sky and saved Nichiren Daishonin's life.

And just to make sure everyone understood a second occurrence took place on the next night, this is all recorded in a Gosho called 'On The Buddha's Behaviour' and it is very exciting to read if you haven't already read it please read it, it is a thriller in itself.

This is an excerpt from that Gosho on the second occurrence that happened.

"On the night of the thirteenth, there was scores of warriors stationed around my lodgings and in the main garden, because it was almost the middle of the month, the moon was very round and full.

I went out into the night garden and there turning towards the moon, recited the Jigage portion of the Juryo chapter of The Lotus Sutra, then I spoke briefly about the merits and faults of the various sects and about the teachings of The Lotus Sutra and I said, 'You the god of the moon participated in the ceremony of The Lotus Sutra did you not, when The Buddha expounded the Hoto chapter, you obeyed his order and in the Zokuri chapter, when the Buddha laid his hand on your head, three times you vowed to fulfil the command to transmit and protect The Sutra, are you not the same god?

Would you have an opportunity to fulfil your vow if it were not for me?

Now that you see me in this situation should you not joyfully rush forward to shield the Votary of The Lotus Sutra and thereby fulfil your vow to The Buddha?

It is incredible that you have not yet done anything, if nothing is done to bring this country to justice, I will never return to Kamakura.

If you intend not to do anything for me how can you continue to shine on complacently, how do you read the following passages from the sutras.

The Daijuku Sutra that the Sun and Moon do not show their brightness.

The Ninno Sutra states both the Sun and the Moon shall act discordantly.

Changing Poison into Medicine

The Saishoo sutra says the thirty three heavenly gods will be enraged.
What is your answer Moon, what is your answer?'
Then as though in answer a large star bright as the morning star fell from the sky and struck a branch of the plum tree in front of me, the soldiers astounded jumped down from the veranda, fell on their faces in the garden or ran behind the house.
Immediately a fierce wind started up, raging so violently that the whole island of Enoshima seemed to roar, the sky shook, echoing with the sound like pounding drums."

This is also recorded in government records of the time, Nichiren Daishonin was proving the truth of his teachings for us all.
This was the purpose of Tatsunokuchi and the purpose of this incident, to prove to us that if we to chant Nam Myoho Renge Kyo with our whole hearts and do Gongyo and practice exactly as the Buddha taught, then the Shoten Zenjin the forces of the universe will definitely work with us and ensure that we can continue our life and fulfil our purpose, when you are up against difficulties chant Shodai with that in mind.
Nichiren Daishonin is saying how his mind was working as he was chanting Nam Myoho Renge Kyo and that is the way our minds should work when we find ourselves in a tight corner.
Chant Nam Myoho Renge Kyo with that determination and with that strength, then there is nothing we cannot overcome.
This is the way the universe will work if we are moving in a positive direction with the intent of our changing poison into medicine and creating Kosen Rufu wherever we go, with that sort of attitude this world can become totally transformed and our task is to go on teaching others about the ultimate truth until we have enough people in the world to prevent disaster through activating the great life force of Buddhahood which exists in every single human being if they only knew it.

Question Three.

Changing Poison into Medicine

"The Guest thereupon flushed with anger, there upon said,
Emperor Ming of The Later Han Dynasty, having comprehended
the significance of his dream of a golden man, welcomed the
teachings of Buddhism brought to China by missionaries leading
white horses.
Prince Shotoku having punished Monanobe No Morina for his
opposition to Buddhism, proceeded to construct Temples and
Pagodas in Japan.
Since that time from The Supreme Ruler down to the numberless
masses, people have worshipped the Buddhist statues and
devoted their attention to the scriptures and as a result, in the
monasteries of Mount Hei and in the southern capitol of Nara, at
the great temples of Onjo-ji and To-ji, throughout the land within
the four seas, in the five areas adjacent to the capitol and seven
outer lying regions, Buddhist scriptures have been ranged like stars
in the sky and halls of worship have spread over the land like
clouds.
Those who belong to the lineage of Shariputra meditate upon the
moon atop of Eagle Peak, while those who adhere to the
traditions of Haklenayashas transmit the teachings of Mount
Kukkutapada.
How then can anyone say that the teachings of the Buddha's
lifetime are despised or that the three treasures of Buddhism have
ceased to exist?
If there is evidence to support such contention, I would like to
hear the facts."

The Guest is really sincerely expressing his belief that Japan was a
religious country.
He is blinded or mesmerised by all the trappings of religion that he
sees in all directions.
The great temples and priests and monks everywhere.
In fact everywhere you looked there were shrines and religious
ritualistic activities.
Japan must be religious, and this is what he sees and in his
complacency he believes Japan must be ok.
On the surface Japan was religious and you only have to see all
those buildings in Japan today to realise that.
Everywhere you turn you will run into temples but underneath the
surface of all that ritual and all those amazing temples there was
hypocrisy and lobbying for power and even killing for the sake of
greed and a lust for power.
That was Mediaeval Japan and in 1260 the situation was
extraordinarily similar to Europe and in England.
Everywhere great cathedrals were being built at about that time.

Monasteries were mushrooming all over Europe but the church itself was becoming deeper and deeper involved in the affairs of this world, in politics.

More and more they were concerned with becoming rich and amassing vast possessions in land and money, so much so that by the fifteenth century, Cardinal Wolsey, a churchman was able to build a palace that was greater than the King.

This was Hampton Court, and the King was so angry with him that to save his head he decided he had better give it to his King.

The King then moved out of Richmond Palace and took his court to live in Hampton Court instead.

This was the situation, immensely rich and puffed up priests and monks, just as in Japan, looked down on the common people.

In the twelfth century Thomas Beckett was murdered on the steps of the alter at Canterbury Cathedral.

This was the culmination of the struggle for power between the church and the King.

In the same century there were two popes at one and the same time.

One in Rome and one in Avignon, both of them puppets of political power.

Meanwhile the ordinary people continued to be subservient to these great priests.

They feared them, and they feared them and obeyed them because they feared the wrath of God which they were taught, that would descend on them if they did not do so.

It is important for us today to consider why it was that religions became so involved in the politics of power and so swept away by greed and amassing material fortune.

The answer is that their religious practice was too weak to motivate a true spiritual reformation in their hearts.

Egoism and the three poisons inevitably remained as the supreme state in their lives and the lives of the leaders and the led.

This is all as Shakyamuni Buddha had predicted.

He had warned that in the period called Zoho, one thousand years and on after he died, Buddhism would become formalised and ritualised and the province of priests and monks and lose the power because of that to truly help the people.

Exactly the same thing applies to the Zoho of christianity.

The Buddhist time periods of Shobo, Zoho and Mappo can be applied to any religion not only Buddhism.

In the case of Europe as cathedrals grew and the priests became more and more magnificent in their robes and their rituals and dogmas became more and more complicated, so the religion

Changing Poison into Medicine

was losing its power to actually help the people in a spiritual sense.
At this particular point of time today when the Nichiren Shoshu Buddhist movement for Kosen Rufu is beginning to expand all over the world, we should take this lesson form history as a warning about to much formality.
It is stupid to only stand on formality.
We should avoid creating anxiety amongst our community of believers because of our concern about meticulous formal details.
People should grow and enjoy faith and practice in their daily lives but nevertheless we must strictly preserve the traditions of Nichiren Shoshu Buddhism as we inherit the great spirit or desire for Kosen Rufu.
Likewise we should gradually establish our own traditions in each country based on the fundamental principles of Nichiren Shoshu Buddhism through discussion and trial and error.
By doing this we will discover the ideal way for the administration of the community of faith unique to our country or to each individual country.
Some tradition, some ritual and formality is necessary but too much is dangerous.
We have to find the balance, The Middle Way.
The best way to find that is based on our practice of Gongyo and chanting Nam Myoho Renge Kyo.
Formality, traditions and rituals represent continuity and stability and give people a feeling of security and even sometimes of eternity, everlastingness.
It is also evidence of the depths of the roots of our faith.
This is why some tradition and ritual is important.
It is something that our movement and its people can be embraced by and move within the framework of.
Without it people can feel naked and lost.
On the other hand why is too much formality dangerous?
Firstly to much importance on formality can be very easily used to glorify those who are permitted to make the rules and lay down the ritual and can be the friend of authoritarianism.
Secondly, people who are weak in themselves like to shelter behind formality.
They can escape from having faith in their own practice of turning poison into medicine.
They can avoid taking ownership and standing alone by the feeling that "if I follow the rules everything must be ok."
It encourages theoretical thinking and doing things for those things sake.

156

Inevitably such people because of their increasing weakness easily become the prey of the authoritarianism that is bred in too much ritual and rule.

It can become a nasty vicious circle and if we look back through history we can see clearly how this has in fact brought religions to ruin in the end.

Today we have Nichiren Shoshu traditions of The Priesthood. Traditions handed own over many centuries in Japan and traditions can be good but also can become really dangerous.

No tradition or formality should exist unless it helps us to deepen our faith and it helps us to maintain unity.

Every formality and ritual should be reviewed from time to time in order to make sure that its existence is for both these points.

We should never ignore the question why.

If someone does not understand in the depths of their heart the answer to a question or the reason for doing things in our community our advance towards our important goal of our personal enlightenment and Kosen Rufu will be resisted.

The spirit will be dulled and diluted.

In 'The West' it is important not to ignore the deductive way of thinking.

There should be a reason for everything and this reason, if it is based on wisdom, should be understandable to all.

For example in Nichiren Shoshu tradition or the most obvious one is the form of Gongyo.

Five prayers in the morning and three in the evening and the way they do it is the tradition based on the teachings of Nichiren Daishonin and contains the wisdom of Nichiren Daishonin and the wisdom of all the successive High Priests.

We should do Gongyo in that form as it deepens our faith and strengthens our unity.

A completely different example is that we carry our beads with two tufts over the left hand and three over the right.

The Priesthood or The Sangha ask the lay people to do the same. It is a small point, and it is there as a symbol of our unity and our willingness to cooperate with our Priests and is very reasonable.

Other traditions should be adapted to the countries culture.

A good example is that there is no need for us to enshrine our Gohonzon in a Japanese style black lacquer Butsudan.

There is no need for us to take our shoes off in order to enter someone's house and do Gongyo unless of course the houseowner requests it.

There is no need to kneel as they do on tatami mats in Japan, if you wish you can sit on a chair.

Changing Poison into Medicine

We do not have to separate men and women as they do in formal meetings in Japan.
This is Japanese custom and tradition, and we must of course use our wisdom in this regard.
Going back to the times of this Gosho what we see is the world is as it was in Japan in the middle ages.
In these times we seem to be tilting and sliding more and more into a state of confusion and darkness.
This is not as it was before in history, it is no good saying this is like it was before such and such a time, it has never been like this before, we should not lull ourselves into a state of complacency by such feelings.
Before there was no threat from global warming and an impending environmental melt down, or of a nuclear holocaust brought about by a war between two huge superpowers.
This in itself makes everything different from any other age in human history.
Before people tended to follow their leaders and most people believed in them, nowadays everyone believes our leaders are floundering about and do not know or have the slightest clue what to do.
Before violence had a target such as violence towards a corrupt hierarchy, maybe a desire to establish some 'ism' by revolutionary means, today it seems it is just destruction for the sake of destruction.
It is blind and groping about in the darkness of despair, it is hitting out at anything and everything, it is not government buildings that are the target, it is small businesses, little shops that people have taken a whole lifetime to build up.
It is neither against the rich or the poor, those who are working or those who are not working, it is neither against the young nor the old, it is destruction for destructions sake.
It arises from the complete confusion that exists in the hearts of many people living today.
This is nothing like it was before, it is totally different to what it was like before.
People who say it is the same are lulling themselves into a state of complacency.
The time is now right for The Gohonzon and for the teachings of Nichiren Shoshu Buddhism.
Now there can be no doubt that what the world needs is the power to transform the hearts of the people, the one great family of humanity.
That power only exists in The Dai Gohonzon and Nam Myoho Renge Kyo of The Three Great Secret Laws.

Changing Poison into Medicine

This is the one and only solution and we can say this increasingly with absolute conviction, we have to spread that understanding to others, we have to open the eyes of the people.

After the outburst of indignation of the traveller in the question, Nichiren Daishonin then continues his argument, his case for the validity of his teachings.

He begins by citing passages from The Lotus Sutra of Shakyamuni Buddha and from The Nirvana Sutra.

This is the answer to this question, here is his answer to question three.

"The Host, anxious to clarify his words replied.

To be sure Buddha halls stand rooftop to rooftop and sutra storehouses are ranged eve to eve.

Priests are as numerous as bamboo plants and rushes and monks as common as rice and hemp seedlings.

The temples and priests have been honoured from centuries past and everyday new respect is paid them, but the monks and priests today are fawning and devious and they confuse the people and lead them astray.

The Ruler and his ministers lack understanding and fail to distinguish between truth and heresy.

The Ninno Sutra for example says,

'Evil monks hoping to gain fame and profit in many cases appear before The Ruler, the heir apparent or the other Princes and take it upon themselves to preach doctrines that lead to the violation of The Buddhist Dharma and the destruction of The Nation.

The Rulers failing to see the truth of the situation, listen to and put faith in such doctrines and proceed to create regulations that are perverse in nature and do not accord with the rules of Buddhist discipline.

In this way they bring about the destruction of Buddhism and of The Nation.'

The Nirvana Sutra states,

'Bodhisattvas, have no fear in your hearts of such things as wild elephants, but evil friends, they are what you should fear. If you are killed by a wild elephant, you will not fall into any of the Three Evil Paths, but if evil friends lead you to your death, you are certain to fall into one of them.'

The Lotus Sutra says,

'There will be monks in that evil age with perverse wisdom and hearts that are fawning and crooked who will say that they have attained what they have not attained, being proud and boastful in heart, or they will be forest dwelling monks, wearing clothing of patched rags, living in retirement, who will claim that they are

159

practicing the true way, despising and looking down on the rest
of humankind. Greedy for profit and nourishment they will preach
The Dharma to laypersons and will be respected and revered by
the world as though they were Arhats who possess the six
supernatural powers. Constantly they will go about amongst the
populace, seeking in this way to slander us.
They will address The Rulers and high ministers, Brahmans and
great patrons of Buddhism, as well as the other monks, slandering
and speaking evil of us, saying 'these are men of perverted views,
who preach the doctrines of heretical sects.'
In a muddied kalpa, in an evil age, there will be many different
things to fear.
Demons will take possession of others and through them, curse
and revile and heap shame on us.
The evil monks of that muddied age, failing to understand The
Buddha's expedient means, how he preaches The Dharma in
accord with what is appropriate, will confront us with foul
language and angry frowns, again and again we will be
banished.'
In The Nirvana Sutra, the Buddha says,
'After I have passed away and countless hundreds of years have
gone by, all the Sages of The Four Stages, will also have passed
away.
After the Former Day of The Law has ended and The Middle Day
of the Law has begun, there will be monks who will give the
appearance of abiding by the rules of monastic discipline, but
they will scarcely ever read or recite The Sutras and instead will
crave all kinds of food and drink to which to nourish their bodies.
Though the wear the robes of monks, they will go about searching
for alms like so many huntsman, spying sharply and stalking softly.
They will be like cats on the prowl for mice and constantly they will
reiterate these words' 'I have attained the state of an Arhat.'
Outwardly they will seem to be wise and good but within they will
harbour greed and jealousy and when they are asked to preach
The Dharma they will conceal it, pretending to be Brahmans who
have taken a vow of silence.
They are not true monks, they merely have the appearance of
monks, consumed by their erroneous views they slander the true
Law.'
When we look at the world in the light of these passages of
scripture we see that the situation is just as they describe it.
If we do not admonish the evil monks, how can we hope to do
good?'

Changing Poison into Medicine

The most important lines of this particular passage are the two last lines.

'If we do not admonish the evil monks, how can we hope to do good?'

Nichiren Daishonin is explaining the reasons throughout this passage as to why he must so strictly admonish these evil monks as he calls them.
He starts quoting from The Lotus Sutra to prove what he has to say because these passages from The Lotus Sutra and The Nirvana Sutra all concern the age of Mappo which is the age in which Nichiren Daishonin was born.
Sometimes we find his attacks on these monks and priests almost too severe, we are sensitive to this sort of thing, we have been brought up in an age of permissiveness.
'Is it really necessary?' we say in our hearts, that Nichiren Daishonin should behave in that way.
'I don't like it, everyone has a right to believe in what they believe.'
This is the way we think today but of course he is not slandering those monks and priests as human beings, he is condemning what they were teaching and preaching, which was leading the people to misery.
This is what he hoped to uproot and in the process save those monks and priests from further slander and causing others in increasing numbers in Japan to slander as well.
These people sincerely believed they were enlightened, they are people with conceited minds, they were judging the teachings of Shakyamuni Buddha and selecting from them.
'We will use this bit here and that bit there, and this bit from this Sutra and this bit from this Sutra.'
This is what we believe with our great minds are the teachings of Shakyamuni Buddha.
These are people of conceited minds and as a result were distorting The Dharma.
This was a terrible thing, this is what Nichiren Daishonin saw so clearly.
This was why Japan was heading for ruination and this was what he was trying to say to everybody.
Studying the Gosho is not playing with theoretical ideology, it is the source of power with which to challenge daily life.
Those who devote themselves to study without practice cannot obtain real benefit no matter how much they know about The Gosho.

161

Changing Poison into Medicine

They cannot draw great good fortune from The Mystic Law.
The ultimate aim of Nichiren Shoshu Buddhism lies in attaining
Buddhahood and for this, practice is indispensable.
A person who boasts about their knowledge of Buddhism and
finds self-satisfaction in the study of abstract theory alone is no
longer a Buddhist much less a follower of Nichiren Daishonin.
Many people of this sort neglect practice and make no effort to
transmit The Law into society or into the future.
They assume a critical attitude towards those who embrace The
Lotus Sutra thereby creating bad karma.
Exactly like those monks, Nichiren Daishonin warns us that we must
not fall into this trap.
The only reason you can fall into it is if you fail to practice as the
Buddha taught.
The Buddha taught three practices not just study, and such
people because they do not do the three practices fail to
change poison into medicine and the three poisons and their
ego's take charge of their lives and as a result what they teach is
totally distorted and we see the same type of people outside of
Buddhism in government.
Politicians, scientists and people in the media, people in society
who may appear cultured, well dressed, charming but in reality
under the surface their lives are filled with the three poisons.
This is the age of the three poisons, the age of Mappo and their
actions in thought, word and deed are based on those poisons.
Let us look at those last lines again.

'If we do not admonish those evil monks, how can we hope to do
good?'

Nichiren Daishonin had to admonish them in order to save the
people and to save them from committing further slander.
If Nichiren Daishonin in 1253 when he declared Nam Myoho
Renge Kyo just said this is the True Dharma ladies and gentlemen
and left it at that nothing would have happened to him
whatsoever.
He could have gone along forming a little sect, people would
have followed him, he would have received no persecution, no
trouble at all.
The reasons the persecutions fell on him like a series of terrible
storms was because he not only said this is The True Dharma, but
he also cited every one of the sects in Japan and said that you
are practicing wrong and distorted teachings.
It is you that are distorting the minds of the people, and this is why
Japan is in such misery.

This was why the persecutions descended upon him.

Nichiren Daishonin was not just concerned with himself he was not just concerned with leading a Buddhist sect, he was concerned about the happiness of everybody and this was why he had to say these things.

He had to admonish those evil monks.

This is true Buddhist mercy, true Jihi.

It comes down in Buddhist terms to the question of what is the greatest good and what is the greatest evil.

The greatest good is to embrace The True Law or Dharma that is The Dai Gohonzon and Nam Myoho Renge Kyo.

The greatest evil, far and away greater than any other evil in Buddhist terms is to slander The True Dharma.

The people of Japan in those days in their ignorance were slandering The True Dharma and desperately suffering the karmic consequences because they were misled by a host of priests and monks.

The greatest good was to tell them this clearly and forthrightly.

If Nichiren Daishonin had preached The True Dharma without condemning the false teachings he would have been cancelling out the greatest good by the greatest evil, by turning a blind eye to the evil that was going on around him.

In the Gosho, 'Admonitions Against Slander,' Nichiren Daishonin deals with this point in some detail, and he quotes from The Nirvana Sutra in the process.

"In The Nirvana Sutra Shakyamuni states,

'If even a good priest sees someone slandering The Dharma and disregards him, failing to reproach him and oust him and punish him for his offense, then that priest is betraying Buddhism but if he takes the slanderer severely to task, drives him off or punishes him, then he is my disciple and one who truly understands my teachings.'

Never forget this admonition against ignoring another's slander of Buddhism.

Both Master and Disciple will surely fall into the hell of incessant suffering if they see enemies of The Lotus Sutra and fail to reproach them. The great teacher Nan Yueh wrote.

'They will fall into hell with evil men. To seek enlightenment without repudiating slander is as futile as trying to find water in the midst of fire or fire in the midst of water.'"

In other words you are merely cancelling out the greatest good by the greatest evil.

We really need to remember this point.

We do not live in a Buddhist country.

We do not have the task of trying to lead a people out of centuries of tradition in sects who follow the wrong teachings in order to open their eyes to see the truth.

Nevertheless if we encounter people who are practicing the earlier teachings of Shakyamuni we have to be extremely firm and forthright in what we say.

If we cannot argue and debate it with detail and documentary proof then we should refer it to someone who can.

In the Gosho all the details are there in order to debate successfully with any such person, Shakyamuni Buddha who taught in The Lotus Sutra said discard all that I have taught before.

He also said that the only teaching in The Age of Mappo that can lead people to enlightenment is The Lotus Sutra.

The other religions in Europe arose quite ignorant of Buddhism. Though there were Buddhist emissaries going as far as Greece in the time of King Ashoka of India. (304-232 B.C.)

Nevertheless due to the ignorance of those teachings and their lack of depth, it does lead for those of us who have followed them, to slander life and of this there can be no shadow of doubt.

We only have to look at the history of Europe to see this so clearly before us.

We must be firm about these principles when we are teaching The True Dharma to others and when we are trying to do Shakubuku we must point out this patiently and firmly.

It has been said that it is a sign of weakness in a religion when they begin to recognise other faiths.

They then start saying that there are many paths to enlightenment, that there is more than one way, this is a very profound observation as this means that a religion is losing its confidence that its teachings are not able to survive the onslaught of other teachings in these contemporary times.

This is all based on the principle of you do your thing and I will do mine.

Like the traveller in this famous treatise we should not be misled by the trappings of religion.

We have to look below the surface to really understand and to realise just how great Nichiren Shoshu Buddhism really is.

In these weak and vacillating times we have to think about this point very, very carefully and we should courageously follow the words and the spirit of Nichiren Daishonin who knowing that all the three strong enemies at once would attack him.

Changing Poison into Medicine

He never spared himself in declaring that what the people were doing, and that what the priests were teaching, were totally wrong and would never lead them down the true path to enlightenment.
His conviction was tremendous and is revealed in these two short Gosho passages.

On Practising The Buddhas Teachings.
"Suppose someone, no matter who, should loudly proclaim that The Lotus Sutra alone can lead people to Buddhahood and that all other sutras far from leading them to enlightenment only drive them into hell, observe what happens if he should thus try to refute the teachers and doctrines of all the other sects.
The Three Powerful Enemies will arise without fail."

The Opening of The Eyes.
"Here I will make a great vow, though I might be offered the rulership of Japan if I will only abandon The Lotus Sutra and accept the teachings of the Meditation Sutra and look forward to rebirth in The Pure Land, though I might be told that my Father and Mother will have their heads cut off if I do not recite the Nembutsu, whatever obstacle I will encounter, so long as persons of wisdom do not prove my teachings to be false, I will never yield!
All other troubles are no more to me than dust before the wind.
I will be the pillar of Japan,
I will be the eyes of Japan,
I will be the great ship of Japan.
This is my vow, and I will never forsake it."

These are amazing words.
They are certainly 'I believe what I feel, and never would I give up The Gohonzon unless some person can prove these teachings to be wrong.'
When Nichiren Daishonin says proved, he means proved in the sense of 'The Three Proofs' of documentary and literary proof, theoretical proof and actual proof in this daily life.
Here we live in a non-Buddhist country, and we teach through persuasion and discussion.
If someone is dedicated to another religion we should leave them if we feel, and they insist that they are happy as a result of practicing it.
This does not mean to say that we should in anyway suggest or agree that there is another ultimate truth other than The Dai Gohonzon and Nam Myoho Renge Kyo.

165

Changing Poison into Medicine

We have to be strong where people are desperately suffering.
This is in the pure interests of true mercy or Buddhist Jihi.
Through the wisdom of The Gohonzon through our practice of
Gongyo and Shodai we should know how to deal with every
different case of Shakubuku.
As long as we are insistent both to ourselves and others that there
is no other teaching for this age that enables people to
overcome their sufferings and enables them to change the
poison of their negative karma into the medicine of good fortune,
to become enlightened in this lifetime, other than to accept The
Dai Gohonzon and Nam Myoho Renge Kyo.
If we waiver on this point we will never Shakubuku satisfactorily.
We shall show the weakness that is being shown by the other
religions and philosophies of this age.
When we are questioned on this point, which of course we will be,
if people say do you really believe that this is the only way?
We always say yes,.
We know of no other and we know that every day we see the
power of The Gohonzon and that nothing else on this Earth
surpasses it.
Never mind whether or not people listen to us, we should teach
The True Dharma.
If someone turns on their heel and walks away it does not matter
because later when that person still sees The Gohonzon working in
your life and the experiences you have of the examples of its
power, they will eventually change their minds.
We should never be afraid of being definite and strong in this
way, on the contrary, if we are weak in this respect then what we
give is an impression of the weakness of our own faith.
It is no good cancelling out the greatest good by the greatest
evil.
We have to be strong and firm, polite and courteous and most
importantly of all merciful and compassionate.
Above all we have to show without saying one word the power of
The Gohonzon working within our own lives.
It is not necessarily a matter of conspicuous benefits.
What is most impressive is the experience of changing poison into
medicine, our own experience of changing our negative karma
into good fortune.
That of struggling and failing and struggling again and eventually
overcoming and transforming our problems.
This is what people are interested in, this power of The Gohonzon
for transformative, positive change in our lives.

Changing Poison into Medicine

There is no other religion in this world with the power to enable people to change their unhappy negative karma, from sadness and darkness and ignorance, to begin to see some light and brilliance in their lives.
To change poison into medicine.
Let us express this with our whole lives.

Question Four.

"The Guest, growing more indignant than ever said, A wise monarch, by acting in accord with heaven and earth, perfects his rule.

A sage, by distinguishing between right and wrong, brings order to the world.

The monks and priests of the world today enjoy the confidence of the entire empire.

If they were in fact evil monks, then the wise ruler would put no trust in them.

If they were not true sages, the worthies and learned men would not look up to them.

But now, since worthies and sages do in fact honour and respect them, they must be nothing less than paragons of their kind.

Why then do you pour out these wild accusations and dare to slander them?

To whom are you referring when you speak of "evil monks"?
I would like an explanation!"

You can feel the indignation of the traveller in the way he says, 'who are you referring to when you speak of evil monks, I would like an explanation!'

The wise monarch today represents government or politicians, and we know that there are so many members of government, ministers and politicians due to the nature of the life they have to lead, are in fact often far from wise.

They have no philosophy no rock on which to base their lives or their conclusions or their decisions.

They are pulled this way one minute and another way in the next, hither and thither, to and fro, back and forth by the political pressures that come on them day after day, week after week and year after year.

If they had The Gohonzon, what a vast difference it would make!
Firstly they would be basing their actions and their decisions on the natural rhythm of the universe, the rhythm of life itself.

Secondly they would have the perception and wisdom to understand and appreciate the minds of the people and their needs.

Thirdly they would have the perception and wisdom to understand the current of the times and the trends of society.

And fourthly and perhaps more important than anything else, they would have the strength within themselves to resist the pressures of political life.

Who will be the first politician of Myoho in our government.
I cannot wait for that day!

He or she or they will increasingly astound and influence their fellow politicians by their unique approach to problems, let us hope we don't have to wait too long.

In this question, Nichiren Daishonin also mentions sages.

Sages today are of course scholars, and we even have a committee of scientists and academics called SAGE that are advising the United Kingdom's government throughout the Covid 19 pandemic, who are knowledgeable, and we hope wise people.

Since world war two there has been a tremendous change in this scholastic world.

Before the war that there were scholars who due to their upbringing and their classical education had been encouraged to develop broad minds, scholars who were able to cast their minds on the wide aspect of life itself.

But since the war education and academic study, like so many other things, has become specialised.

Children and young people are now directed down a narrow channel and this channel continues on through university and into life itself.

We lack scholars, as we lack leaders with this broad outlook and understanding of life as a whole, as a backcloth to the specialist subject they deal with.

We have tended to become very narrow in the educational world and the scholarly world due to the educational system which has grown in the post war United Kingdom.

This is a tragedy, nothing should interfere with education but unfortunately education itself comes under political pressure.

A scholar like the wise monarch should be able to feel due to their wide understanding the rhythm of the times, otherwise they are liable to make false judgements.

Who again is going to be the first great scholar of Myoho here in the United Kingdom or the first great educational reformer and I cannot wait for that day to arrive either.

As long as influential people in society, scholars or government leaders are narrow in their outlook they cannot and never will truly understand the rhythm of the times and therefore the conclusions that they reach and the philosophy and teachings that they spread or the acts that they make are inevitably going to be narrow and rigid also.

If the minds of societies leaders are impure or narrow then inevitably society itself will be impure and narrow and, just as Buddhism teaches, that this means that the land will be impure also.

Why is it that this narrowness of views on the part of leaders should restrict the people themselves after all the people have their own minds?

Firstly because the narrow minds of societies leaders lead to the imposition of a moral code.

Their view on life rather than being natural must be imposed by precepts or commandments, a code of conduct.

Secondly it leads to a rigid system of laws.

Thirdly it inevitably leads to a tighter and tighter bureaucracy or bureaucratic control over the people.

This is like three layers of a very heavy overcooked cake, and this has now happened for centuries.

If you look at the history of Europe this has occurred in so many countries and we see the results of it carrying on today.

Out of this restriction and narrowness natural life force is lost.

People feel confined and fettered.

They become distressed and sometimes even desperate, their natural life force becomes lower and lower and lower.

And through this they cannot so easily face challenges when there are really serious ones or steer the right course for the happiness of their countries.

No power or resilience exists anymore and this apathy that results from it breeds even more evil in the form of a lust for power and a privileged few.

We see this all over the world and there is no need to give more examples.

In my country of The United Kingdom we have kept our freedom better than most, so we really need to make sure that we do not allow it to be shaved away anymore.

How can we produce wise monarchs and sages in this age?

Having heard these arguments that Nichiren Daishonin is stating in this Gosho, it is impossible without a correct and all embracing philosophy which such people can base their lives and actions.

It is such a philosophy which aerates that heavy solid cake we were talking about earlier.

The teaching of such a philosophy is the mission or role of a Buddha or in Japanese terminology a Shonin or sage, a supreme or enlightened teacher.

Such a person is able to stand back and through their own enlightenment teach the true way of life which is in rhythm with the natural law of the universe.

Looking back over history there have been not so many cases where such a person appeared but certainly you could say that in the reign of King Ashoka of India, who was a most enlightened

Buddhist King, the state of his lands and kingdom was supremely prosperous and happy.

Really you cannot help coming to the conclusion that there is only one all embracing philosophy which can truly apply itself to every human problem and condition today and that is the teaching of Nam Myoho Renge Kyo.

There is no other and we feel so uncomfortable about that sometimes.

It goes against our British nature which is allowing everybody to be free to do what they like, but still that should not prevent us from believing that there can only be one real truth and that there is only really one way to get at it and that is through Nichiren Daishonin's teachings embodied in Nichiren Shoshu Buddhism.

This is what The Buddha Shakyamuni with his great and worldly wisdom taught nearly three thousand years ago.

Any wise monarch or sage will be so if they are putting their life in rhythm with the life of the universe itself.

The key lines of this question are those last two.

"Who are you referring to when you speak of evil monks? I would like an explanation!"

This Nichiren Daishonin proceeds to give in the answer and the answer is a justification through documentary proof of Nichiren Daishonin's attack on the Nembutsu or Pure Land sect.

Later in the Gosho he also refutes other sects and we do not need to go into these other refutations in great detail as it is unlikely that we are going to have to do battle in a debate with a nembutsu follower.

It was extremely important that Nichiren Daishonin should give detailed proof of the validity of what he was saying because in those days in Japan and over the next seven hundred and fifty years there were plenty of Japanese Nichiren Shoshu Buddhists who had to engage with the followers of The Nembutsu in their country in debate about the true teaching.

Nevertheless if we listen to this answer it gives us the spirit and conviction of Nichiren Daishonin, and we should bear in mind all the time that nembutsu is after all only representative of all false and incomplete teachings in the world today.

Let us now look at the answer.

"The host said: At the time of the Retired Emperor Gotoba, there was a priest named Honen who wrote a work entitled the Shenchaku shu or The Nembutsu Chosen Above All.

He contradicted the sacred teachings of The Buddhas Lifetime and brought confusion to the people in every direction.

The Shenchaku shu states, 'Regarding the passage in which the Meditation Master Tao-cho distinguished between The Sacred way teachings and The Pure Land Teachings and urged people to abandon the former and immediately embrace the latter:

First of all, there are two kinds of Sacred Way teachings, The Mahayana and The Hinayana.

Judging from this, we may assume that the esoteric Mahayana doctrines and the true Mahayana teachings are both included in the Sacred Way.

If that is so, then the present day sects of Shingon, Zen, Tendai, Kegon, Sanron, Hosso, Jiron and Shoron, all these eight schools are included in The Sacred Way that is to be abandoned.

The Dharma Teacher Tan Luan in his Oju ron chu states; 'I note the Boddhisattva Nagarjuna's Jujubibasha ron says: "There are two ways by which a bodhisattva may reach the state of non-regression.

One is the difficult to practice way and the other is the easy to practice way."

"The difficult to practice way is the same as The Sacred Way, and the easy to practice way is the Pure Land Way.

Students of the Pure Land sect should first of all understand this point.

Though they may previously have studied teachings belonging to The Sacred Way, if they wish to become followers of The Pure Land teachings, they must discard The Sacred Way and give their allegiance to The Pure Land teachings.'

Honen also says: "Regarding the passage in which the priest Shantao distinguished between correct and sundry practices and urged people to abandon the sundry practices and embrace the correct practices:

Concerning the first of the sundry practices, that of reading and reciting sutras, with the exception of the Kammuryoju Sutra and the other Pure Land sutras, the embracing, reading and recitation of all sutras, whether Mahayana or Hinayana, exoteric or esoteric, is to be regarded as a sundry practice.

Concerning the third of the sundry practices, that of worshipping, with the exception of worshipping the Buddha Amida, the worshipping or honouring of any other Buddhas, bodhisattvas or deities of this world is to be regarded as a sundry practice.

In the light of this statement, I declare that one should abandon such sundry practices and concentrate upon the practice of the Pure Land Teachings.

What reason would we have to abandon the correct practices of The Pure Land teachings which insure that, out of a hundred persons, all one hundred will be reborn in The Pure Land, and cling instead to the various sundry practices and procedures, which could not save even one person in a thousand?

Followers of The Way should ponder this carefully!"

Honen further states: "In the Jogen nyuzo roku or Chen yuan Era Catalogue of the Buddhist Canon we find it recorded that, from the 600 volumes of the Daihannya Sutra to the Hojoyu Sutra, the exoteric and esoteric sutras of The Mahayana or the great vehicle total 637 works in 2,883 volumes.

The phrase from the Kammuryoju Sutra of 'reading and reciting the great vehicle' should be applied to all these works.

You should understand that, when The Buddha was preaching according to the capacity of his various listeners, he for a time taught the two methods of concentrated meditation and unconcentrated meditation.

But later, when he revealed his own enlightenment, he ceased to teach these two methods.

The only teaching that, once revealed, shall never cease to be taught is the single doctrine of The Nembutsu."

Honen also states: "Regarding the passage which says that the practitioner of the Nembutsu must possess three kinds of mind. It is found in the Kammuryoju Sutra.

In his commentary on that sutra Shantao says, 'Someone may ask: "If there are those who differ in understanding and practice from the followers of the Nembutsu, persons of heretical and mistaken belief, how should we confront them?"

I will now make certain that their perverse and differing views will not cause trouble.

These persons of evil views with different understanding and different practices are compared to a band of robbers who call back the traveller who has already gone one or two steps along their journey.' In my opinion, when this commentary speaks of different understanding, different practices, varying doctrines and varying beliefs, they are referring to the teachings of The Sacred Way."

Finally, in a concluding passage, Honen says, "If one wishes to escape quickly from the sufferings of birth and death, one should confront these two superior teachings and then proceed to put aside the teachings of The Sacred Way and choose those of The Pure Land.

And if one wishes to follow the teachings of The Pure Land, one should confront the correct and sundry practices and then proceed to abandon all of the sundry practices and devote ones entire life to the correct practices."

When we examine these passages, we see that Honen quotes the erroneous explanations of Tan Luan, Tao cho and Shantao, and establishes the categories of The Sacred Way and Pure Land teachings, the difficult to practice and easy to practice ways.

He then takes all the 637 works in 2,883 volumes that comprise The Mahayana Sutras of The Buddhas lifetime, including those of The Lotus Sutra, Shingon along with all the Buddhas, bodhisattvas and deities of this world, and assigns them all to the categories of The Sacred Way teachings, the difficult to practice way and the sundry practices, and urges people to "discard, close, ignore and abandon" them.

With these four injunctions he leads all people astray.

And on top of that he groups together all the sage monks of the three countries of India, China and Japan as well as the students of Buddhism of the ten directions, and calls them a "band of robbers," causing people to insult them!

In doing so, he turns his back on the passage in the three Pure Land Sutras, the sutras of his own sect, which contains Amida's vow to save the people "excepting only those who commit the five cardinal sins or who slander the correct teaching."

At the same time, he shows that he fails to understand the warning contained in the second volume of The Lotus Sutra, the heart and core of the entire body of teachings The Buddha expounded in the five periods of his preaching life, which reads, "If a person fails to have faith but instead slanders this Sutra when their life comes to an end they will enter the hell of incessant suffering."

And now we have come to this latter age when people are no longer sages.

Each enters their own dark road, and all alike forget the direct way.

How pitiful that no one cures them of their blindness!

How painful to see them vainly lending encouragement to these false beliefs!

And as a result, everyone from the ruler of the nation down to the common people believe that there are no true sutras outside the three Pure Land sutras, and no Buddhas other than The Buddha Amida and his two attendants.

Once there were men like Dengyo. Gishin, Jikaku and Chisho who journeyed ten thousand miles across the sea to China to acquire the sacred teachings, and there visited the mountains and rivers to pay reverence to Buddhist statues and carry them back.

In some cases they built holy temples on the peaks of high mountains in which to preserve those scriptures and statues; in other cases they constructed sacred halls in the bottoms of deep valleys where such objects could be worshipped and honoured.

As a result The Buddhas Shakyamuni and Yakushi shone side by side, casting their influence upon present and future ages, while the bodhisattvas Kokuzo and Jizo brought benefit to the living and the dead.

The rulers of the nation contributed districts or villages so that the lamps might continue to burn bright before the images, while the stewards of the great estates gave their fields and gardens as an offering.

But because of this book by Honen, this Shenchaku shu, the lord of teachings Shakyamuni, is forgotten and all honour is paid to Amida, The Buddha of the Western Land.

The transmission of The Dharma from Shakyamuni Buddha is ignored, and Yakushi, The Buddha of the Eastern Region is neglected.

All attention is paid to the three Pure Land sutras in four volumes, and all the other wonderful scriptures that Shakyamuni expounded throughout the five periods of his preaching life are cast aside.

If temples are not dedicated to Amida, then people no longer have the desire to support them or pay honour to the Buddha's enshrined there; if monks are not practitioners of the Nembutsu, then people quickly forget all about giving those monks alms.

As a result, the halls of the Buddha fall into ruin, scarcely a wisp of smoke rises above their moss covered roof tiles and the monks quarters stand empty and dilapidated, the dew deep on the grasses in their courtyards.

And in spite of such conditions, no one gives a thought to protecting The Dharma or to restoring the temples.

Hence the sage monks who once presided over the temples leave and do not return, and the benevolent deities who guarded the nation depart and no longer appear.

This has all come about because of this Shenchaku shu of Honen.

How pitiful to think that, in a space of a few decades, hundreds, thousands, tens of thousands of people have been deluded by these devilish teachings and in so many cases confused as to the true teachings of Buddhism.

If people favour what is only incidental and forget what is primary, can the benevolent deities be anything but angry?

Rather than offering up ten thousand prayers for remedy, it would be better to simply outlaw this one evil doctrine that is the source of all this trouble!"

This is really exciting.
It is exciting because of its preciseness and at the same time its absolute certainty of the righteousness of what he was saying.
Everything is carefully documented, everything is carefully stated against documentary proof.
At this stage in this Gosho he is not concerned with actual proof which Nichiren Daishonin himself said was the most important form of proof, but with documentary proof in order to refute the Nembutsu sect for good and all.
The most important lines are right at the beginning of the answer.

"He contradicted the sacred teachings of Shakyamuni."

This is Mappo, when this Gosho was written it was in the very first centuries of Mappo.
This is exactly what Shakyamuni had predicted two thousand years before that of the loss of his, Shakyamuni's Pure Dharma or Law, in the age of Mappo, when the world would be in a state of chaos and destruction.
Japan was in this state of chaos, the same state of chaos that the world is in today.
The priests in those times were dressed like soldiers rather than priests.
There was an extraordinary situation about one hundred years before this time when the priests were involved in incessant violence and fighting against each other to protect their own power and privileged position in the land.
This was an amazing situation for Buddhism to find itself in.
This was the world into which Nichiren Daishonin was born.
These monks and priests concern was with profit and power more than anything else, and we can see the same thing in our own European history.
The days of the Great Cardinal Wolsey when the religious power was totally intertwined with secular power, in the case of the history of the monasteries in the United Kingdom, we saw it and see it.
The church became hugely rich through exploiting their knowledge over the people and with these land and riches they were able to lend to the King and even sometimes blackmail the King so that they would be powerfully established politically in the country.

Religion was totally impure and mixed up with politics.

Even today the bishops sit in the House of Lords with a vote.

This in its turn led later to in more recent years, the condoning of war.

Priests on both sides preaching the love of god and the righteousness of the cause for which their country was fighting.

Time and again this has occurred in European history.

When people are under the influence of the wrong teachings, a vicious cycle of evil is set up.

The three disasters and seven calamities arise, and this causes the people to want to escape from life as it is.

Then escapist teachings and religions appear.

Today there are other means of escape, drugs, drink, raves and incessant music, sex, mysticism, there is a plethora of sects and cults in this country, even divorce is a means of escape.

This is the karma that is passed on from generation to generation and this also weakens the life force steadily from generation to generation.

The weakness of religion still afflicts us to this day.

Maybe quite a number of people reading this book never really practiced christianity, maybe they did, either way christianity and its weak points are still rooted in us and in our culture.

What is the thing that we suffer from most?

At the root of so many things is guilt.

Guilt is bred from the teachings of christianity as made by the church and not by Jesus Christ himself, this is where guilt has arisen from.

It is very difficult for people from the east to understand how powerful guilt is in our lives and how evil it is.

It holds an incredible grip on most western lives.

Guilt is utterly negative.

Guilt exhausts life force.

Guilt is purposeless.

Thankfully we are fortunate enough to have found The Gohonzon and to begin to understand the teaching of Honin myo based on the law of cause and effect.

The teaching of Honin myo which says, it does not matter what has happened before.

The lower six worlds are part of human life you cannot escape from them.

What matters is to make the great causes now to elevate your Buddha state and turn all those lower worlds into influences to propel your life forward towards your awakening and enlightenment.

Out of these distorted and incomplete teachings also came the class war.

It was the priests who established authoritarianism, it was the priests who taught that human beings were superior to all other forms of life, it was the priests with their knowledge who looked down on the people and taught others who said they were religious and had knowledge to look down on the people.

This is where it has all arisen from.

Everything can be traced back in the history of this world of ours to the wrong religion and philosophy.

All our afflictions of today in this country and elsewhere arise from nowhere else but this single point.

Another important passage in that long answer is.

"And now we have come to this latter age, when people are no longer sages, each enters their own dark road, and all alike forget the straight way, how pitiful that no one cures them of their blindness, how painful to see then vainly lending encouragement to these false beliefs and as a result, everyone from the ruler of the nation down to the common people believes that there are no true sutras outside the three Pure Land sutras, and no Buddhas apart from the Buddha Amida and his two attendants."

In a Gosho called, 'A Decreasing Span of Life,' Nichiren Daishonin explains that it is inevitable, as human beings develop intellectually, so will their capacity for evil actions grow.

In other words the three poisons take over.

This is the cause of people developing arrogant and conceited minds, using their superior knowledge to have power and influence over others.

We have already talked about many examples of this occurring. This is the age of Mappo which Shakyamuni Buddha predicted would be filled with the three poisons because as the world advances and intellectual capacity grows so unfortunately does the ego.

It is vital to master and control this terrible tendency.

This tendency which is insidious and creeps in on life and society almost without anyone realising it.

We must find the philosophy which is wiser than the cleverest person and greater and deeper and wider than the most profound knowledge and I know of no other philosophy except that of The Dai Gohonzon and Nam Myoho Renge Kyo and the teachings of Nichiren Daishonin embodied in Nichiren Shoshu Buddhism which meets these requirements.

Changing Poison into Medicine

It may be said of all the worlds philosophies, systems of thought and religions that though they were meant to precisely direct the current of the age, they are no longer capable of controlling basic human nature.
It may be said that humanity is now unable to supress evil desires and has fallen prey to the ego.
Such philosophies, concepts and religions have been proven to be as transient as the Moon and to fade just like the setting Sun.
They are unable to cope with the extreme speed with which the times and peoples values change, or with the diversity of change inherent in human culture.
As a result they have become bereft of the power to provide their respective peoples, let alone the entire human race, with a precise direction in life.
Humanity has lost control of itself because of the weakness of religion and the philosophies and the teachings that people now follow, due to these teachings inability to keep pace with the incredible speed in which the times are changing and developing.
This began hundreds of years ago when the church refused to believe that the world was spherical, despite all the proof that was given to it, this is one example of how far this goes back in time and human history, it could not keep pace with the times.
The churchmen of those days could not understand how they could support this philosophy of a round world instead of a flat one.
It sounds ridiculous in these times, but it continues today.
Contraception in certain branches of the church is still said to be wrong, totally wrong under any circumstances, yet it is available in vast quantities for everybody, and there is a population explosion problem.
Also parts of the church still deny the basic rights of LGBTQ+ communities around the world.
What does this lead too?
To those who are sincere and seriously minded, it can only lead to guilt or fear where sex and sexuality is concerned.
Through this narrow mindedness, through this attempt at control over people's lives, hearts and minds, guilt once again is nurtured in human life.
Likewise, if we look at the arts, sciences or economics of today, these are ridden with and corrupted by the three poisons and because of this they cannot always contribute to peoples fundamental happiness.

Changing Poison into Medicine

For example in the arts due to a growing obsession with sex, death and violence, these desires are stimulated in human life and so these erroneous world views spread.
Certainly no happiness is caused through it in the true meaning of the word.
In economics the motive of profit breeds greed and at the same time the motive of collectivism breeds apathy and takes the challenge out of life.
In science we see people encouraging consumers to spend and waste.
Products are built deliberately with a limited life to encourage further spending.
Worst of all there are an enormous number of people and money involved in the production of weapons of mass destruction and in particular nuclear devices.
All who are involved in the construction of such weapons of mass destruction are doing the devils work.
How can we straighten the body of society and remove these poisons?
The only way is once again to spread The True Dharma and an understanding of the law of life.
To establish the ultimate truth in every land just as the title of this Gosho implies, to establish absolute respect for life above all else.
In history there are lots of examples of people and movements which start with pure intentions and end up being distorted.
When the philosophy of capitalism was expounded first of all it was expounded with sincerity by such people as Adam Smith, they really believed that it was right for the people of the planet but in time this capitalism was pursued purely for the sake of profit and for the sake of power and greed.
Karl Marx also had pure intentions.
He expounded a philosophy that he firmly believed would bring happiness to the people, but his teachings became the tool of politicians who wanted to gain power and hold onto it.
Power has a terrible attraction towards the evil way.
How can we ensure that people with such pure and noble intentions can follow the course on which they have embarked and not have all they teach torn asunder and used for an evil selfish end?.
Again there is no other way than Nam Myoho Renge Kyo and Nichiren Shoshu Buddhism.
There is no other power within human life which is strong enough to sustain following a course that is enlightened, positive, good and righteous.

Changing Poison into Medicine

We have said many times that there have been many philosophies in this world but not one of them gave a practice which had the power to sustain it.

These philosophies were nothing but empty ideas but in the case of Nichiren Daishonin and his school of Nichiren Shoshu Buddhism, he has given us the practice to produce this power with which to sustain a course of the greatest good to ourselves and all people around us.

To an awakening and enlightenment and wisdom for all peoples regardless of nationality, age, race, gender and sexuality.

Towards the end of this answer Nichiren Daishonin says.

"If people favour peverse doctrines, forget what is correct, can the benevolent deities be otherwise than angry?

If people cast aside doctrines that are all encompassing and take up those that are incomplete, can the world escape the plots of demons.

Rather than offering up ten thousand prayers for remedy, it would be best to simply to outlaw this evil doctrine that is the source of all the trouble."

Every ill is traceable to the wrong religion or teaching.

Only we, such a few in number in this country, have the ability to spread The True Dharma to establish the ultimate truth in this land.

We are part of one amazing human movement that is spreading its influence all over the world, with one desire, that is to see people happy and to spread a teaching that can achieve a lasting peace on Planet Earth.

People naturally desire peace on this planet above all else, their dream is for the flowering of a human culture from the soil of perpetual peace in this world.

It is only natural that people desire to live happily to the end of their lives.

Humanity is aware of the barbarity and cruelty of war, but peace can never be attained by passively waiting for it.

In order to secure the right to happiness, each and every individual of every race, nationality, gender and sexuality, must now become awakened to the growing necessity to proclaim their demands for peace.

Neither peace nor a culture of peace can be born only from concepts.

People must realise that a firm foundation of true peace and culture of true peace can be constructed only through actions.

Through a practice of a profound and steadfast faith or principle which lays the greatest stress on the absolute respect for life itself.

Neither publicity nor idealism but action in its real sense is required for this cause today.

Let us make friends and Shakubuku.

Let us share our thoughts about the state of this world with others. Even if not all of these friends can chant Nam Myoho Renge Kyo, let them see a life force that exists in us, and they may begin to believe in us, to respect what we are doing and to give us their support even though because of their karma they are unable to practice at this time.

Let us persevere and there will also be people who will practice with us on this incredible journey called Kosen Rufu.

Since the time when Nichiren Daishonin submitted Rissho Ankoku Ron to remonstrate with Hojo Tokiyori the de facto leader of Japan, there have been many other disasters in Japan, culminating in the Great Kanto Earthquake in 1923.

This was the worst earthquake in Japanese history and destroyed thousands and thousands of homes and lives in the Tokyo and Yokohama area.

It is very difficult for us to visualise the devastation inflicted on the people in this comparatively earthquake free part of the world.

Finally the culmination of all of Japan's disasters from the time of Rissho Ankoku Ron was World War Two.

In the last year of this war, every single city in Japan was bombed to pieces.

The allies began with the main cities, then spread outwards to every other city in the entire length and breadth of Japan.

Our minds tend to concentrate on the atomic bombs which were the final stroke that were dropped on Hiroshima and Nagasaki.

The death and severe and serious injury from the bombing was horrendous.

In that final and terrible bombing, six hundred thousand people died or were seriously maimed and injured.

These were civilians.

This was in Japan itself.

No less than three million homes were destroyed by fire or explosives and ten million people were made homeless.

It is so very difficult to visualise such a situation.

Ten million people homeless, living in holes in the ground or under rough shelters in the midst of absolute desolation.

You could say that these ultimate disasters in Japan occurred because Hojo Tokiyori refused to listen to what Nichiren Daishonin was teaching.

When he sent this treatise to the government, rather than taking notice of it they instead stepped up persecution against him.

All because he was trying to establish the ultimate truth, and this was against all the established religions and teachings in Japan of that time.

This is a very sobering thought.

These disasters occurred time and again throughout Japanese history culminating with the greatest and worst of all in the twentieth century and up to this day, that of the atomic bombing of Hiroshima and Nagasaki.

The only time nuclear weapons have ever been used on a civilian population in the history of humanity on Planet Earth.

This was the karma of the Japanese people.

While reflecting on the karma of the Japanese people it also good to reflect on the karma of our own people which also contains shadows and darkness as well as some good fortune.

What was Nichiren Daishonin trying to point out to the ruling authorities of that day in Rissho Ankoku Ron?

Firstly he was saying that the people had been misled into following false and erroneous teachings.

He particularly singled out the teaching called Nembutsu which had become the most popular religion in Japan and millions had flocked to it.

The reason being that it was a form of escapism from the misery that surrounded everyone in Japan at that time in those medieval days.

Nembutsu taught that there was a paradise waiting for people in the Pure Land in The West after death and if they chanted the Nembutsu chant of Nam Amida Butsu then they would be sure to go there after they departed from this world.

This seemed to those people the only hope in those devasting times.

These teachings were spread by priests and monks, and they actually distorted the teachings of the historical Buddha Shakyamuni and even indeed denied the sutras.

Therefore the monks and the priests and all the people who followed them, which was the majority of the people in Japan, were actually committing slander against the ultimate truth or The True Dharma.

Now things are different in Japan thanks to the Nichiren Shoshu Buddhist movement which began in earnest after the second world war ended when propagation of religion was freed for the first time in Japan's history and is now allowed and permitted in the new constitution drawn up with the guidance of the occupying forces.

For the first time Japan could hear about Dai Gohonzon and Nam Myoho Renge Kyo on a wide scale.

Of course it had existed in The Head Temple at Taiseki Ji for many years and every so often attempts had been made to propagate it but always this resulted in persecution.

After world war two for the first time propagation could begin freely and without hindrance and as a result of this hundreds of thousands of practitioners gradually began to appear and practice in Japan chanting Nam Myoho Renge Kyo and setting their lives in rhythm with The True Dharma or the law of the universe.

The results can be seen gradually appearing in Japan today and steadily over the years following world war two.

The transformation in Japan is incredible now compared to the picture of devastation described for you earlier.

At the same time of the spread of the teachings of Nichiren Shoshu Buddhism and Nam Myoho Renge Kyo in Japan, through the compassionate force of the universe itself, which is always working in a positive, creative and harmonious way, the teachings of Nichiren Shoshu Buddhism has now spread from Japan overseas.

It is now being followed and practiced in increasing numbers in many countries around the world.

It was through the tremendous exertion, belief and conviction of The High Priests of Nichiren Shoshu and the practitioners in Japan that these teachings were carried overseas and were enabled to blossom and grow.

At the same time it was Nichiren Shoshu who pointed out that the tragedies and disasters that existed in medieval Japan, for which the only remedy was for people to follow and practice the True Dharma, now applies to the whole world.

This situation exists to this present day.

The disasters of medieval Japan are now everywhere in every corner of the globe.

In accordance with the teachings of Nichiren Daishonin, just as the benevolent forces of the universe left Japan in those medieval times there could be a danger of those benevolent forces leaving the entire planet in our time.

This extremely sobering thought is the driving force behind our great efforts to teach more and more people the truth of the law of life and to open their eyes to an understanding of that truth.

Rissho Ankoku Ron is still an incredibly important document in these current times not only for Japan but for the whole world.

Fortunately in our times power in many countries is not in the hands of despotic rulers as was the case of Japan in the middle ages, but of course in some countries of the world it still remains the case.

Changing Poison into Medicine

In democracies where they exist, the people are in the end the sovereign power and it is the people therefore who in these modern times should be awakened to the ultimate truth and in turn awaken others to it rather than it being necessary for the ruler of the land such as Hojo Tokiyori to be Shakubuku'd as in those days.

We are the people.

We happen to be through our good fortune, those who have heard about it first and begun to put it to the test and prove it in our daily lives.

It can be no one else but our task to open the eyes of others, our fellow citizens in the United Kingdom alongside those other practitioners of Nichiren Shoshu Buddhism who live in other countries across the globe.

This is our role and purpose in life more than anything else.

This is the great purpose of the movement of transforming poison into medicine.

To create world peace which we call Kosen Rufu.

Like some of the people that we try to teach The Dharma to the traveller in this tale of Nichiren Daishonin's in this thesis, gets incredibly angry at Nichiren Daishonin's conviction.

He grows increasingly resentful as Nichiren Daishonin condemns the established orthodoxy and order in Japan at that time.

By the time the traveller asks the fifth and sixth questions in Rissho Ankoku Ron, he was really furious because everything that he had seen in the existing order in Japan had been condemned by Nichiren Daishonin's words.

Question Five.

"This time the guest was truly enraged and said:
In the ages since our original teacher The Buddha Shakyamuni preached the Three Pure Land Sutras, the Dharma Teacher T'an Luan had originally studied the four treatises but abandoned them and put all his faith in the Pure Land teachings.
Similarly, the Meditation Master Tao Ch'o ceased to spread the multifarious doctrines of the Nirvana Sutra and devoted all his attention to propagating the practice that leads one to the western Pure Land.
Shan Tao discarded the sundry practices and established the single practice of the Nembutsu, and the supervisor of monks Eshin collected essential passages from various sutras to form his work, making the single practice of the Nembutsu the essence of his teaching.
Such was the manner in which these men honoured and respected the Buddha Amida, and uncountable numbers of people as a result were able to gain rebirth in the Pure Land.
Of particular note was the sage Honen, who as a child entered the monastery on Mount Hiei.
By the time he was seventeen, he had worked his way through all sixty volumes of Tendai literature and had investigated all the eight schools and mastered their essentials.
In addition, he had read through the entire body of the sutras and treatises seven times and exhausted all the works of exegesis and biography.
His wisdom shone like the Sun and Moon, and his virtue exceeded that of the earlier teachers.
In spite of all this, he was in doubt as to the proper path to emancipation and could not make out the true meaning of nirvana.
Therefore he read and examined all the texts he could, pondered deeply and considered every possibility, and in the end put aside all the sutras and concentrated on the single practice of the Nembutsu.
In addition he received confirmation of his decision when Shan Tao miraculously appeared to him in a dream, and he proceeded to spread his doctrines amongst friends and strangers in all four corners of the land.
Thereafter, he was hailed as a reincarnation of Bodhisattva Seishi, or was revered as Shan Tao reborn.
In every quarter people of eminent and lowly birth alike bowed their heads in respect, and men and women from all over Japan sought him.
Since that time, the springs and autumns have succeeded each other, and the years have accumulated.

And yet you insist upon putting aside the venerable teachings of Shakyamuni Buddha contained in the Pure Land sutras and wilfully speak evil of the passage describing the oath of the Buddha Amida.

Why do you try to blame the sacred age of Honen for the disasters of recent years, going out of your way to slander the former teachers of the Pure Land doctrines and to heap abuse on the sage Honen?

You are, as they saying goes, deliberately blowing back the fur and hunting for flaws in the leather, deliberately piercing the skin in hopes of drawing blood.

From ancient times to the present, the world has never seen such a speaker of evil!

You had better learn a little caution and restraint.

When you pile up such grave offenses, how can you hope to escape punishment?

I am afraid even to sit here in your company.

I must take up my staff and be on my way!

The host, smiling, restrained his guest and said.

Insects that live on smartweed forget how bitter it tastes; those who stay long in privies forget how foul the smell is.

Here you listen to my good words and think them wicked, point to a slanderer of the Dharma and call him a sage, mistrust a correct teacher and take him for an evil monk.

Your confusion is great indeed, and your offense anything but light.

Listen to my explanation of how this confusion arose and let us discuss the matter in detail.

Shakyamuni Buddha expounded the five periods of doctrines, established the order in which they were preached, and divided them into the provisional and true teachings.

But Tan Luan, Tao Ch'o, and Shan Tao embraced the provisional teachings and forgot about the true ones, went by what had been taught in the earlier period of the Buddha's life and discarded what was taught later.

They were not the kind of men who delve into the deep places of Buddhist doctrine.

Honen in particular, though he followed the practices advocated by these earlier men, was ignorant as to the source from whence they came.

How do we know this?

Because he lumped together all the 637 Mahayana scriptures in 2,883 volumes, and along with them all the various Buddhas and bodhisattvas and the deities of this world, and urged people to "discard, close, ignore and abandon" them, with these four injunctions corrupting the hearts of all people.

Thus he poured out perverted words of his own invention and took absolutely no cognizance of the explanations put forth in the Buddhist scriptures.

His is the worst kind of baseless talk, a clear case of slander.

There are no words to describe it, no way to censure it that is not too mild.

And yet people all put faith in this baseless talk of his, and without exception pay honour to his Shenchaku Shu.

As a consequence, they revere the three sutras of the Pure Land and cast all the other sutras aside; they look up to one Buddha alone, Amida of the Land of Perfect Bliss, and forget about the other Buddha's.

A man such as Honen, is in truth the archenemy of the Buddha's and the scriptures, and the foe of sage monks and ordinary men and women alike.

And now his heretical teachings have spread throughout the eight regions of the country; they have penetrated every one of the ten directions.

You became quite horrified when I blamed an earlier period for the disasters that have occurred in recent years.

Perhaps I should recite a few examples from the past to show you that you are mistaken in your feelings.

The second volume of the Maka Shikan quotes a passage from the Shih chi or Records of the Historian which says:

"In the closing years of the Chou Dynasty, there were persons who let their hair hang down, went about naked to the waist, and did not observe the rites and regulations."

The Guketsu, in the second volume, explains this passage by quoting from the Tso chuan or Commentary on the Spring and Autumn Annals as follows: "When King P'ing of the Chou Dynasty first moved his capital to the east, he saw men by the Yi river who let their hair hang down and performed sacrifices in the fields. Someone who had great understanding said: 'In less than a hundred years this dynasty will fall, for the rites are already neglected.'

From this it is evident that the portent appears first, and later the disaster itself comes about.

The Maka Shikan passage goes on to say: "Juan Chi was a man of extraordinary talent, but let his hair grow like a mass of brambles and left his belt undone.

Later the sons of the aristocracy all imitated him, until those who behaved in a churlish and insulting manner were thought to be acting quite naturally, and those who were restrained and proper in their behaviour were ridiculed as mere peasants.

This was a sign that the Ssu Ma family (The Rulers of the Western Chin Dynasty) would meet with their downfall."

Similarly in, The Nitto junrei ki or Record of a Pilgrimage to China in Search of the Dharma by the Great Teacher Jikaku records that in the first year of the Hui ch'ang era (841) Emperor Wu tsung of the T'ang Dynasty commanded the priest Ching Shuang of Chang ching ssu temple to transmit the Nembutsu teachings of the Buddha Amida in the various temples, going about from one temple to another without ever ceasing.

In the second year of the same era, soldiers from the land of the Uighurs invaded the borders of the T'ang empire.

In the third year of the same era, the regional commander in the area north of the Yellow River suddenly raised a revolt.

Later, the kingdom of Tibet once more refused to obey orders from China and the Uighurs repeatedly seized Chinese territory. On the whole, the conflicts and uprisings were like those that prevailed at the time when the Ch'in Dynasty and the military leader Hsiang Yu were overthrown, and the towns and villages were devasted by fire and other disasters.

What was even worse, Emperor Wu tsung carried out a vast campaign to wipe out Buddhist teachings and destroyed a great many temples and monasteries.

He was never able to put down the uprisings and died in agony shortly after.

In view of these events, we should consider the fact that Honen lived in the time of the Retired Emperor Gotoba, around the Kennin era (1201-1204).

And what happened to the retired Emperor is evident before or very eyes.

Thus T'ang China provided an earlier example of the fall of an Emperor, and our own country offers similar proof.

You should neither doubt that this nor consider it strange.

The only thing to do now is abandon the evil ways and take up those that are good, to cut off this affliction at the source, at the root!"

Nichiren Daishonin said both in this thesis and in many other Gosho that the ultimate truth must be able to satisfy The Three Proofs, that of documentary proof, theoretical proof and most important of all, actual proof in daily life.

In question four, Nichiren Daishonin was dealing with documentary proof against the Nembutsu teachings, the biggest heretical sect in Japan at that time.

191

These were the very people that stirred up the authorities against him and persecuted and attacked Nichiren Daishonin from time to time.

Nichiren Daishonin knowing this, had incredible courage and absolute conviction in his role and purpose in life, in writing this thesis at all.

He was well aware that it would bring down the strength of the authorities against him.

Nevertheless in this question and in the subsequent one, question six, he relentlessly pursues his attempt to teach or create understanding in his opponent in the dialogue as to the ultimate truth.

This particular question is concerning rather more theoretical and actual proof in the answer to it than documentary proof.

In this answer to the question number five, Nichiren Daishonin first of all proves that the teachings of the man called Honen who spread the Nembutsu are in fact distorted and inferior and against the teachings of the historical Buddha Shakyamuni.

Secondly he begins to refute the teachings of Honen by theoretical proof and then finally actual proof in the form of looking back at the history of China and Japan.

Nichiren Daishonin's approach is very direct, very confident and straight speaking, he never flinches in his determination to achieve his aim.

On the other hand he never gets angry, and he is always courteous even though he maybe firm, he is always compassionate and confident.

These really are an example of the way we also should teach the Dharma and react to the questions and even the anger of the people who we are talking to.

To be firm, confident, courteous, never getting angry, always polite.

There is no debate or dialogue that has ever occurred in the whole eight hundred year history of Nichiren Shoshu that hasn't resulted in a victory for the True Dharma or teachings and there have been many in that history.

We know that the teachings of Nichiren Daishonin and Nichiren Shoshu Buddhism are complete and all embracing, therefore if we are patient we can always succeed in helping people to understand provided they are prepared to listen.

If they are not prepared to listen there is nothing we can do about it except wait until one day when they are.

This is truly the way of Shakubuku.

Maybe sometimes we think we can never do this ourselves, but the truth is that we can.

Maybe not as well as Nichiren Daishonin did as he talked to this traveller in this thesis.

Shakubuku when it is sincere and when it is based on our compassion and our determination to open the eyes of the other person and to help them to overcome their misery or their sufferings, then those words that we say flow directly from our Buddha state.

This was the teaching of The Buddha.

The words come from our Buddha nature, therefore what have we to fear, why shouldn't we be confident, we are doing the Buddha's work, we are the envoys of the Buddha when we Shakubuku.

Therefore our words are the words of the Buddha.

We need never fear or lack confidence in our ability to do so, even though we may have only been practicing a week, or even a month or two, still it is possible to give an experience of what you have understood through the practice so far and penetrate deeply into the heart of the person who is listening.

"The host, smiling, restrained his guest and said: Insects that live on smartweed forget how bitter it tastes, those who stay long in privies forget how foul the smell is."

Nichiren Daishonin believed in straight speaking and in using words that would really penetrate the life of his listener and I think these words are a good example of that.

Nichiren Daishonin is showing how easy it is for people to take religion and accept religion blindly.

These perverted views which can be spread through inferior teachings seem to become the established order, they seem almost to be common sense, yet they cannot be logically justified in anyway whatsoever, but still people will accept them blindly without questioning.

This is the amazing part of life and the power of religious and philosophical matters.

People seem to think that religion and philosophy ought to be illogical and mysterious and of course this is ridiculous.

If religion is the truth of life, then it must be totally, completely and logically explainable.

This is what is behind these earthy comments at the beginning of that particular passage.

"But Tan Luan, Tao Ch'o, and Shan Tao embraced the provisional teachings and forgot about the true ones, went by what had been taught in the earlier period of the Buddha's life and discarded what was taught later.

They were not the kind of men who delve into the deep places of Buddhist doctrine.

Honen in particular, though he followed the practices advocated by these earlier men, was ignorant as to the source from whence they came.

How do we know this?

Because he lumped together all the 637 Mahayana scriptures in 2,883 volumes, and along with them all the various Buddha's and bodhisattvas and the deities of this world, and urged people to "discard, close, ignore and abandon" them, with these four injunctions corrupting the hearts of all people.

Thus he poured out perverted words of his own invention and took absolutely no cognizance of the explanations put forth in the Buddhist scriptures.

His is the worst kind of baseless talk, a clear case of slander."

Honen was the propagator of the Nembutsu teachings in Japan, they had begun in fact in China.

He founded the sect that followed the Nembutsu teachings called Jodo, or The Pure Land School and they taught people to ignore all the teachings of Shakyamuni Buddha including The Lotus Sutra which Shakyamuni Buddha himself had said was supreme amongst his teachings and to concentrate only on three sutras which talked about the pure land.

Honen was slandering the Buddha with such teachings, yet people continued to flock to him in a Buddhist land.

Honen was intelligent, he was probably quite a charismatic person and most important of all he was intelligent and was able to impress the more simple people of those times.

Previously Nichiren Daishonin explained how the monks who propagated false teachings were able to impress people with their knowledge of mundane things.

The monks and the priests of those days were most expert in such matters as building, planning cities and agriculture and so on.

It was this that really impressed the people.

We can see the same thing today.

A person with a magnetic media personality can have incredible power and through various other ways, like the written word and so on, it is possible for these people to exert great influenceeven though their teachings or what they are trying to put across is not necessarily sound.

Changing Poison into Medicine

Look at America's recent history of a media star millionaire becoming President.
People can become mesmerised by this.
They became mesmerised by Honen, just the same as they can become mesmerised by a great media personality, so that his distorted views of The Dharma seemed to become normal to them, a tradition.
The world today is still full of cults and sects of many different sorts, some of them are not terrible or evil in what they are doing, but there are many that really are an evil influence, extorting money, spreading distorted views of life, not giving any actual proof, nor for that matter any other sort of proof of their validity.
Yet people still follow.
The most terrible case recently of course is the Islamic State death cult, or ISIS, which has indoctrinated thousands of people and committed the most terrible atrocities in the middle east and around the world.
This is incredible but it is true.
The influence of philosophy and religion based on the completely wrong view that religion should be completely illogical and mysterious is colossal, even in this technological age that we live in today.
Why is this?
The answer is the people who are desperate, unhappy, miserable and bewildered by the state of the world, will therefore grasp at anything and they are open to such influences.
They lose any sense of comparing one religion or philosophy with another because of this desperation, they can just plunge in and hang on.
There is also a tendency to avoid discussion about religion and philosophy, people feel out of their depth.
How many cases have there been when families hear about a family member starting to practice Nichiren Shoshu Buddhism then raise tremendous objections, often these people are not particularly religious at all.
The ones who become most agitated are people who are not religious or practiced any religious properly.
Often those who are practicing some other religion like christianity or islam are more broad minded, but the ones who don't practice any faith feel guilty.
This is why their agitation is so great.
They feel when they hear that their family member is practicing Buddhism, which they don't understand and know very little about, that they have failed them in some way.

They feel guilty that they should have studied religion or philosophy more themselves or they feel agitated just out of pure ignorance of religion and philosophy in a general sense.

Most of all some people are totally unable to see the connection between religion and philosophy and the state of a country.

They think of it as a personal and private matter just involving inward prayer and giving some spiritual help and nothing else.

The great principle of Esho Funi in Buddhism points out clearly that what is in the hearts of the people will be reflected in their environment, what is the hearts of the people reveals itself in the environment or the society or country in which they live.

This is such an amazing principle that teaches that if you are in hell then your environment will reflect hell.

If you are in anger, your environment will reflect anger and if you are in Buddhahood the highest state of human life then your environment will reflect Buddha.

Honen's reputation at this medieval time in Japan was almost like Jesus Christ here in the west.

He was a mythical wonderous figure and although he was already dead there were many legends about him.

It was these Nembutsu followers, believing in this man, who were enraged by Nichiren Daishonin's Rissho Ankoku Ron who attacked his small cottage in Matsubagayatsu, near Kamakura and tried to kill him.

Many of the other persecutions that followed were also instigated by them.

We see the same thing in history in other people who were trying to do good.

Jesus Christ was persecuted by the jews and those who criticised christianity in The Middle Ages after his passing, were also blindly persecuted with such horrendous inventions such as The Inquisition or burning people at the stake.

This was all in the cause of obliterating those who dared to question anything to do with the established religion of the day.

In the history of the spread of Nichiren Shoshu Buddhism there has always been persecutions as well as Shakubuku or teaching others.

The inferior teachings had to be refuted in order to establish The Ultimate Truth.

These great people, Nichiren Daishonin, Nikko Shonin and the other High Priests of Nichiren Shoshu and most recently High Priest Nikken Shonin, who have been terribly persecuted have sheltered us and enabled us to meet and to receive The Gohonzon in this present day and age in far more peaceful circumstances that ever existed before.

Changing Poison into Medicine

It is the truth today that wherever you look in society, whether in politics, or economics, or science, or even in education, there is always corruption to one degree or another.
This is because humanity has had no rock or philosophy on which to really base their actions.
We have all grown apathetic about this situation as we have been living in it for such a long time now, we often feel nothing can be done about it and so we get used to just accepting it.
Sometimes we just cannot be bothered and react this way to the truth, to societies actions, to the wrongs that we can see all around us.
In the third chapter of The Lotus Sutra, taught nearly three thousand years ago, Shakyamuni Buddha said this.

"They dwell in hell so long that they come to think that it is natural as playing in a garden and the other evil paths seem like their own home."

This is a human tendency.
An amazing situation arises when those who try to change what smells, or the established order of the day, are generally attacked by society because they disturb the status quo when those who go with it are rewarded.
For example if you take a young teacher, they may passionately rebel against what they see as the cause of the smells of the corruption and problems in the education system and they try to change it and they fail.
Maybe they try again, and they fail and in the end because they want the security of their job and they passionately believe in their role as a teacher no matter what, they stop complaining.
Let us look forward to a time when there are educators who basing their lives on The Buddhism of Nichiren Daishonin can instigate some form of change in the educational system as we see it today into a far more humane and compassionate one.
It is a human tendency to accept what we find around us, the established way.
However and thank goodness, there is always youth, young people, it is always the young people who try their best to seek something new.
Their desire to change things that they believe to be wrong and of course they are not always right, but they have the youthful energy, a powerful driving force, and if properly directed by a sound and all-embracing philosophy and practice, they can follow the true way to change our society and ultimately Planet Earth.

Changing Poison into Medicine

The driving force of any revolution, including a spiritual revolution, is usually young people.
Let us look at the passage again,

"A man such as Honen, is in truth, the deadly enemy of The Buddha's and The Scriptures, and the foe of sage monks and ordinary men and women alike."

In the end all social problems, Nichiren Daishonin is saying, can be traced back to a religious source, to erroneous, inferior or incorrect religious or philosophical teachings.
For example, the class struggle in this country of the UK and the evils of the class system have grown out of an authoritarian church and patriarchy with their superior attitude going back to its earliest days towards those who were ordinary people.
If you go to Fountain Abbey in Yorkshire, you can see the glory of the accommodation of the monks and the priests, as compared to the lower orders, or the ordinary people like us, who lived in the darkness below.
God is superior to everyone and therefore the priest who serves god is superior.
This was the attitude that led to the class troubles that effect our society up until the present day.
The best pews in church were reserved for those who could afford them.
You had to pay a high rental for a front row seat at every service.
Further back, before the industrial revolution, before that system came in, the front rows were always for the nobility and the local squires.
Where was christ's compassion in the social ostracism of people who were insane, or the very poor, such as occurred in the eighteenth century.
People were segregated because of their awful circumstances into fearful institutions with no hope from life whatsoever, you only have to read Dickens to learn all about it.
Nichiren Daishonin said people who were teaching inferior teachings were the most evil people in the world, whether they were consciously doing so or not.
Religion should never be approached blindly.
It should be discussed freely and openly but still in the hearts of the people there is the feeling of what do we have to do with it, or we do not understand it, or they worry about the wrath of god descending on them.
The freedom of religion is not just the freedom of worship but is also the freedom of discussion.

This is what should be actively encouraged by Nichiren Shoshu Buddhists and do not worry about whether you feel people are going to react well or not.

Just try, and by trying you sow the seed and open up an area of interest which may not blossom until much later.

Because of Nichiren Shoshu Buddhism's confidence in the power of The Gohonzon and its ability to satisfy the three proofs, especially actual proof, it provides us with the framework for debate which has been used in all the debates that have occurred down through history.

This framework is in the form of the fivefold comparisons and the five guides to propagation, but the conviction in the power of The Gohonzon which we have because of our actual proof of its transformative power in our actual lives enables us to approach debate in this way.

In a non-Buddhist country we do not have to use this to the same extent as they do in Buddhist countries.

The fivefold comparisons proves, in terms of the correctness of the teaching, why Nam Myoho Renge Kyo is correct or The Ultimate Truth.

First of all, in comparing Buddhism with non Buddhism, and that Buddhism is the correct teaching.

Secondly, comparing Mahayana Buddhism against Theravada/Hinayana Buddhism, where The Mahayana is the correct teaching.

Thirdly, comparing the true teaching, which is The Lotus Sutra, against the provisional or pre Lotus Sutra teachings, where The Lotus Sutra is the correct teaching.

Fourthly, comparing the essential teaching in The Lotus Sutra, which is he Juryo chapter, against the theoretical chapters, where the essential teaching is correct.

Fifth and finally comparing The Buddhism of The Sowing, which is Nichiren Daishonin's Buddhism, against the Buddhism of Shakyamuni, which is known as The Buddhism of The Harvest, where The Buddhism of Nichiren Daishonin or Nichiren Shoshu is correct and therefore the teaching for this age of Mappo.

In each progressive debate throughout history, this framework or approach has been used and is irrefutable.

The five guides to propagation are,

Firstly, the teaching should be correct for the age.

This comes out of the fivefold comparisons above.

Secondly, that the people have the intellectual capacity to accept it.

Thirdly, that the time is right.

Changing Poison into Medicine

Certainly the time when Japan was devasted after the second world war was right.
Certainly the time when people are most receptive to it is now in the west when there is so much environmental havoc and misery in all directions.
Fourthly, that the country or society should be considered in those teachings.
In other words, that the teaching should be propagated in accordance with the culture of that country.
Fifth and finally, that previous teachings should be understood so that it could be refuted in debate.
The confidence we have in The Gohonzon, which all The High Priests of Nichiren Shoshu have had, down through the ages, has led to such a clear approach to what we call Shakubuku.
Let us now look at another sentence.

"China provided an earlier example on how The Pure Land Teachings, brought about the fall of an Emperor and our own country offers similar proof."

Here Nichiren Daishonin moves on from theoretical proof and very briefly gives actual proof based on actual happenings in the history of China and Japan.
By now he has his guest, the traveller, thinking deeply.
Some of the rage has subsided, sufficiently so for the traveller to ask another question.

Question Six.

"The guest looking somewhat mollified said, 'though I have not yet probed deeply into the matter, I believe I understand to some degree what you are saying.

Nevertheless in both Kyoto the capital and in Kamakura the headquarters of The Shogun, there are numerous eminent Buddhist leaders and key figures in The Clergy and yet none of them have so far appealed to The Shogun concerning this affair or submitted a memorial to the throne.

You on the other hand, a person of humble position, think nothing of spewing out offensive accusations.

Your assertions are open to question and your reasoning lacks authority.'

The Host said:

'Though I may be a person of little ability, I have reverently given myself to the study of The Mahayana.

A blue fly, if it clings to the tail of a thoroughbred horse, can travel ten thousand miles and the green ivy that twines around the tall pine, can grow to a thousand feet.

I was born as the son of the one Buddha, Shakyamuni and I serve the King of the scriptures, The Lotus Sutra, how could I observe the decline of The Buddhist Law and not be filled with the emotions of pity and distress.

Moreover The Nirvana Sutra states:

"If even a good Priest sees someone slandering The Law and disregards him, failing to reproach him, to oust him, or to punish him for his offence, then you should know that The Priest is an enemy of The Buddhist Law, but if he is willing to reproach the person, to oust him, or to punish him for his offence, then he is my disciple and one who truly understands my teaching."

Although I may not be a good priest, I certainly do not want to be accused of being an enemy of The Buddhist Law, therefore in order to avoid such charges, I have cited a few general principles, given a rough explanation of the matter.

In the past at the time of The Gennin Era (1224-1225) as a result of a petition submitted to the throne time and again by the two temples of Enryaku Ji on Mount Hiei and Kofuku Ji in Nara, an Imperial command and a letter of instruction were handed down ordering that the wood block used in printing Honen's Shenchaku shu be confiscated and brought to The Great Lecture Hall at Enryaku ji Temple, there they were burnt in order to repay the debt owed to The Buddha's of the past, present and future.

In addition, orders were given that the menials who are attached to The Kanjin-in Shrine, should dig up and destroy Honen's grave in Kyoto.

Changing Poison into Medicine

At this time Honen's disciples, Ryukan, Shoko, Jokaku, Sassho and others were condemned to exile in distant regions and were never pardoned.
In view of these facts, how can you say that no one has submitted a complaint to the authorities concerning these matters."

Despite all of Nichiren Daishonin's arguments the traveller is still, at least sentimentally attached, to the established order of things or the teaching of Nembutsu as founded by Honen.
It is difficult for human beings to give up previous beliefs or established views.
Some of us have found it difficult to cut the attachment to christianity.
Not because we believe in christianity once we have embraced The Gohonzon, but because there are sentimental ties.
Perhaps people find they miss the services, the beauty of them and the hymns, or perhaps the great buildings, the cathedrals and the churches.
Perhaps it is because ever since they were little toddlers, they have said the lord's prayer at their mothers side.
All sorts of sentimental reasons can make people cling to what is in fact not the ultimate truth, even though the ultimate truth is explained and known to them.
Nichiren Daishonin, to convince the traveller, explains that Honen had in fact already been rejected by the authorities of Japan in 1224.
That was only thirty years before this thesis was written, yet in that thirty years a hundred and eighty degree turn had been done and the people had embraced the Nembutsu despite the explanations of its erroneous teachings thirty years before.
In fact Honen's disgrace was very complete.
He was exiled.
He was even given his posthumous name or his name after death, before he died, which was the ultimate disgrace.
After his death his gravestone was destroyed, and his body was dug up and it was thrown into the sea.
This was immediately after Honen died only twenty five or thirty years before Nembutsu spread in those terrible times when Nichiren Daishonin was living.
The human being can be very fickle.
Let us study a paragraph from the answer.

Changing Poison into Medicine

"The Host said, though I may be a person of little ability, I have devoted and reverently given myself to the study of The Mahayana.
A blue fly, if it clings to the tail of a thoroughbred horse, can travel ten thousand miles and the green ivy that twines around a tall pine can grow to a thousand feet."

Nichiren Daishonin compares himself there to the worst and most despised of all insects the horrible blue fly that buzzes around the dustbin, but he points out that if it clings onto the tail of a thoroughbred horse it can travel enormous distances.
In saying that Nichiren Daishonin is pointing out that you do not have to be of high social status in order to discover and teach the truth of life.
Nichiren Daishonin as it were, stuck to the tail of the thoroughbred horse, which was The Lotus Sutra.
This was his self enlightenment, that Nam Myoho Renge Kyo, which he understood with his whole life, was in fact in the orthodox flow of Buddhism and was contained in the depths of The Lotus Sutra.
He had then studied for so many years so he could prove this and understand and explain the documentary proof for his self enlightenment as a young man to The Law of Myoho Renge Kyo.
Because this law was in his heart, it dictated all his values and all his actions based on those values.
We can see that in the whole history of his life and what he was able to achieve in it.
Likewise, because we have found The True Law or The Gohonzon and are awakened to it, that law begins to dictate our actions based on our values derived from the law of Nam Myoho Renge Kyo.
For this reason many of you have got this book and are reading it to study more about this great, Pure Law or Dharma.
If people hold the wrong law or teachings or philosophy in their hearts then inevitably their values are equally wrong and distorted.
Therefore their actions to are distorted.
Their actions will not be for their greatest happiness if they go against the true law of life but will be for their greatest unhappiness instead.
The value of a person's actions depends entirely on the law or belief or world view that is in their hearts, this also applies to society as a whole.
To find the correct law and to base your life on it is of absolute, total, and ultimate importance.

Changing Poison into Medicine

Sadly that is so little understood in this world today.
In The Gosho, Nichiren Daishonin wrote.

"Since The Law is supreme, the person is respect worthy and since the person is respect worthy, the land is sacred."

In The Lotus Sutra it says,

"To attain this Law of Myoho Renge Kyo is of greater benefit than all the jewels of the universe."

From then on your thoughts and therefore your actions are based on the ultimate truth of life, for this reason if not for any other we need to Shakubuku.
Looking around us and seeing how few of us understand the ultimate truth of life and how as a result of that peoples values are wrong or distorted and their actions always follow suit.
Through sowing the seed of The True Law of the true understanding of life in the hearts of people they can then find that their actions are leading them to a happier life, this is the greatest and most profound reason for Shakubuku.
Let us study another paragraph from the answer to the question above.

"I was born as the son of the one Buddha Shakyamuni and I serve the King of scriptures, The Lotus Sutra.
How could I observe the decline of The Buddhist Law and not be filled with emotions of pity and distress."

This may be a little confusing, but Nichiren Daishonin had to be very careful about what he said about himself otherwise his followers would have suffered even worse persecution and possibly himself also.
It was not until much later after his exile to Sado Island that he actually declared himself to be The Buddha of this age of Mappo.
In this case he calls himself the one son of The Buddha Shakyamuni.
If we have gratitude, which is what Nichiren Daishonin is referring to here, for all the benefits we have gained as we started to practice, how can we honestly prevent ourselves from spreading those benefits to others and teaching others how to gain them themselves, other people's suffering surely must move us to do that.
Shakubuku is proof of whether we are true disciples of Nichiren Daishonin and whether we really understand our mission in life.

Changing Poison into Medicine

This is the spirit of 'Fu ji shaku shinmyo' which is a phrase in the Jigage portion of Gongyo which we recite daily.
It means 'yearning to see The Buddha, we do not begrudge our lives.'
Yearning to see the Buddha nature rising in our life, we give our whole life in return, devoting ourselves to Nam Myoho Renge Kyo and spreading The True Dharma in this world to the best of our ability.
Whenever you say that phrase in Gongyo it is a good point to check whether in that particular Gongyo you feel that you are giving yourself wholeheartedly because that is this spirit which will bring the greatest joy of life and living.
As long as we are begrudging our lives, we may begrudge our time, maybe begrudge studying and reading this book or having to go to meetings where we meet other practitioners or doing Shakubuku, then of course we cannot experience the full joy that this practice can bring us.
Benefits bring joy but the greatest joy comes from giving your time and energy wholeheartedly and without resentment in return.
This is the proof of the pudding, this is the spirit of 'Fu ji Shaku Shinmyo'
All the great people throughout the history of Nichiren Shoshu like Nikko Shonin who succeeded Nichiren Daishonin as High Priest, The Three Martyrs of Atsuhara and in recent years High Priest Nikken Shonin and up to the present day with the present High Priest Nichinyo Shonin, all have this spirit.
They all gave or give their lives whole heartedly to practice and spreading The Dharma.
Let us look at another paragraph.

"If even a good priest sees some one slandering The Law and disregards him, failing to reproach him, to oust him, or to punish him for his offence, then you should know that the priest is an enemy of the Buddhist law, but if he is willing to reproach the person, to oust him or punish him for his offense, then he is my disciple and one who truly understands my teachings."

This is a very important point.
This paragraph that sounds so strict but is in the spirit of pure Buddhist mercy or Jihi, pure compassion.
If someone slanders someone else who is actually embracing The True Law or The Gohonzon, The Lotus Sutra actually says that sickness will occur in that slanderer in this life and heavy sickness in the next.
This is the law of cause and effect, of slandering The True Law.

Changing Poison into Medicine

This does not mean that everyone who is sick slanders the law, but this is the effect when people make such a cause.
There can be other causes of sickness so therefore unless we stop people who are slandering the law we have no mercy or compassion.
The distorted teachings will grow because of those persons actions and they themselves will suffer more.
This is especially important in our relationships with our fellow Nichiren Shoshu Buddhists.
We have to take action, if for whatever reason slander, or in Japanese 'Onshitzu,' gets a grip on someone who is slandering another practitioner.
It also applies outside of our community of believers to anybody that is slandering life or The True Law.
People who do not spread the teaching once they have received it themselves are allowing more space for the inferior and incorrect teachings and misunderstandings of life to grow.
The effect of not practicing Shakabuku is that you are allowing the world to head for disaster that little bit more quickly rather than arresting that downhill rush which we see in the world today.
The poisons in life are growing and are then reflected in the wars and conflicts, global pandemics and environmental destruction and chaos that we see on our Planet Earth at this great crossroads in human history into which we have been born.
In every respect we have to chant Shodai to do Shakubuku.
Shakubuku is a matter of, as Nichiren Daishonin himself shows in this writing, straight and sincere speaking.
It is cowardly if we see someone suffering because of slander and not to do anything about it.

In the Gosho 'The Opening of The Eyes,' Nichiren Daishonin writes.

"If someone is about to kill your father and mother, should you not try to warn them?
If an evil son is insane with drink and threatening to kill his father and mother, should you not try to stop him?
If some evil person is about to set fire to the temples and pagodas, should you not try to stop him?
If your only child is gravely ill, should you not try to cure him with moxibustion treatment?
To fail to do so is to act like those people who do not try to put a stop to the zen and nembutsu followers in Japan.
As Chang-an says 'If one befriends another person but lacks the mercy to correct him, he is in fact his enemy.'

207

Changing Poison into Medicine

I Nichiren, am Sovereign, Teacher, Father and Mother to all the people of Japan but the men of the Tendai sect who do not refute the heretical sects are all great enemies of the people, as Chang-an noted, 'he who makes it possible for an offender to rid himself of evil, is acting like a parent to him.'"

This passage is really important for all of us practitioners of Nichiren Shoshu Buddhism and is in itself the spirit of Nichiren Daishonin.
He would brave anything in order to save people from suffering and his courage was truly incredible.
He truly was a lion amongst men.
When we read such a passage and we see how Nichiren Daishonin lived it in every respect, our gratitude should be enormous.
Our gratitude for receiving The Gohonzon and for those who brought it to us and in the case of those earlier days, braved incredible persecution so that we are able to practice today.
This should make us feel gratitude in the third prayer of Gongyo.
This should drive our determination to try to live the words of Nichiren Daishonin and carry on his heritage.
In return we are bound to get some sansho shima or obstacles.
The negative force of life is bound to try to interfere.
When we think about doing Shakubuku something shuts our mind to it, we always have that tendency.
Nichiren Daishonin said that this is the proof that this is The True Law, the fact that it immediately incites opposition from the negative force of life in the most subtle ways.
There is a Gosho on this topic or point in 'Letter from Sado.'

"In the past he despised the votaries of The Lotus Sutra and ridiculed The Sutra itself, sometimes with exaggerated praise and sometimes with contempt.
He has met all eight of these terrible sufferings for such acts against The Lotus Sutra, which is as magnificent as two jewels combined, two moons shining side by side, two stars conjoined, or one Mount Hua placed atop another.
Usually these sufferings would torment a person over many lifetimes, appearing one at a time, but Nichiren has denounced the enemies of The Lotus Sutra so severely that all eight descended upon him at once.
His situation is like that of a peasant heavily in debt to his Lord and others, as long as he remains on the estate, they are likely to defer his debts from one year to the next, rather than mercilessly hounding him.

But as soon as he tries to leave, everyone will rush over and demand that he repay everything at once.
Thus The Sutra states, 'It is due to the blessings obtained by protecting The Law that one can diminish his sufferings and retribution.'"

This is Nichiren Daishonin talking about himself and how because he so strongly castigated the false teachings, all the retribution possible fell upon him in the form of the negative or devilish force of life, those forces which are always working against the positive and enlightened side.
Also in the last part of that passage, talking about the person who has been living in the same place for years who has got credit from the bank and various trades people.
Everything is quite peaceful but the moment they stand up and says they are going to move, all the creditors are there at the door and the bank is on the phone everyday asking them to repay the loan in full.
This is the truth of life, it is the same with us.
We are like that person when we start to practice and move our lives more positively forward than ever before, inevitably that negative force comes up and tries to stop us.
This is the natural force of life which we call 'Sansho Shima,' but always sansho shima can be overcome.
Only fools run away or panic and give up.
Those who are wise perceive this truth of life and rejoice because it means that truly they are following the correct teaching of The Buddha, the correct path in life.
Nichiren Daishonin himself took the brunt of everything.
We today spread the teaching under his, as it were, umbrella but of course in our own individual lives we do find this opposition is still working against us.
If it did not Nichiren Daishonin is saying that this would not be The True Law that we are spreading in the world today.
We ourselves are happy or unhappy because of our karma.
It is through practicing Shakubuku, Nichiren Daishonin taught on many, many occasions, that we can change our unhappy karma and enter a higher state of life.
No wonder the devilish force of life resists as it does, as it tries to stop us from advancing.
This is proof of the power of Shakubuku, to change karma in itself. To change our poison into medicine.
Shakubuku is not something invented by Nichiren Shoshu, it is the will and testament of Nichiren Daishonin because out of Shakubuku we can become happy and change those aspects of

Changing Poison into Medicine

our karma which has caused us untold misery and through Shakabuku we can awaken people one by one until we change the unhappy karma of humanity and create the harmonious world that everyone is so desperately seeking in these dark times as we head towards the abyss of environmental melt down.

Question Seven.

The guest, continuing to speak in a mild manner, replied:
'One could hardly say that Honen is the only one who disparages sutras and speaks ill of other priests, since you do the same thing yourself.
However, it is true that he takes the 637 Mahayana scriptures in 2,883 volumes, along with all the Buddha's and bodhisattva's and the deities of this world, and urges people to "discard, close, ignore and abandon" them.
There is no doubt that these four injunctions are his very words; the meaning of the passage is quite clear, but you keep harping on this one little "flaw in the jewel" and severely slander him for it.
I do not know whether he spoke out of delusion or out of true enlightenment.
Between you and Honen, I cannot tell which is wise and which is foolish, or determine whose assertions are right and whose are wrong.
However, you assert that all the recent disasters are to be traced to the Senchaku shu, speaking quite volubly on that point and elaborating on the meaning of your assertion.
Now surely the peace of the world and the stability of the nation are sought by both ruler and subject and desired by all the inhabitants of the country.
The nation achieves prosperity through The Buddhist Law, and The Law is proven worthy of reverence by the people who embrace it.
If the nation is destroyed and the people are wiped out, then who will continue to pay reverence to the Buddha's?
Who will continue to have faith in The Law?
Therefore one must first of all pray for the safety of the nation and then work to establish The Buddhist Law.
Now if you know of any means whereby disasters can be prevented and troubles brought to an end, I would like to hear about it.'

As you see the travellers attitude has changed considerably and he is getting much calmer and for the first time he acknowledges Honen's errors.
This was the teaching that denied all of Shakyamuni's sutras and taught the existence of a pure land in the western part of the universe and made reference to three sutras of Shakyamuni where he mentioned the existence of this legendary heaven or land.
You can see that towards the end of that first paragraph the traveller is getting thoroughly confused and says between you

and Honen, I cannot tell which is wise and which is foolish, or determine whose assertions are right and whose are wrong.
Today in the 21st century, that question could be put by many people too.
Who is right?
Who is wrong?
What is right and what is wrong?
With all the plethora of teachings and philosophies and information that pours into our lives in this so called information age, which we can read, research and investigate so easily in a moment, at the click of a smart phone, we still seem to be in a state of absolute confusion.
Along with these advances in technology, the times have also been changing rapidly from an age of materialism to an age of the mind.
From an age of the mind to an age of life.
People have now begun to awaken to the fact that true happiness only exists within your life itself, not from some exterior cause or object.
Let us now declare that the age in which your greatness was measured by fame or wealth is now completely over.
The leading characters of this new age of ordinary people are ordinary people.
That is, you and me and that includes the vast expanse of the world's population of human beings, which encompasses the whole of planet Earth.
Changing times have always caused confusion in people's minds and quite naturally, the established order is now being shaken.
There are still plenty of people in this world following that old, outdated philosophy of consumerism and materialism and still believing that they can obtain happiness through material possessions.
On the other hand, there are others who are pressing forward to find the truth and to awaken themselves from this slumber and these numbers of people are steadily increasing day by day.
This is a wonderful thing for us Nichiren Shoshu Buddhists.
We are at a point of change, where people are dithering, thinking, wondering which way to go in order to find true happiness and live with a truly harmonious lifestyle.
Everyone is beginning to seek to understand a new way of living because of the effects of the environmental meltdown.
The ever nearer, ever closer climate crisis.
The extinction event that people fear.

Changing Poison into Medicine

Everyone is beginning to sense that humanity as truly at a crossroad and are seeking a viable alternative to consumerism and materialism.
Recently, it seems there is something of a religious or spiritual revival, a new seeking spirit is growing in the life of the people.
It is not very strong yet but nevertheless it exists.
It has been happening now since the turn of the millennium or even before with its roots in the sixties post second world war.
There has definitely recently been a revival in the seeking mind especially in young people as the physical world around us seems to be slowly crumbling into the self destruction of the climate crisis, as we advance into this historic Anthropocene age.
There are people of courage who are trying to grope their way out of the fog of the old beliefs and philosophies and
knowing beyond a shadow of doubt that true happiness does not arise simply and solely from material possessions and wealth.
This is now the age of the mind.
What is right?
What is wrong?
The age of the mind is ordinary people seeking to find the truth.
We Nichiren Shoshu Buddhists who practice Nichiren Daishonin's Buddhism are convinced that The Gohonzon is the ultimate truth that people are seeking in the depths of their lives.
How do we know this?
Because we prove it in our lives to ourselves and others every day, one day at a time.
There is no doubt that our British characteristics of wishing to be tolerant and our sense of fair play often makes us feel that we should not knock anyone else's beliefs.
What we would prefer to say, in our hearts, is that there are many ways to the ultimate truth and if you feel happy doing what you are doing please go on with it.
Please go on saying that but not with the idea that Nam Myoho Renge Kyo is one of the many alternative ways to reach enlightenment.

Nam Myoho Renge Kyo is enlightenment.
Nam Myoho Renge Kyo is not a path to enlightenment, it is enlightenment in itself.

I do not think we have heard the word enlightenment used so often in the religions of christianity, judaism or islam, very rarely is such a term mentioned.
Certainly enlightenment is not contained in the creed of materialists, capitalists, socialists, communists and so on.

Changing Poison into Medicine

In other religions they talk of earning the grace of god, the favour of some omnipotent power which is outside of yourself.

In the same way as the materialists are desiring power through material possessions which they draw from outside themselves. Whereas Nichiren Shoshu Buddhism teaches that enlightenment is already inherent in you.

Just work hard at it and clear the cobwebs of negative karma away, change your poison into medicine and you will discover it. Shakyamuni's Buddhism, Judaism, Christianity, Islam and Hinduism are truly, from Nichiren Daishonin's perspective, paths to the one enlightenment.

They are not enlightenment.

They do not reveal the ultimate truth, which is Nam Myoho Renge Kyo, which is the enlightened or Buddha Nature in all life in the universe.

All these other religions, certainly not by chance, appeared around about the same time in various parts of the world.

They all reached their zenith between about a thousand or one thousand five hundred A.D., and they all began to decline and lose their hold on the lives of the people as the result of the growth of science and materialism.

There can be many roads to the one truth.

All rivers flow into the ocean.

Each one of these religions is leading towards the ultimate truth but none of them teach the existence of the ultimate truth existing in every single human being by the very nature of their make up as entities of life in this universe.

Of course it is right not to interfere with somebody if they say that they are happy practicing whatever it is they are practicing.

If they are happy and wish to continue with it we should not worry because without a doubt it is better than nothing.

Without a doubt it is opening up their religious seeking minds.

Without a doubt they are moving along the path towards the discovery of the ultimate truth, but never should we demean The Gohonzon or Nam Myoho Renge Kyo by saying that Nam Myoho Renge Kyo is one of many roads to the ultimate truth.

It is absurd when you think about it as of course Nam Myoho Renge Kyo is the ultimate truth, the true entity of life and the true aspect of reality.

It is not a road to go anywhere.

Nam Myoho Renge Kyo is the destination and what is more we prove it in our lives everyday a day at a time.

Nam Myoho Renge Kyo is like the great ocean into which all the rivers of the world flow.

Changing Poison into Medicine

We should remain friends with those who maybe practicing other philosophies and every so often we try to Shakubuku them, but never should we get upset or angry.
We should always remain courteous and patient even though we never cease to chant that one day they will find the ultimate truth for themselves.
Nichiren Daishonin sets this example in Rissho Ankoku Ron.
Towards the end of Rissho Ankoku Ron he says.

"It seems to me that when people are in this world they all fear what their lot will be in the life to come.
So it is that some of them put their faith in heretical teachings or pay honour to those who slander The Law."

This is really deep insight into the human mind.
None of those religions which we have referred to can really explain the function of death, therefore the fear of death always exists.
Those other religions and particularly Honen's religion or The Pure Land sect taught that if you just did your best in this life whatever your circumstances are, and keep faith in his teachings, then after death you would be reborn in the pure land in the western part of the universe.
This is just the same as Christianity, Islam, Judaism, Hinduism, even Theravada Buddhism.
They all talk about a paradise or a heaven or a nirvana in some form or another.
Something which is outside of this awful world.
Death then always remains an enigma, something unknown, something to be feared and because of this these religions have held the people without actually developing their lives.
Destiny is therefore the will of god and in Shakyamuni's Buddhism in the way it was distorted, destiny was the will of the Buddha.
There was no way out of it, you were born in the world of animality that is where you stayed until many, many, many lifetimes you elevated your life to something better, this is no great solution to improving your life in this world.
This led to the apathy which encouraged further disasters and destruction.
Right at the end of the question, the traveller says to the host.

"Now if you know of any means whereby disasters can be prevented and troubles brought to an end, I would like to hear about it."

If only Hojo Tokiyori had really answered in that way in reality.
Japanese history might have been incredibly different.
The Buddhist Law would have flourished seven hundred and fifty
odd years ago in Japan and instead of falling into darkness
culminating in the outbreak of world war two, the karma of the
Japanese people could have been completely different.
If only Hoji Tokiyori had really thought like that, perhaps the Far
East would have never been effected by that war and many
things would have been different today.
These if only's are hypothetical and are of little account because
all that has happened in those nearly eight hundred years is now
a matter of history.
Hojo Tokiyori did not listen to Nichiren Daishonin.
The Buddhist Law was not established nearly eight hundred years
ago.
All that is the past but for us the important thing is that the
message of Rissho Ankoku Ron is not in the least bit old history.
It is not something of the past, indeed it lives today as it has never
lived before.
The governments and peoples of today should heed Rissho
Ankoku Ron and act on it now and this has now, in these
contemporary times, become even more urgent and vitally
important than ever before.
Today it is not Japan that is on the verge of destroying itself in the
middle ages, but it is the whole world that now faces imminent
destruction.
We must teach the great principles of Nichiren Shoshu Buddhism
wherever we go whether or not people listen.
Whether or not they seem likely to practice, as in no way are we
able to judge who will practice and who will not practice.
Even the beginnings of an understanding of the fact that life is the
most precious treasure in the universe and should be respected
above all else or that humanity and its environment are
completely and utterly inseparable, even the beginning of an
understanding of such great principles as this or an understanding
of karma or the universal law of cause and effect will all make a
profound difference to a person's life whether or not they actually
practice Nichiren Shoshu Buddhism.
Once a person has heard of the law of cause and effect or the
fact that life is eternal as taught in this Buddhism, they cannot fail
than begin to think and in many cases this will partially open their
eyes and their minds and deeply effect their actions even though
they maybe not always realise it.
In the concept of Kosen Rufu of the world, the support of people
who can see something of the greatness of Nichiren Daishonin's

Changing Poison into Medicine

Buddhism through its principles is extremely important, whether or not they commit themselves to practice.
This is a matter or not of whether their karma is right to do so.
Their influence, those who can see the greatness of the principles, think about it and let it affect their life if even only a little, is of incredible importance from the point of view of the future peace of the world.
Together with those who are actually practicing, they will help to tilt the balance of this world towards the positive, enlightened rather than the negative, ignorant forces of life which have been the predominate force up to this present time in the history of humanity.
To help us win such support is indeed the great purpose of our efforts in talking to people about Nichiren Shoshu Buddhism and more importantly showing actual proof of the practice by them seeing the evolution and changes that occur in our life and our behaviour as a human being as we turn our poison into medicine.
Let us look at a part of Nichiren Daishonin's reply to question seven.

The host said:
"There is no doubt that I am the foolish one, I would never dare to claim to be wise.
However, I would just like to quote some passages from the Sutra,s and offer some brief thoughts.
Concerning the means for insuring order in the nation, there are numerous passages in both Buddhist and non-Buddhist texts, and it would be difficult to cite them all here.
Since taking up the study of Buddhism, however, I have frequently given thought to this matter, and it seems to me that prohibiting those who slander The Law and paying respect to the priests and followers of the correct way is the best way to assure stability within the nation and peace in the world at large."

This statement expresses the theme running through the whole of Rissho Ankoku Ron.
That slander of The True Law or The Lotus Sutra or in other words slander of life itself is the surest way to ruin a nation, or even a Planet.
What really is slander of The True Law?
It is not only slandering The Gohonzon and slandering those who are practicing Nichiren Shoshu Buddhism, this is the specific meaning of slandering The True Law or Dharma.
There is also a general meaning which is anything which denigrates or harms life or causes unhappiness.

Changing Poison into Medicine

This is slander of The True Law in the general sense, and this of course is what the whole world is suffering from at this moment in time and history.

Life itself is The True Law, Myoho Renge Kyo, which is life in all its myriad, and wonderous workings.

Today wherever you look in the world there is slander of life.

To take a few examples, there are brilliant people involved in technology which pollutes the air we breathe, and all the environment around us.

There are powerful nations capable of great cultural development, who instead are wasting their energies on war against those nations that are weaker.

There are scientists, family people with spouses and children that work feverishly day in and day out on weapons of mass destruction.

There are businesspeople who give to charity with one hand and grab hordes of vital commodities denying them to the poorer and less developed countries in order to bring the price high and make great profits from them.

The list is endless, such people are either blind, ignorant and utterly stupid or if they are not so, they are nothing else but evil.

This is why we must teach the great principles of Nichiren Shoshu Buddhism wherever we go whether people will listen or not, whether or not they actually practice.

We must step by step open the eyes of the people everywhere and eradicate slander of life especially through blindness, ignorance and stupidity and this is our mission as Nichiren Shoshu Buddhists.

There are evil people who will not listen to what Buddhism teaches or what anyone else who is trying to achieve a peaceful world say.

They even try to destroy the movement of those, who with their whole heart's, desire a peaceful and happy world.

These people in Buddhism are called 'Icchantika,'

This is a Sanskrit word 'Icchan' which means faith and 'tika' which means not containing.

In other words Icchantika means or translates as containing no faith or truly evil or containing strong evil desire.

The Icchantika are human beings who are totally at the mercy of the dark, deluded, negative force of life, totally ruled by the fundamental darkness inherent in life itself.

When the two groups of those who practice and those who support the great principles of Nichiren Shoshu Buddhism grow stronger and stronger, when finally they then outweigh the

219

influence of the Icchantika, a critical mass is achieved or reached.

The natural balance of our Planet is then tilted or tipped towards the light and enlightenment or toward the Buddhahood inherent in life itself, or in other words Myoho Renge Kyo has fused with the life of humanity itself.

We can then, at last, succeed in achieving Kosen Rufu or World Peace and live in harmony with ourselves and our environment, as we have finally changed for ever the poison into medicine.

Achieved through each individuals personal transformation, and then this eventually encompasses the whole of humanity itself, thus creating a new era or age of enlightenment and happiness in human history.

This is the natural progression or evolution of our species towards revealing its fullest potential or highest and best condition of being or life, taking our place in the natural order of the galaxy and the universe, which is eternally evolving in this way.

We do not know what an individual's state of life and karma is, there are many stories of how someone has Shakubuku'd somebody who they never thought in a thousand years would ever practice, on the other hand there are stories of people who you thought would practice, which you find to your bitter disappointment, do not.

We cannot judge.

That is why we try to spread the teachings wherever we go whether or not people will listen to what we say, speak to all , speak to everybody, whenever there is a chance.

The Icchantika are those who slander without remorse.

They are those human beings who reject any morals and teachings who spit back in the faces of those who are trying to achieve a better world.

If we think of recent history and past history we can see the people who truly in all their actions are subtly introducing influences of evil in all their contacts with others.

They know what they are, and they revel in it with no thought of repentance or shame.

Repentance in Buddhism is known in Japanese as Zange.

Zange means to feel the utmost regret with your whole life.

In Shakyamuni's Buddhism repentance is explained in its application to people who are not practicing Buddhism.

There were five kinds of repentance or Zange for people not practicing.

One was to respect The Three Treasures of The Buddha, The Dharma & The Priesthood (Sangha) even though they did not practice.

The second was to respect seniors in years and experience.
The third was never to ignore or despise other people or use them for selfish ends.
The fourth was never to kill creatures more than is necessary than to sustain life.
And the fifth was to try to deeply understand the law of karma or cause and effect and thus try to follow the correct way.
Through understanding the principles of Nichiren Shoshu Buddhism more and more people even without practice can begin to observe those five ways of not slandering The Dharma or Law and start to make good causes in order to overcome their previous slander and thus influence the world in a positive way.
In the west christianity introduced confession, or confession to a priest and I am sure this may give some people a sense of some wellbeing like getting a load off your mind, but confession cannot change anything deep in your life.
It is not powerful enough to change your karma.
A priest to start with is a human being, they cannot discharge or remove that deep inherent cause lodged in a person's life that causes them to do those things about which they are confessing to in the first place.
Nichiren Daishonin explains Zange as follows in the Gosho.

"Sit up straight and ponder the true aspect of your life, if you do deep zange your past sins will melt like frost and dewdrops in the sunshine of your wisdom."

Viewed from the aspect of eternal life every single one of us must have slandered life or The True Law at one time or another and remember that slander can be by thought, word or action.
Worst still is that we may still be doing it even though we are now practicing Buddhism.
Maybe we are complaining and blaming others for things that happen to us that we do not like.
Maybe we are sometimes hating people.
Maybe we are criticising destructively.
Maybe we are hurting people by some of our remarks.
Maybe we are even hurting people occasionally by causing bodily harm to them in a fit of anger.
If we seem to be getting no benefits, if we seem not to be changing our karma, if nothing seems to be moving forward in our lives, if we cannot change our poison into medicine, then you should think about slander.
We should really think twice every time we moan and complain and blame others or if we hate others, even for a moment.

Every time we do it we are perpetuating our karma of slander.
Zange is the practice to recognise that we are actually
slandering.
Zange causes us to actually face it and as we chant The Daimoku
& Shodai to realise that with the whole of our life.
Then if we really realise this deeply, regret wells up from the very
depths of our lives and fills our entire being.
We then realise that we are still perpetuating that karma maybe
every day, making more causes which will bring even more
negative effects.
After that we feel gratitude despite the fact that we have
committed all this slander and that we are still doing it sometimes.
We are fortunate enough to have met The Gohonzon so that we
can change this karma and we chant Shodai strongly having
done zange for actual proof that the compassion of the Buddha
actually exists in us, even in those areas where previously we have
committed this slander.
Why does zange work?
It really does work, there is not one person I know who has done
deep zange and not been enabled to make changes in their life
as a result.
Why is it important?
The point about zange is that we tap the very depths of our lives
and for the first time ever, through acknowledging those bad
causes that we ourselves have made, we open up the depths of
our lives, for the first time we are no longer hiding anything.
We are not hiding anything from The Gohonzon, and we are not
hiding anything from ourselves even though we may have
suspected it existed and turned a blind eye to it and denied it.
We recognise it with our whole heart and face it and admit it.
This releases the poison that has been locked in our lives,
probably for many, many, years and in some cases lifetimes.
We rid ourselves of it and as a result of that we reveal The
Gohonzon that is within our lives lying behind all those clouds of
poison.
The Sun of the Buddha nature or The Gohonzon is always shining
in our lives which so often lies behind the poison clouds of slander.
A shallow zange is not particularly valuable or effective.
It may be better than nothing, but really zange must fill your
whole being, your whole life.
Your whole life filled with regret with what you have done and
then that's it, it is done, no more guilt.
Really chanting strongly to change that horrible karma and rid
that poison from our lives once and for all and to see the Buddha

nature as actual proof, occurring where it has never occurred before.

If you stole a watch from somebody ten or twenty years ago, zange is not saying to Gohonzon when you chant 'I am really sorry I did this'

Zange is seeing the cause that you made by that act, the hurt and pain that you caused in some one's life.

Feeling it right in the very depths of your life and longing to see that person again so that you can make amends and give them ten thousand watches in return if you could only do so.

This is zange right in the depths of your being, in the depths of your life.

Sadly the Icchantika cannot even begin to feel the need for apology of any sort, shallow or deep.

We have to really fight against the influence of the true deep slanderers of 'The True Dharma,' or Myoho Renge Kyo, the Icchantika.

The point is, as Nichiren Daishonin is saying, the world in which we live in today even perhaps in our own country, even in our own town, is gradually and insidiously being dragged down by these people who are warping and distorting the minds of ordinary people.

Nichiren Daishonin is saying that the Icchantika are the fundamental cause of the three calamities and seven disasters appearing in this world by their negative and destructive influence.

They are sapping the life force and natural wisdom from the people and breeding hopelessness, apathy and frustrated violence.

They follow such dogmas as, 'nothing can be done about it all,' 'Grab, grab, grab while the going is good,' 'You maybe dead tomorrow,' 'Let's destroy this system and lead a violent revolution against it,'

We have seen it all before in history.

We forget that there is a devilish or evil influence working amongst certain people who bring about such situations in society.

Icchantika are nothing else but people who in fact are totally influenced by the devilish and destructive force of life.

They are often in disguise.

They may even appear benign and benevolent outwardly, but their actions are to dupe and deceive others causing them to slander themselves in their ignorance.

Nichiren Daishonin says in the Rissho Ankoku Ron to people who practice Buddhism and knowing that Buddhism is totally against talking life, he uses the word kill.

It is necessary to kill the life of these devilish people, of course not physically, but to kill the evil in their minds and their influence.
The word kill is used without a doubt to emphasise the unbelievable danger that these people cause to humanity.
By what means can their evil minds be killed without physical violence?
What is necessary is for people's minds to be awakened so they can see the distortion of the truth which such people are trying to impose in the minds of others.
The principles which we believe in, the dignity of life and so on, are those very principles which can open the eyes of people so that they are no longer duped and deceived, even if they do not practice Nichiren Shoshu Buddhism, this undermines the position of influence which such people hold.
That they should lose their followers and be isolated.
In ancient Japan, to kill meant to refuse offerings to such priests and monks who were evil.
In those days there were priests and monks who carried begging bowls around into which people made their offerings of food and also gave them clothing and shelter.
The old system was to open people's eyes to them and to their evil ways so that the asking for offerings were refused and their influence was destroyed.
Of course it is never easy to Shakubuku such a person, so long as they are serving the devilish influences in life, worse still the devilish force will do its utmost to protect them.
Naturally when they die they will fall into the hell of incessant suffering, but even so we have to try and after their influence has been reduced, it will be necessary for those who know them to persuade them to practice.
This is what the word kill means in this context.
Nichiren Shoshu Buddhism is of course totally compassionate, totally against the taking of life, but that compassion is like the compassion of a strict father as well as the compassion of a gentle mother.
There is nothing grey in Buddhism, everything is clear, black or white.
Killing is taking influence away from these people so that they can no longer hold the minds and hearts of ordinary people.
The Icchantika actually destroys goodness.
In the Gosho Nichiren Daishonin writes,

"Evil and goodness are the two laws of right and left from the time of kuon ganjo (infinite past)"

224

Changing Poison into Medicine

In other words evil is inherent in life, especially in the six lower worlds which every living creature as well as human beings possess.

Even in the state of Buddha all the other worlds still exist otherwise a Buddha would not be a human being.

The lower worlds exist in us all and only through the Buddha state is it possible to turn these lower worlds into consistently positive influences, or to change poison into medicine.

The Law of Life contains good and evil and what is more it is up to each individual human being which they choose, good or evil, for a lifetime, for a day, for a year even for a moment.

Most people want to choose good.

The number of people who willingly wish to choose evil, the Icchantika is comparatively small, but the power of evil is so strong that it can easily drag down those who desire to lead a good life.

People in this age really need the power of The Gohonzon, they need to activate their Buddha nature in order to overcome this inherent and incredibly strong tendency towards evil, so we must Shakubuku wherever we go whether people will listen or not.

Up to this time certainly in this country of Great Britain and all the other countries of the world, the ultimate truth, the supreme dignity of life has not yet been established.

Life as the most precious of treasures in the entire universe is not yet really understood.

It is we who practice who have to establish it through the great principles of Nichiren Shoshu Buddhism and the teaching of Nichiren Daishonin in the Gosho and through the great power of The Gohonzon working in our life.

People have got used to gain at the expense of others, and this leads to suppression of other individuals or whole groups of individuals.

This leads to human suffering.

Gain at the expense of others.

We see it everywhere, we fiddle our taxes and the result of that on a large scale is that taxes have to be increased.

Shoplifting is rife and a menace in the retail world, what is the result?

It means an increase in prices for everyone else, it may be only very small, but it is an increase added to all the other increases which eventually causes the people to have difficulties financially.

People expect pay for no work, there are many cases of people drawing pay when they are actually lying in bed at home.

This is a way of life especially perhaps in the west.

Changing Poison into Medicine

This is not the way of The Gohonzon.
The way of The Gohonzon is that benefit equates with effort, reward is always through effort.
We know this only too well as we do not get the benefits of The Gohonzon without making great effort ourselves.
In Buddhism the benefits of The Gohonzon are never, ever at the expense of others.
In our society benefits are expected speaking generally at the expense of others in one way or another.
In the Gosho 'The Gift of Rice,' Nichiren Daishonin says.

"Life itself is the most precious of all treasures, even the treasures of the entire universe cannot equal the value of a single human life."

This is one of the guiding principles of Nichiren Shoshu Buddhism, that is the supreme dignity of life and its eternal nature and that it is founded on a strict law of cause and effect.
These principles can have a considerable effect on the lives of the people.
Every day in Gongyo in the Jigage section, we recite the words, 'Butsu-go jip pu ko.'
Which translates as 'The Buddha's words are true not false.'
In other words the dignity of life should be a reality in our daily lives, in our behaviour, in everything we do, not just an ideology.
To respect others, to respect nature, to respect our environment, to respect everything that surrounds us before anything else in all our actions.
Those who become aware of this principle and practice can find the power through The Gohonzon to do this.
They consistently see their whole karma changing and even those who become aware of it and do not practice can definitely enhance their way of life and their effect on this world.
Above all else our task is to fight against the slanderers of The True Dharma and this, as you are now at the beginning of your understanding, is the greatest and most humane action that anybody can possibly take.
To kill your own devilish nature is the first step.
Through using the power of The Gohonzon to change the poison of our negative karma into the great medicine of revealing our true selves, our Buddhahood.
We use these negative forces in our own lives as the fuel of our enlightenment, thus changing the poison into medicine.

After we succeed in killing our own devilish nature we then can kill
it in others through Shakubuku, no greater or nobler task could
possibly exist.
It is a straight battle in this world of ours between good and evil,
there are no grey areas.
To kill or to be killed, this is the truth of it.
Do we win and avoid the imminent destruction of our natural
environment and perhaps our very existence on this planet, or do
we fail?
Nowhere in the Gosho does Nichiren Daishonin prophesise this
destruction.
If we really keep the fighting spirit in our hearts and really
Shakubuku then there is no reason on earth why this apocalyptic
vision of the future should occur.
We have to steadily get on with the job of Shakubuku wherever
we go and whether people listen to us or not.
In the same passage from the Jigage section of Gongyo as
'Butsu-go jip pu ko.'
It reads.
'Nyo-to u chi sha. Mot to shi go gi. To dan ryo yo jin. Butsu-go jip
pu ko.'
Which translates as.
'You, persons of wisdom, rid yourself of all doubts about this, cut
them off once and for all, the Buddha's words are true, not false.'
Perhaps from now on when we recite these words in Gongyo we
can remind ourselves that this should be our spirit, our fighting
spirit, to kill and not be killed.
What does to kill mean?
These strong words mean to kill the slander in people's lives and
minds but first and foremost in ourselves.
The people in this day and age are Sovereign, we now live in a
democratic system of government where ultimately the power
resides with the people, in the Gosho, 'Propagation by The Wise,'
Nichiren Daishonin said.

"Buddhism can be correctly propagated only by a person of
unsurpassed wisdom, this is why Shakyamuni summoned
Bodhisattva Jogyo and entrusted it to him."

That person of unsurpassed wisdom is The Buddha of This Age,
Nichiren Daishonin and though we may not feel like it, so far as
our own local circumstances are concerned, we are the people
of unsurpassed wisdom because we practice day in and day out
with The Gohonzon drawing out the qualities of our Buddha
nature and revealing it in our lives.

Changing Poison into Medicine

This is quite a thought and often we feel we have got no wisdom at all, but in fact because we practice correctly we have.
If we really trust The Gohonzon we can definitely cope in debate with any single person that we may encounter, whatever field of society they may come from.
Nichikan Shonin the 26th High Priest of Nichiren Shoshu propounded three ways to protect The Teachings.
First is through the absolute unity of The Priesthood and the lay peoples, fighting together side by side for Kosen Rufu.
The second is for The Priesthood only.
That every High Priest must absolutely protect the purity of The Dharma or teachings and the treasures of Nichiren Shoshu, of which the foremost one is Dai Gohonzon.
The third one is for us Lay persons only.
To protect The High Priest and protect the teachings through ever wider propagation amongst the people.
With reference to the last one concerning lay persons only, we must protect through our chanting of Shodai.
This gives us the life force and the wisdom to do Shakubuku so more and more people can begin to understand The Dharma.
We can also protect through taking the lead in our own unique and particular environment in our particular field of society.
We should look at our particular field or particular environment and our particular role in that environment which only we can possibly be responsible for, we can take the lead through teaching others about this Buddhism, through letting people understand its principles.
For example, as a partner and a mother in your home, and those who visit it, amongst your children, in your neighbourhood or community, in the school your children attend.
If you are a mechanic, you can take the lead again at home, again in the community, in your workplace, amongst your work colleagues, maybe within your trades union and in many different ways.
As a scientist again you can take the lead in your home, in your town or city, in your place of work.
As an artist you can take the lead in the culture that you are a part of whatever medium you work with.
In so many different ways each person can be of influence through the power of The Gohonzon and the practice working in their lives.
There have been many revolutions in history and every or nearly every one of them has caused the loss of an incredible number of lives.

In our revolution called Kosen Rufu not a single life is lost and not a
single life is harmed in any way.

As the great movement for Kosen Rufu advances in almost every
country of the world there will be more and more people who are
influential in various fields of society who will begin to embrace
The Gohonzon and The Dharma of Nichiren Shoshu.

Politicians, scientists, doctors, teachers, artists and so on.

On the other hand we must be very clear that unlike christianity
and unlike other religions, Priests and Lay leaders will never, ever
enter politics.

Politics and religion according to the teachings of Buddhism must
be kept separate always and entirely.

Otherwise the religious movement itself becomes subject to
political pressure and we have seen plenty enough of this in
history already and we have seen the effects of this in christianity
down through the ages, through the past two thousand years or
so, of course there will be practitioners who work in politics,
people who are already in politics who will start to practice.

Those who have started to practice who may want to then enter
politics and they will inevitably have influence, as would any other
person in their field of endeavour and will bring points of view that
others could not possibly think of.

Most important of all it is those people in a political area who must
defend to the very last the freedom of speech, worship and
fundamental human rights.

The task of the religious movement is to spread the teachings
amongst the people who are in turn the electorate.

Those people are then able to begin to really think for themselves
based on sound wisdom and compassion and wise judgement
and choose the right course and the right representatives in
parliament.

Also Buddhism should never supress other religions, this has been
seen in the past through priests of certain faiths wielding political
power.

Nichiren Shoshu Buddhism is passionately concerned with
freedom of religion.

If others challenge Buddhism, we must challenge them back in
the form of debate and discussion.

People are entitled to believe what they like to believe in, our task
is to set the principles of Nichiren Shoshu Buddhism alongside the
principles they believe in and they in the end have to judge
which is the set of principles which they should be following.

We should never be arrogant, never be irritated because others
decide to continue with their own religion or philosophy.

Changing Poison into Medicine

Indeed we should encourage them by saying please go ahead and we will work alongside you for peace, because through our friendship they can begin to see the greatness of Nichiren Shoshu Buddhism working in the daily lives of those who practice it.
If there is separation between us, if there is a whole wall between us, how can they ever see the actual proof shining brilliantly in the lives of those who practice with The Gohonzon.

Question Eight.

"The Guest said, 'If we are to put an end to these people who slander The Law and do away with those who violate the prohibitions of the Buddha, then are we to condemn them to death as described in the passages of the sutras you have just cited?

If we do that, then we ourselves will be guilty of inflicting injury and death upon others and will suffer the consequences will we not?

In the Daijuku sutra the Buddha says "If a person shaves his head and puts on clerical robes then whether that person observes the precepts or violates them, both gods and men should give him alms, in doing so they are giving alms and support to me, for that person is my son, but if men beat and abuse that person, they are beating my son, and if they curse and insult him, they are reviling me."

If we stop to consider, we must realise that, regardless of whether one is good or bad, right or wrong, if he is a priest, then he deserves to have alms and nourishment extended to him.

For how could one beat and insult the son and not cause grief and sorrow to the father?

The brahmans of the Bamboo Staff school who killed the Venerable Maudgalyayana have for a long time been sunk in the hell of incessant suffering.

Because Devadatta murdered the nun Utpalavarna, he has for a long time gasped in the flames of the Avichi hell.

Examples from earlier ages make the matter perfectly clear, and later ages fear this offense most of all.

You speak of punishing those who slander The Law, but to do so would violate the Buddha's prohibitions.

I can hardly believe that such a course would be right.

How can you justify that?"

Nichiren Daishonin's purpose in posing this question as made by the guest to his host is to clear up confusion over this point of how and what tactical steps to take to stop the slander which was rife in the land of Japan at that time and of course is rife throughout the world today.

The only effective way, which he leads into is Shakubuku.

Even a person who is thoroughly evil must be saved, this would be 'The Buddhist Way.'

We have to establish a relationship between all people and The Gohonzon or do our best to do so.

Even what is known as a reverse relationship to The Gohonzon will eventually end in that person embracing it, the important thing is the relationship.

Changing Poison into Medicine

In Shakyamuni's time there was a ruler called King Ajatshatru who refused to listen to the teachings of the Buddha, largely because of the machinations of the evil cousin of Shakyamuni, Devadatta. King Bimbisara who was Ajatshatru's father was Shakyamuni's sponsor.

Nevertheless the son Ajatshatru would not listen and for a long time he led a wild and evil life, killing his father and constantly waging war on his neighbours and slaughtering vast numbers of people.

In the end he came out in fearful, stinking boils all over his body and as a result of that, it brough him up short in his tracks and caused him to stop and reflect, through that self-reflection he began to realise that this must be karma, or cause and effect, the result of his past evil deeds and actions.

He then went to Shakyamuni Buddha to accept the teachings of Buddhism and the story ends with him extending his life by forty years.

This began with a reverse relationship with the Buddha, he slandered Shakyamuni due to being incited by Devadatta.

In the end it was that relationship that was the important thing because when he did come up against it this caused him to stop and think, reflect on his life, he then realised that he must do something about it to save himself from a hellish existence.

He then embraced the Buddhist teachings.

We have no need to fear when we are doing Shakubuku whether or not people listen to what we say when we are talking about Buddhism, the most important thing is the establishment of the relationship between a person and The Gohonzon.

Even if at the beginning it is a relationship that is slanderous.

That slander is in that person's life anyway.

It has to come out before they can find true happiness and contentment.

In the end our responsibility is to kill the evil mind of the slanderer and of course this also means that we do not have the right to kill anybody for the sake of Buddhism.

Life is like a crystal, it turns the colour of whatever light is shone onto it, if you shine a blue light onto a crystal, it appears to be blue and if you shine a red light onto a crystal it appears to be red, so to kill somebody is like destroying the crystal itself.

What is needed is to shine the right colour light onto the crystal.

All human life, whatever the behaviour of that individual person, is treasure from the perspective of The Dharma or all the Buddhist teachings.

We tend to condemn people, we can condemn a race, a type of people, a category of people, this is the awful human tendency arising from the lower worlds.
In fact it is the colour of the light that may be causing them to behave in an ignorant or unpleasant way.
We must be absolutely clear that from the perspective of the Buddhist teachings or Dharma, we are totally against harm or hurt or killing of life and we are totally against slander of life.
This is the enemy of life, the evil force in life which we have to do battle with and should do battle with every day, both in ourselves and where necessary when we see it working in other people.
In this respect, as an example, it is great that the UK has ceased to use capital punishment, whatever the argument for or against, capital punishment is destroying life and life is the most precious of treasures.
Going back to this question.
In the Daijuku sutra the Buddha says,

"If a person shaves his head and puts on clerical robes then whether that person observes the precepts or violates them, both gods and men should give him alms, in doing so they are giving alms and support to me, for that person is my son.
But if men beat and abuse that person, they are beating my son, and if they curse and insult him, they are reviling me."

This all sounds a bit confusing in the light of what we have already been considering and this is why Nichiren Daishonin included this particular paragraph in the Rissho Ankoku Ron.
Instead of thinking about priests let us think about one of our great cathedrals, York Minster, which is a fantastic and beautiful building, it is full of marvellous examples of craftsmanship and human skills.
Inside there are priceless carvings and stained glass windows which are famous throughout the world, there are also works of art and priceless gold and silverware and other treasures.
Because of this beauty people tend to honour and respect a religion.
People go to temples in Buddhist countries, and they are magnificent, and they are over awed by it and feel this must be something great.
This is in fact absurd.
If the teachings of the religion are weak, or ignorant, no matter how beautiful the building they are going to is, it will be of no ultimate value to this world, or to the people concerned.

Changing Poison into Medicine

We can respect history, artistry, and the craftsmanship contained in a cathedral but not the teachings or what it represents.
We can apply the same thinking to the Pope.
He may be a compassionate and courageous man and this we must respect but this does not mean to say we should respect what he preaches as he rallies and preaches against abortion, contraception and divorce.
This is very shallow and for many very controversial.
Buddhism teaches that these three things are only evil if they are motivated by the three poisons of greed, anger and ignorance.
To make a general rule for all humanity can be cruel and destructive and destroy the peoples happiness.
Going back to the Daijuku sutra, which was quoted earlier, because a person dresses in the traditional robes of a priest does not mean to say that what he thinks says and does is necessarily respect worthy.
We can respect their intention but not what they teach and if it is slander we have to try to change their mind.
The robes of a Nichiren Shoshu Priest are symbolic of the equality with the lay people.
The robes carry a number of square patches, this is to remind and is symbolic of the fact that at one time the priests of Nichiren Shoshu were incredibly poor and that they are ordinary people who suffer the ups and downs of this life just as much as anyone else does.
They share the sufferings of the people of this world on an absolutely equal basis in relation to The Gohonzon, this is a very wonderful thing.
Sometimes we are called 'The Children of The Buddha,' so what is a child of the Buddha?
The 26th High Priest of Nichiren Shoshu Nichikan Shonin said,
A child of the Buddha is the person who practices 'yu-myo sho-jin'
In the Hoben pon of Gongyo we say.
'jin gyo sho-butsu, Mu-ryo do ho. Yu-myo sho-jin. Myo-sho fu mon.'
Yu-myo means valiantly, sho-jin, means untiringly seeking The Buddha.
Therefore Yu-myo means steadfast faith in The Gohonzon and sho-jin means chanting Shodai untiringly.
To take faith in The Gohonzon and do nothing is evil, to take faith and to take action is good, using those terms of evil and good in respect of the evil force of life or the negative force of life and the positive, enlightened force of life.
Nothing, meaning taking no action for turning your own poison into medicine or to change society in this world for the better.

235

Changing Poison into Medicine

Let us try to live up to this term we repeat in Gongyo many times daily, 'Yu-myo sho-jin,' trying to advance a little bit every day.
In the answer that follows this particular question Nichiren Daishonin explains further that censure of the person slandering is not against the person or the priest, it is against what he teaches, slander of The True Law of Life.
In this respect they are not children of the Buddha if the words that are emitted from their mouths are not the words of the Buddha, so in the answer to question eight the host says.

"The host said, You have clearly seen the passages from the sutras that I have cited and yet you can ask a question like that, are they beyond the power of your mind to comprehend?
Or do you fail to understand the reasoning behind them?
I certainly have no intention of censuring the sons of the Buddha, my only hatred is to the act of slandering The Law.
According to the Buddha's who lived prior to Shakyamuni, slanderous priests would have incurred the death penalty but in the sutras preached since the time of Shakyamuni, priests of this type have merely been prevented from receiving alms.
Now if the people within the four seas and the ten thousand lands, all those who belong to the four kinds of believers, if only they would cease giving alms to wicked priests and instead will all come over to the side of the good, then how could we have any more of these troubles rising to plague us, these disasters coming to confront us."

This is really a crucial point.
Nichiren Daishonin is pointing out to the ruling authorities of those times, that they were still supporting priests who were spreading teachings that were evil and could lead people to unhappiness.
The ruling authorities or The Shogunate were revering tradition and history and the beauty and treasures of the great temples in Japan at that time, but they were not examining the teachings themselves.
Then he goes on to point out that before Shakyamuni's day, before Buddhism, evil priests were actually killed physically.
We know this because there are many stories in Shakyamuni's Buddhism where he gives examples of people suffering intensely because of killing a priest in the past.
From Shakyamuni's time onwards, from the inception of Buddhism onwards if an evil priest did not respond to Shakubuku and the true teachings then offerings to him were stopped, the treasures of life were denied to him.

The treasures that provide accommodation, clothing and food stuffs and as a result of that their influence was reduced and ultimately destroyed.

It was killing the evil in them, causing them to self reflect.

Let us look at the true meaning of this term Shakubuku that we use so often.

Shaku means to break or refute or instead of break you could say sever or cut off, buku means to cause to follow.

This means to 'kill' a slanderous mind and to stop offerings, the source of life, like cutting off with a sword.

Slander as we now know is acting against The True Law, Myoho Renge Kyo, acting against life itself.

Distorting or going against the true teachings of The Buddha, which are all concerned with the inherent dignity of life.

We use the term Shakubuku here in the UK in quite a loose way because it is such a fascinating word to use.

Strictly speaking Shakubuku is only necessary in a Buddhist country where people have a strong attachment, over generations in families, to teachings which are slanderous and distorted or to formalities and rituals which are equally slanderous but practiced in the name of Buddhism, doing these things because their grandfathers and grandmothers and great grandfathers and great grandmothers did it, clinging to things superstitiously or sentimentally for fear of offending their relatives or their ancestors. Fears of demons and devils and all the other ways in which such distorted teachings, which are far from the truth, had to resort to in order to hold the people.

In the Gosho it clearly explains that in a non-Buddhist country where there is no deliberate distortion we use what is known as Shoju as the method of propagation.

Shoju is as different from Shakubuku as fire is from water.

Shoju means by persuasion, by discussion, and by example.

Shoju means that we understand and can relate to the erroneous thoughts of the person whom we are talking to, that we do not necessarily and categorically say that they are wrong, but we draw then gradually to understand the truth through those three means of persuasion, discussion and example.

Of those three, example is by far the most convincing.

It is the way we change that convinces parents, brothers, sisters and friends to practice because it is proof of the power of The Gohonzon.

It is the power of The Gohonzon which is the most important thing that we should talk about.

The actual proof, the experience of that power.

Nichiren Daishonin himself said the three proofs were all important, literary, theoretical and actual but by far the most important he said, is actual proof.

This actually shows in this daily life the infinite power of The Gohonzon at work, and this is something that other religions cannot necessarily show, this is the best way to cause people to begin to practice.

Through the example of our faith and practice which quite naturally is manifested in our daily lives.

Contemporary society has lost its correct view of life and humanities place in it.

In such circumstances it is an inevitable tendency for people to seek out True Buddhism which reveals the absolute law, which is neither a partial view nor just an ideology but provides people with the means to actually transform the reality of their lives.

Therefore by awakening yourselves to your profound mission and establishing your roots in society based on the principle that faith and practice are equal to daily life we must become respected citizens who steadily and untiringly make a wonderful contribution to our communities and to society in general.

What we achieve in our personal lives, in our families, in our communities is the actual proof which many people, though they do not know it in their conscious minds, are waiting for.

Beyond this aspect of transformation of our personal lives lies Nichiren Daishonin's will and testimony for the great desire and goal of Kosen Rufu, that of establishing an eternally peaceful world through this transformation within human life itself.

The fundamental basis of our practice is Jigyo and Keta. That is practice for ourselves, and also practice for others.

This applies not only to our individual lives but also on a collective basis to society as a whole.

This is the meaning of Kosen Rufu, the change in society itself.

So as an individual we may chant Shodai to The Gohonzon perhaps for harmony in our family and we achieve it and that is great, but we have to look beyond that in a collective sense to how we can begin to actually change society through the inner change in each individual.

Our goals and determinations are not just confined to ourselves and our problems and our family and our world, they also apply to our community, our neighbourhood, our towns and cities and the whole country and in the broadest sense the whole world or Planet Earth.

Changing Poison into Medicine

As long as human beings continue to be apathetic and do nothing, the world will be like it is now and it will get even worse. There could even be more global pandemics like Covid 19 as we spiral into the vortex of the ever growing destruction of the climate crisis leading to an extinction event which is currently being talked about and maybe another war between the superpowers of China and America could erupt

When human beings decide to change the world, they can change it, and with the power of The Gohonzon we are the best people to take the lead in this endeavour and movement.

We must change it because Nichiren Shoshu Buddhism is the only nucleus for peace between peoples and harmony with our environment that exists now and in the future.

A Japanese historian who has painstakingly worked out that between the years 1500 B.C. and 1860 A.D. there had been no less than 8000 treaties for peace negotiated in the world and their duration has averaged no more than two years.

Peace can never be attained through the negotiations of politicians, it can only be achieved through the change in the hearts of human beings.

This is what the practice of Nichiren Shoshu Buddhism is all about. The reason why long term peace has never been achieved is because of the incredible power of egoistic nationalism which is motivated by the innate fundamental darkness of life and the three poisons of greed, anger and ignorance, which breeds fear that arises from it, which is the cause of so much trouble in this world.

People refuse to believe that others have a right to be equal with them, this is a fact.

This tendency arises and is the root cause of all armed conflicts and civil conflicts, national arrogance and pride on both sides. People in their heads understand the equality of all races and of all human beings theoretically but when it comes to the crunch and it effects their own personal lives, they choose to become blind to that fact because of fear and lack of trust.

Nations are spending vast amounts of money every day on armaments because of their suspicion and doubt of other human beings.

The most important thing for the world at this time and in this Anthropocene age is the growth and development of a philosophy which is founded absolutely on equality and the dignity of life, which gives the power to human beings to control the negative and destructive aspects of human nature and their minds.

239

Nothing else has that power except Nichiren Daishonin's Buddhism as practiced in The Nichiren Shoshu School of Buddhism or The Fuji School of Buddhism and the power of The Dai Gohonzon, which is The Great Mandala inscribed for the enlightenment of all living beings, only this power can create the unification of the human race.

The only way to achieve this on a wider scale is more Shakubuku and we are so incredibly fortunate to have found such a mission and purpose in this life.

Nichiren Daishonin in the Gosho says that inherent enlightenment appears in the universal forces called Bonten and Taishaku, whilst inherent ignorance or delusion is represented by The Devil of The Sixth Heaven using the old Buddhist terminology.

The truth is that the leaders of this world are either one or the other, there is no grey area.

Either they have the good, positive force of Bonten and Taishaku working within and through them, or they have the negative and destructive force of The Devil of The Sixth Heaven, it depends entirely on what they base their lives and actions on.

If the philosophy on which they base their life and actions is not polluted by the three poisons of life, then Bonten and Taishaku will work in them, but if the three poisons are in the least bit, working in their lives, the Devil of The Sixth Heaven takes over.

Shakyamuni predicted so long ago in The Lotus Sutra that as Kosen Rufu progresses, many great leaders will appear in society who through the practice to The Gohonzon can overcome the three poisons by changing them into good medicine and reveal their enlightened Buddha nature and lead people to happiness. Three thousand years ago Shakyamuni stated that in The Lotus Sutra.

This is an incredible thought and out of us now and those who practice in the future, great leaders in all fields of society, science, medicine, politics, the arts will appear at the appropriate time.

Question Nine.

"With this, the guest moved off his mat in a gesture of respect, straightened the collar of his robe and said.

'The Buddha's teachings vary greatly, and it is difficult to investigate each doctrine in full, I have had many doubts and perplexities, I have been unable to distinguish reason from unreason, nevertheless, this work by the venerable Honen, this Shenchaku shu does in fact exist and it lumps together all the various Buddha's, Sutras, Bodhisattva's and deities and says that one should discard, close, ignore and abandon them.

The meaning of the text is perfectly clear and as result of this Sages have departed from The Nation, the benevolent deities have left their resting places, hunger and thirst fill the world and disease and pestilence spread abroad.

Now, by citing passages from a wide variety of scriptures, you have clearly demonstrated the right and wrongs of the matter, therefore I have completely forsaken my earlier mistaken convictions as my ears and eyes have been opened on point after point.

There can be no doubt that the stability of The Nation and the peace of the world are what all people from the ruler down to the common people long for and rejoice in.

If we can quickly put an end to the alms given to these Icchantika and ensure that continuing support is instead given to the host of true priests and nuns, if we can still these white waves that trouble the ocean of the Buddha and cut down these green groves that overgrow the mountain of The Law then the world may become as peaceful as it was in the golden age of Fu Hsi and Shen Nung and The Nation may flourish as it did under the sage rulers Yao and Shun.

After that, there will be time to dip into the waters of The Law and to decide which are shallow doctrines and which are deep and to pay honour to the pillars and beams that support the house of the Buddha.'"

At last the guest is beginning to understand and accept what the host has been teaching, who is now winning the battle of Shakubuku, and he realises that the only way to save the nation at that time was to stop making offerings to those who are teaching evil.

Today if you look at the whole world the situation is in a sense quite similar but on a much larger, a much grander and much more horrifying scale.

Changing Poison into Medicine

There are many, many religions and philosophies and even more cults throughout the world and because of this people are understandably very confused and suspicious on the whole of religion in general.

They distrust religion and especially they distrust more and more the way in which religions are run.

There have been so many cases of extortion, enforced separation from families, brainwashing and worse still horrors in the name of various cults calling themselves religions.

This situation of course, has made it very difficult for people to decide or even begin to understand what religion is all about.

The only way we can convince people that what we practice is good and right and worthwhile and great is by showing the power of The Gohonzon, this is the unique asset which we have. This is why we must go out into society and show actual proof to an ever widening circle of friends and acquaintances.

This is our priceless treasure of The Gohonzon and its great power. This is undeniable through the actual experiences of a million people in this world who now practice Nichiren Shoshu Buddhism. It is about this that we should speak and lay emphasis on more than anything else in Shakubuku, not empty theory but actual proof of this power at work in our lives, no one else has The Dai Gohonzon of The Three Great Secret Laws.

This is why other religions have often to rely on blind faith or on superstition, on instilling fear, or on downright deceit and trickery. This is such an incredible treasure, this is what we must emphasise. The Gohonzon at work in the lives of ourselves and our friends.

Do not try to prejudge whether a person will practice or not, open our arms wide and bring anybody in who shows even the slightest glimpse of interest in making this world a better place to live in, or the slightest glimmer of interest in them changing their unhappy circumstances.

The spirit of Nichiren Daishonin, that we can realise through reading the Gosho, is never to lose a friend, our spirit should be the same, even if a person does not listen, even if they go away, let us keep in touch with them, of course not every day or every week or every month but every so often give them a call.

What is an ideal world?

The higher religions in this world find it very difficult to describe this and usually it seems to be a world apart from this real world.

They talk about a pure land, a utopia, a paradise or a heaven of some sort and this applies to Theravada Buddhism also, but The Lotus Sutra totally denies this concept.

The Lotus Sutra makes four great points.

The first is that this mundane world is itself the Buddha's land.

Secondly that everything depends on the life condition, on the hearts and minds of the people.

Thirdly, if those hearts and minds are filled with good fortune and wisdom, society will be a place of happiness and prosperity and the land will be rich and fruitful.

Fourthly, if that good fortune and wisdom is not there, evil will rule. There is no grey area, one or the other.

In the Gosho, 'The Person and The Law,' Nichiren Daishonin says.

"Since the Law is supreme, the person is worthy of respect, since the person is worthy of respect the land is sacred."

In a society that is not based on the rock of 'The Ultimate Law of Life,' it is very easy for gentle or passive people to be led in a way that makes them little better than animals.

Totally controlled by government or oligarchies, or by tyrannical dictators or indeed sometimes by power hungry religious clergy.

People have always been striving for a paradise, in Europe, people believed when religion lost its power that this paradise could be achieved through reformation of the social structure of countries.

Sharing everything, equality for all, and so on, which led to socialism and communism, but these isms have not changed the happiness of the people.

It does not actually and fundamentally change the hearts and minds of humanity.

To establish happiness and prosperity for the people there must be a philosophy that is absolutely rooted in humanity itself.

This is the greatness and universality of Nichiren Shoshu Buddhism. It follows that political science, if it is to give happiness to the people, must also have its roots in a philosophy that teaches the absolute dignity of life.

Because we base our lives on The Gohonzon and by experiencing its power in our daily lives we quite ordinary people can have the temerity to make determinations for five, ten or twenty years ahead, we can do such things, but what politician can really make a determination ten, twenty or even five years ahead?

Most of them are unable to think more than this year or at least no further than the next general election.

This is because the pressures of life confuse and upset and rock them off their feet, they have no real humane philosophy on which to base their lives and therefore they lack the wisdom and courage to look so far ahead, and we all suffer as a result.

Hemmed in by all these problems they simply cannot see any solutions.

Gradually now, the people are becoming sovereign as democratic ways spread further throughout the world but even a democracy cannot function properly unless the people exercise their prerogative.

That they are prepared to think for themselves, and they are prepared to make wise judgements on the issues of the day and then have the courage to voice their views and make sure in one way or another that those views are heard.

Through the wisdom and the courage that The Gohonzon brings forth from human life there is no doubt that gradually such a human movement will arise everywhere.

Where people will truly be taking part in democratic procedures and the government of their land.

Wisdom, Compassion and Courage is essential.

It is difficult to believe that this can come from anywhere else but practice with The Dai Gohonzon of Nichiren Shoshu Buddhism.

Those who practice with The Gohonzon just as The Lotus Sutra said will gradually become the leaders of society because people will see the wisdom of their actions, even though they cannot bring themselves to practice.

Let us really hope that many people who practice this Buddhism in the future will move out and play their part in politics and their local communities and neighbourhoods, taking the lead to help people find a happier more fulfilling way of life.

The ultimate purpose of politics must be to save ordinary people from unhappiness based on a spirit of true compassion.

Sadly at the moment politicians still use people, they still manipulate them for their own egoistic satisfaction.

Let us really determine to increase our Shakubuku efforts so that we can get this movement advancing at a more rapid rate than it has up to this day.

Every movement has to begin.

Every movement has to grow but it must also gradually accelerate otherwise it will lose momentum when it hits obstacles and difficulties.

Let us chant Shodai with the determination that more and more people can unleash their unique potential and put it into action in whatever field of society they wish to do so.

In the perfect balance of Nichiren Shoshu Buddhism we should remember that Shakubuku is not just for others, but it is also for ourselves.

It is not just for Kosen Rufu and the peace of the world.

It is so that we can change our own poison into medicine and attain Buddhahood, which is the purpose of the whole practice of Nichiren Shoshu Buddhism.

Changing Poison into Medicine

This great writing that is Rissho Ankoku Ron is all about slander. We too have slandered in this life and in past lives and even perhaps today, we have hurt or harmed life in one way or another, especially our own.

Perhaps persecuting or even thinking ill constantly of others. Worse still if it was towards those who practice with The Gohonzon, slander is always the cause of the worst sufferings that we go through, and we must learn to understand this.

We cannot turn a blind eye to the fact that we also have created deeply unhappy karma because we have slandered and harmed life or worse still that we have actually slandered The Gohonzon or other believers in The Gohonzon in past lives.

If we have used our minds and our tongues and our bodies through our actions for evil in such a way, what cause must we make in order to overcome that unhappy karma?

It can only be to use our minds, our tongues and our bodies for good and there is no greater good than being able to bring someone to The Gohonzon so that they too can begin to reveal their Buddha state and change their own poison into medicine. This why Nichiren Daishonin taught that the only sure way to change karma is through Shakubuku.

We need to think of this and not gloss it over, it is not just Shakubuku for this amazing dream of Kosen Rufu, it is Shakubuku so that we can overcome the effects of slander in our lives and find true happiness, without any fears and anxiety, true peace and contentment.

If we are going to change our karma we have to use our minds, our tongues and our bodies for good, for the greatest goodness which is Shakubuku otherwise we can never achieve our own awakening or Buddhahood or enlightenment and we can never rid ourselves of whatever slander there may be in us.

Of course it varies, some it may be heavy, some it may be lighter but for sure there is some slander there, not one single person can say that they have never harmed or hurt anybody or life in general, not one single person.

This is the karma that we have to overcome, and we do it through Shakubuku.

This document called Rissho Ankoku Ron is pure treasure for human beings everywhere.

We really have to have conviction in this ourselves.

If we doubt this document then we need to read it again and again because this document also explains in the greatest detail the validation for all that The Buddha of This Age, Nichiren Daishonin is saying.

Changing Poison into Medicine

Let us make sure that none of us will join that brigade of people who because their faith in their own religion is so weak maintain that there are many different ways to enlightenment, many different paths, none of us should fall into that trap.

It is true that there are many paths to The Dai Gohonzon but for us who have the amazing and unbelievable good fortune to have found The Gohonzon ahead of most of the human race it is important that we clearly understand to the very depths of our lives that Nam Myoho Renge Kyo is not a path.

Nam Myoho Renge Kyo and The Dai Gohonzon are the ultimate truth.

Nam Myoho Renge Kyo is it!

It is not a path to anywhere and it is very important that we have absolute conviction in that, if we do not have it then we should continue to study and read Rissho Ankoku Ron and chanting Shodai until we do.

Everything is explained in this document.

After this final answer to the traveller, he is totally convinced.

"The host exclaimed in delight.

The dove has changed into a hawk, the sparrow into a clam! How gratifying!

You have transformed yourself through your association with me, a friend in the orchid room, just as the mugwort growing in the hemp field becomes straight.

If you truly give consideration to the troubles I have been describing and put entire faith in these words of mine, then the winds shall blow gently, the waves will be calm, and in no time at all we will enjoy bountiful harvests.

But a person's heart may change with the times, and the nature of a thing may alter with its surroundings.

Just as the moon on the water will be tossed about by the waves, or the soldiers in the vanguard will be cowed by the swords of the enemy so, although at this moment you may say you believe in my words, I fear that later you will forget them completely.

Now if we wish first of all to bring security to the nation and to pray for our present and future lives, then we must hasten to examine and consider the situation and take measures as soon as possible to remedy it.

Why do I say this?

Because of the seven types of disaster described in the Yakushi Sutra, five have already occurred.

Only two have yet to appear, the calamity of invasion from foreign lands and the calamity of revolt within one's own domain.

And of the three calamities mentioned in the Daijuku Sutra, two have already made their appearance.

Only one remains, the disaster of warfare.

The different types of disaster and calamity enumerated in the Konkomyo Sutra have arisen one after the other.

Only that described as marauders from other regions invading and plundering the nation has yet to materialise.

This is the only trouble that has not yet come.

And of the seven disasters listed in the Ninno Sutra, six are now upon us in full force.

Only one has not yet appeared, the calamity that occurs "when enemies rise up on all four sides and invade the nation."

Moreover as the Ninno Sutra says, "When a nation becomes disordered, it is the spirits which first show signs of rampancy. Because the spirits become rampant, all the people of the nation become disordered."

Now if we examine the present situation carefully in the light of this passage, we will see the various spirits have for some time been rampant and many of the people have perished.

If the first predicted misfortune in the sutra has already occurred, as is obvious, then how can we doubt that the later disasters will follow?

If, in punishment for the evil doctrines that are upheld, the troubles that are yet to appear should fall upon us one after another, then it will be too late to act will it not?

Emperors and Kings have their foundation in the state and bring peace and order to the age; ministers and commoners hold possession of their fields and gardens and supply the needs of the world.

But if marauders come from other regions to invade the nation, or if revolt breaks out within the domain and peoples lands are seized and plundered, how can there be anything but terror and confusion?

If the nation is destroyed and families wiped out, then where can one flee for safety?

If you care anything about your personal security, you should first of all pray for order and tranquillity throughout the four quarters of the land, should you not?

It seems to me that, when people are in this world, they all fear what their lot may be in the life to come.

So it is that they put their faith in heretical doctrines and pay honour to slanderous teachings.

It distresses me that they should be so confused about right and wrong, and at the same time I feel pity that, having embraced Buddhism, they should have chosen the wrong kind.

With the power of faith in their hearts, why must they recklessly give credence to heretical doctrines?

If they do not shake off these delusions that they cling to but continue to harbour distorted views, then they will quickly leave this world of the living and surely fall into the hell of incessant suffering.

Thus the Daijuku Sutra says: "Though the ruler of a state may have for countless existences in the past practiced the giving of alms, observed the precepts and cultivated wisdom, if he sees that my teaching is in danger of perishing and stand idly by without doing anything to protect it, then all the inestimable roots of goodness planted through the practices just mentioned will be entirely wiped out.

Before long, the ruler will fall gravely ill, and after his life has come to an end, he will be reborn in the great hell.

And the same fate will befall the ruler's consort, his heir, the high ministers of state, the lords of cities, the village heads and generals, the magistrates of the districts, and the government officials."

The Ninno Sutra states: "If persons destroy the teachings of the Buddha, they will have no filial sons, no harmony with their six kind of relatives, and no aid from the heavenly deities and dragons. Disease and evil spirits will come day after day to torment them, disasters will descend on them incessantly, and misfortune will dog them wherever they go.

And when they die, they will fall into the realms of hell, hungry spirits and animals.

Even if they should be reborn as human beings, they will be destined to become soldiers or slaves."

Retribution will follow as an echo follows a sound or a shadow follows a form.

Someone writing at night may put out the lamp, but the words he has written will still remain.

It is the same with the effect of the deeds which we carry out for ourselves in the threefold world.

The second volume of The Lotus Sutra says: "If a person fails to have faith but instead slanders this sutra, when his life comes to an end, he will enter the Avichi hell."

And in the Fukyo chapter in the seventh volume it says: "For a thousand kalpas they underwent great suffering in the Avichi hell."

In the Nirvana Sutra we read: "If a person separates himself from good friends, refuses to listen to correct teachings and instead embraces evil teachings, then as a result he will sink down into the

Avichi hell, where the size of his body will become eighty four thousand yojanas in total length and breadth."
When we examine this wide variety of sutras, we find that they all stress how grave a matter it is to slander The Law.
How pitiful that all people should go out of the gate of the correct teaching and enter so deep into the prison of the heretical doctrines.
How stupid, that they should fall one after another into the snares of these evil doctrines and remain for so long entangled in this net of slanderous teachings.
They lose their way in the mists and miasmas and sink down amid the raging flames of hell.
How could we not grieve?
How could we not suffer?
Therefore you must quickly reform the tenets you hold in your heart and embrace the one true vehicle, the single good doctrine of The Lotus Sutra.
If you do so, then the threefold world will become the Buddha land, and how could a Buddha land ever decline?
The regions in the ten directions will all become treasure realms, and how could a treasure realm ever suffer harm?
If you live in a country that knows no decline or diminution, in a land that suffers no harm or disruption, then your body will find peace and security and your mind will be calm and untroubled.
You must believe my words, heed what I say!
The guest said: Since it concerns both this life and the lives to come, who could fail to be cautious in a matter such as this?
Who could fail to agree with you?
Now when I examine the passages you have cited from the sutras and see exactly what the Buddha has said, I realise that slandering is a very grave fault indeed, that violating The Law is in truth a terrible offense.
I have put all my faith in one Buddha alone, Amida, and rejected all the other Buddha's.
I have honoured The Three Pure Land Sutras and set aside the other sutras.
But this was not due to any distorted ideas of my own conception.
I was simply obeying the words of the eminent men of the past.
And the same is true of all the other persons in the ten directions.
But now I realise that to do so means to exhaust oneself in futile efforts in this life, and to fall into the Avichi hell in the life to come.
The texts you have cited are perfectly clear on this point and their arguments are detailed, they leave no room for doubt.

From now on, with your kind instruction to guide me, I wish to continue dispelling the ignorance from my mind.

I hope we may set about as quickly as possible taking measures to deal with these slanders of The Law and to bring peace to the world without delay, thus insuring that we may live in safety in this life and enjoy good fortune in the life to come.

But it is not enough that I alone should accept and have faith in your words, we must see to it that others as well are warned of their errors!"

At last the guest has completely understood that the only way to rid the land of its problems and troubles is to reject inferior and erroneous teachings and concentrate the lives of everybody in the land on the ultimate truth.

He points out in those paragraphs that it is the people who are led astray by the priests and monks who have been teaching those inferior and incomplete sutras.

The only way to overcome the problem in actuality is for both the government and the people to stop making offerings to such priests and monks.

This is a very important point because at that time the ruling authorities were solidly sponsoring such sects as zen, jodo and shingon.

It was these sects and the priests and monks in charge of them who in turn were persuading the government to persecute Nichiren Daishonin.

In the final paragraphs, which you have just read, Nichiren Daishonin also warns that urgent steps have to be taken to stop erroneous and heretical teachings from spreading any further, otherwise he says, the two remaining calamities or disasters which are predicted in the earlier sutras of the Buddha, which will befall those people or countries who are slandering The Lotus Sutra or the law of life, will inevitably occur.

Those two remaining disasters which had not yet appeared, though all the others had, are civil war and invasion by a foreign power.

In emphasising this point through his understanding of all the teachings of Shakyamuni Buddha, Nichiren Daishonin was making a very important prediction.

In fact the ruling authorities of those times, or the Kamakura Shogunate, completely ignored Rissho Ankoku Ron but exactly as predicted both these disasters of civil war and invasion from a foreign power took place exactly as he said they would, validating in the process everything that he had said in Rissho Ankoku Ron.

Changing Poison into Medicine

Civil war broke out whilst Nichiren Daishonin was in exile on Sado Island after they had tried to behead him on the beach at Tatsunokuchi.

It is incredible to note that in the case of the foreign invasion, the first step towards it took place exactly seven years and seven months from the date on which Rissho Ankoku Ron was presented, that first step being the arrival of The Mongol emissaries arriving in Japan with an ultimatum.

Then amazingly enough, since Japan rejected the ultimatum, the first invasion by The Mongols, took place exactly fourteen years after the Rissho Ankoku Ron was written and submitted to The Shogunate and the second invasion took place exactly twenty one years after Rissho Ankoku Ron was written and submitted.

Bearing in mind the relationship between the number seven and the seven characters of Nam Myoho Renge Kyo and our understanding of the importance of actual proof and this figure, we can see that the rhythm of life works in both great happenings and disastrous happenings.

These happenings of foreign invasion occurred and manifested themselves, measured in time and multiples of seven, multiples of Nam Myoho Renge Kyo.

Through this we can really see the rhythm of the law of life at work.

"The host exclaimed in delight.
'The dove has changed into a hawk, the sparrow into a clam! How gratifying!

You have transformed yourself through your association with me, a friend in the orchid room, just as the mugwort growing in the hemp field becomes straight.

If you truly give consideration to the troubles I have been describing and put entire faith in these words of mine, then the winds shall blow gently, the waves will be calm, and in no time at all we will enjoy bountiful harvests,

But a person's heart may change with the times, and the nature of a thing may alter with its surroundings.

Just as the moon on the water will be tossed about by the waves, or the soldiers in the vanguard will be cowed by the swords of the enemy, so, although at this moment you may say you believe in my words, I fear that later you will forget them completely.'"

'You have transformed yourself through your association with me, a friend in the orchid room, just as the mugwort growing in the hemp field becomes straight.'

Changing Poison into Medicine

In this sentence Nichiren Daishonin is emphasising the importance to our lives of the people with whom we associate.

It is a human tendency to be strongly influenced by our environment but equally as Buddhists we know that through the principle of Esho Funi, the inseparability of self and the environment, we too can have great influence on our environment.

Nichiren Daishonin is saying that it is important that through the power of our practice we establish a good environment containing good friends and influences and especially of course The Gohonzon itself.

Most people today want to live happy and peaceful lives, they long in their hearts for this but it is the environment which playing on their desires causes them to plunge down the wrong track.

Not only people but it is the same with countries, there is a chain reaction.

One country following the wrong philosophy of life will cause another country and then another country and then another country to go the wrong way for the peoples happiness and we can see this today in the events that surround us.

In the way of our own country following the lead of the United States, it is now deeply involved in nuclear arms proliferation and also we entered the wars in Syria, Libya, Iraq and Afghanistan when the United States took the lead and we followed with many other western nations.

Also today in the way that Japan is under incredible pressure from the western nations led by the United States and their foreign policy to rearm to an extent that its constitution does not allow, forcing changes in the constitution by the Japanese Government to enable Japanese forces to fight overseas for the first time since world war two by passing its now recent and notorious "War Laws."

And through the passing of these "War Laws" undermining its famous pacifist constitution enshrined in article nine which was a treasure of peace for all of humanity.

Thus enabling Japanese forces to fight alongside the American armed forces against China if another war breaks out in the region.

The whole purpose of Nichiren Shoshu Buddhism is to gradually overcome peoples adherence to such erroneous philosophies and teachings throughout the world.

To open the eyes of the peoples of the world to the ultimate truth of life so as people, they can unite together to stop this disastrous trend of warmongering on our one and only planet Earth.

Changing Poison into Medicine

There is nothing more important than the fundamental law of life and the universe, which means life itself and the right to live that life in peace with all other living beings.

The most important question is how we can preserve and nurture life through establishing world peace.

We know that up until now humanity has experienced many, many failures to make this most noble ideal a reality and made many mistakes.

We can only overcome this tendency to fail by embracing this fundamental law of life and the universe and learn to live in harmony with it.

We have the great good fortune to have become awakened and enlightened to this law before many others have even heard or know about it.

Because of our good karma we have been able to embrace this law ahead of most of the human race.

As human beings we are deeply interdependent and related in our daily lives and our own personal circumstances to our environments, in other words we are all deeply related to the society in which we all live and work.

If humanity is to become truly peaceful and happy it must change those aspects of our societies which cause unhappiness and human suffering.

Since this relationship to our environment is symbiotic it is essential that all our actions are based on faith in The Gohonzon, which embodies the principle of Ichinen Sanzen.

If we look at the stark reality of today's world we see the rise of nationalism in many nations, a rise in racism and xenophobia and egoism.

It is a fact that each nation has its own laws and culture and these we must respect but at the same time we can follow our own path.

The path of the great law of life itself.

Nam Myoho Renge Kyo.

The Mystic Law of Life and the universe.

This has to be the most realistic path to follow in order to experience absolute happiness in our lives and to pass it on to others, to accomplish this it is vital that we develop ever greater and deeper faith, then we ourselves become a manifestation of this Mystic Law of Life.

Through the great Buddhist principles of Esho Funi and Ichinen Sanzen we can transform our world and make the noble ideal of a harmonious world and of world peace for all living beings a reality.

Changing Poison into Medicine

The great document and treatise or manifesto of The Buddha,
Rissho Ankoku Ron is saying exactly the same thing.
We can become as ordinary human beings a manifestation of
The Mystic Law, hence all our actions will be based on the
wisdom and compassion of that Law or Dharma.
These are bound to reflect throughout our society.

"Now if we wish first of all to bring security to the nation and to
pray for our present and future lives, then we must hasten to
examine and consider the situation and take measures as soon as
possible to remedy it.
Why do I say this?
Because of the seven types of disaster described in the Yakushi
Sutra, five have already occurred.
Only two have yet to appear, the calamity of invasion from
foreign lands and the calamity of revolt within one's own domain.
And of the three calamities mentioned in the Daijuku Sutra, two
have already made their appearance.
Only one remains, the disaster of warfare.
The different types of disaster and calamity enumerated in the
Konkomyo Sutra have arisen one after the other.
Only that described as marauders from other regions invading
and plundering the nation has yet to materialise.
This is the only trouble that has not yet come.
And of the seven disasters listed in the Ninno Sutra, six are now
upon us in full force.
Only one has not yet appeared, the calamity that occurs "when
enemies rise up on all four sides and invade the nation."

In one part of the world or another people are being afflicted by
the three calamities and the seven disasters, in fact the whole
world is experiencing one of the three calamities, that of
pestilence or epidemics as we are currently, at the time of this
book being written, in the grip of the global Covid-19 pandemic.
This is inflicting untold suffering and death for many people and
their families and loved ones around the world.
This is perpetuating the unhappiness of the people everywhere.
The three calamities as expressed in the Daijuku sutra are,
inflation, warfare and pestilence.
The seven disasters as expressed in the Yakushi sutra are,
epidemics, foreign invasion, civil war, unseasonable storms,
unseasonable droughts, changes in the heavens that have a
deep and profound effect on nature and the natural world, and
eclipses.

255

Nichiren Daishonin is saying that unless we keep moving towards Kosen Rufu these disasters will never abate on the contrary they will increase.

The only solution is Shakabuku and teaching others about the existence of the ultimate truth.

Speaking generally, people are naturally very short sighted, they cannot see below the surface of the problems which beset our planet today.

Because they cannot see below the surface they are unable to change the root cause of these problems and thus achieve a lasting peace and harmony.

It is like a weed, unless you get to the root, however much you cut it down, it will always grow again.

For example, people think that disarmament is the solution to armed conflict and to bring about a lasting peace but in fact it is not, unless the root cause for human beings to arm themselves is removed and eradicated from this world, the three poisons lying in the depths of every human life which cause wars and all these other devilish acts which are occurring across the globe today, causing untold misery and unhappiness, will continue.

Even if disarmament was achieved, inevitably unless the root cause is eradicated people will start to rearm again.

We have already mentioned the exactness in terms of time of Nichiren Daishonin's predictions of civil war and foreign invasion at that time and these were a cornerstone or a fundamental cause for Kosen Rufu.

As a result of those predictions exactly being fulfilled, they validated the wisdom and truth contained in Rissho Ankoku Ron. Immediately they resulted in Nichiren Daishonin's pardon by the government.

Through this he was able to retire to Mount Minobu and there he lay the foundations for Kosen Rufu by training his disciples and inscribing The Dai Gohonzon, all of which took place in the last eight years of his life.

'Moreover as the Ninno Sutra says, "When a nation becomes disordered, it is the spirits which first show signs of rampancy. Because the spirits become rampant, all the people of the nation become disordered."

Now if we examine the present situation carefully in the light of this passage, we will see the various spirits have for some time been rampant and many of the people have perished.

If the first predicted misfortune in the sutra has already occurred, as is obvious, then how can we doubt that the later disasters will follow?

Changing Poison into Medicine

If, in punishment for the evil doctrines that are upheld, the troubles that are yet to appear should fall upon us one after another, then it will be too late to act will it not?"

Here when Nichiren Daishonin is talking about evil spirits becoming rampant he is referring to erroneous, incorrect and inferior teachings.
These sap peoples life force and unbalance their lives and as a result create chaos and disorder in society and the environment itself.
In the Gosho, 'The Person and The Law,'

"Since the Law is supreme the person is worthy of respect, since the person is worthy of respect, the land is sacred."

To establish a peaceful and prosperous, happy land, The Dharma or teaching must be supreme.
Are there any peaceful, prosperous and happy lands in all the world at this time in human history?
Each and every problem in the world today can be traced back to erroneous, incorrect and inferior teachings.
What are the pillars of Nichiren Shoshu Buddhism when related to human life, when these teachings of the ultimate truth actually become integrated with our daily life?
They are freedom, equality and dignity.
Dignity meaning the supreme dignity of each and every individual life form and especially of human life.
Although each of these principles is separate in itself they are all actually interdependent.
For example, freedom for some cannot be at the expense of other people's lives, likewise, equality, must be based on the dignity of each individual life and the dignity of people's lives again must not be at the expense of freedom and equality of other people's lives.
They are all interchangeable.
They are the unshakeable three pillars of a Buddhist democracy.
Let us look at dignity first because this rests at the base or support for the other two.
The supreme dignity of each individual person's life is the main pillar of a Buddhist democracy.
Many people in the world talk about the dignity of life but sadly it is mostly pure theory or ideology.
Without the right philosophy and a practice that is powerful enough to enable one to live that philosophy, to maintain the dignity of every single individual life is virtually impossible.

257

Jesus Christ taught the dignity of life, but the proof of the pudding is in the eating.

The christian practice has lacked the power to sustain that course so that as a result generally speaking, christianity has been a history of war and violence.

Today we suffer from the hangover of this in the way of a state of mind and the actions of our people.

Where is the dignity of life in the racist behaviour of football fans? Where is the dignity of life in the wars we waged in Iraq, Afghanistan, Libya and Syria and currently, by proxy, in Palestine and Yemen?

The only way supreme dignity of life can be preserved and respected and sustained is through following a philosophy and practice which enables you to reveal the highest life state of human life.

Without this, the devilish force of life will always win the battle.

The supreme act of dignity is for someone who is filled with this highest state of human life to help others to reveal the same state.

Shakubuku is therefore without a doubt the highest and most noble and pure action.

A supreme act of humanity, to express and draw out the highest state of human life from others, enabling them to establish the supreme dignity of their life, with all the great qualities of enlightenment and Buddhahood that go with it.

Secondly let us look at freedom.

In this country today the concept of freedom is still freedom from the dogma and the commandments and the moral code of christianity, it is also freedom from the class system, which goes back to christian feudal times, and became the framework within which the christian moral code was conducted but in fact these two are only partial freedoms.

Buddhism points out that in the light of the law of causality these are only comparatively shallow external freedoms.

They will not be long lasting unless the root cause of the evils of the class system and the moral code and its attraction to people is removed.

What is the root cause?

Again it is erroneous, inferior and incomplete religious teachings which because of their inadequacy had to resort to a moral code based on fear and hierarchical and patriarchal domination.

What is the solution to this?

All phenomena and therefore our environment are in a state of constant flux, true freedom is developing the power within yourself to have freedom from the influence of external conditions, whether they be social, political or religious if they are against the supreme dignity of your own life, and also finding freedom within the battle with oneself.

This means freedom from control by your shallow desires or the dark side or fundamental darkness of life, freedom from the chains of our unhappy karma and freedom from the sufferings of life.

This inner transformation can only be attained by a religion that has the power to bring out the highest state of human life, that of enlightened Buddhahood.

Equality is also preached in christianity.

All human beings are stated to be equal before god and indeed born in his image, but the question is does god appear to create human beings equally?

Despite that politics, economics and so on have additionally preached equal rights for everybody but in fact we know very well this has proved to be pure theory, throughout our history. Buddhism points out the truth that in fact everyone is different, that there are great inequalities because of karma, peoples natures to are different.

Everyone has different abilities and a different potential.

It is not surprising therefore that although it is supposed to be based on christian ethics, western neo liberal democracy has emphasised freedom far more than the difficult problem of equality.

Wherever we look we see inequality.

Employers, employees, rich against poor, racial inequalities, in every field of society there are acute inequalities and as a result we see frustration and anger, riots and wars but even despite all that we are still not equal.

If we look on the other side of the sociological scene we see Chinese state 'communism' which has found itself to be emphasising equality rather than freedom, equality in material wellbeing.

However the truth of the matter is that to impose this principle of equality on people who are innately different has resulted in a rigid and restrictive social system.

This has restricted peoples freedom and as a result we see the same on the other side of the coin, frustration and anger.

You can see in the case of both Western Christian Neo Liberal Democracy on the one side and Chinese Atheistic Materialist 'Communism' on the other side that in these two religions of The East and The West, freedom and equality do not bed down at all and work against each other and they are two extremes.

The truth in the light of Nichiren Shoshu Buddhism is that freedom inevitably concerns the individual, whist equality relates to society as a whole.

How do we harmonise these two?

If we can harmonise freedom and equality then you will produce dignity.

We can see this fundamental problem in our western society of how to harmonise these two extremes in order to obtain supreme dignity.

Nichiren Shoshu Buddhism and The Lotus Sutra teaches us about The Ten Worlds and about The Mutual Possession of The Ten Worlds, it teaches us that Buddha exists even in those in the life state of hell and that hell exists in the Buddha state.

Though we may appear to be unequal and naturally different, we can all achieve the highest state of human life which is awakened and enlightened Buddhahood.

Furthermore Buddhism teaches us that the differences between us are of supreme importance.

The cherry, plum and peach tree all look the same in the winter, gnarled and bare and rather ugly, yet in the spring, each produces its own particular blossom and fruit, which though different are supreme in themselves.

It is on this awareness of the supreme dignity and unique potential of each very different individual that the wisdom of Nichiren Shoshu Buddhism can create a true democracy.

The perfect whole, which is both equal and free.

It is the same as a body with its limbs, fingers and toes, heart and hair and eyes and many different parts yet making up the perfect and harmonious one single body.

If politics, sociology and economics are always based on true compassion, always motivated by the determination to preserve and foster and encourage the development of the supreme dignity of each individual life through developing human life's highest state, people will then be able to give their own unique potential in full too the whole human family.

We will be able to achieve a truly happy and absolutely democratic society in each country and in the whole world based on these wonderful Buddhist principles.

In the end the spirit of Rissho Ankoku Ron is to create such Buddhist democracies in each country and ultimately in the whole world based on these three pillars of Freedom, Equality and Dignity.

"Emperors and Kings have their foundations in the state and bring
peace and order to the age.
Ministers and commoners hold possession of their fields and
gardens and supply the needs of the world.
But if marauders come from other regions to invade the nation, or
if revolt breaks out within their domain and peoples lands are
seized and plundered, how can there be anything but terror and
confusion, if the nation is destroyed and families are wiped out,
then where can one flee for safety.
If you care anything about your personal security, you should first
of all pray for order and tranquillity throughout the four quarters of
the land, should you not?"

Emperors and Kings refers today to leaders of society and
ministers and commoners are the people.
Fields and gardens refer to our daily work and the state refers to
whatever level you like to take, it could be a community or a city
or a whole nation or the entire world.
Nichiren Daishonin is saying here that the whole purpose of
politics should be to provide a happy daily life for the people, a
life in which they can feel thoroughly fulfilled because the
structure of society allows them each to contribute to it.
The frustrations of this life are very largely because people find it
impossible to contribute in their own unique way.
Nichiren Daishonin's Buddhism is defining a society in which the
social structure is fused and totally integrated with humanity in
general.
Politics, economics, the sciences, the arts, education and culture
are all integrated and in harmony with the lives of ordinary
people, all aiming towards giving a fulfilling and happy life to
each and every single person, allowing them to fully realise their
own unique potential.
What do we actually see in the west today?
If you take western neo liberal capitalism which really views a
social structure (state) as a necessary evil and therefore they
always try to keep it as small as possible, and this goes to its
greatest extreme in a military dictatorship which creates intense
bureaucratic control.
The will of the few is imposed on the many and it was against this
that the revolutions of the nineteenth century took place and as
a result there is a great gap between rich and poor and between
the educated and the uneducated.
Adam Smith's original thinking was that humanity should be free
and that if left free, god would harmonise peoples various

activities in a very natural way but in fact things did not work out that way.

Looking at socialism which aims to create a very large scale social structure so that all people can share in the benefits of that society equally.

The tendency of such weighty and bureaucratic structures tend to restrict the freedom of the individual and as a result bring waves of apathy and dependency.

From a Buddhist viewpoint capitalism and socialism are two extremes and because of this what we see today is a great polarization of society between these two political views.

What is needed from a Buddhist perspective can best be described as a 'Humanistic Socialism' based on a true democracy.

Firstly the people would administer themselves aiming towards developing each individual's full potential so that each person can lead a fulfilling life.

Secondly, the extent to which each person gives their full potential through the effort they make is what measures the reward which they earn, that is to say, the extent of reward relates exactly to the extent of each individuals effort.

This a reflection of the principles of Buddhist practice with The Gohonzon.

It is very easy to say how on earth can we unravel what exists today and produce such a society based on these principles of Equality, Freedom and Dignity of Life?

What sort of social structure has to be created so that every human beings voice can be heard if they so wish, so that everyone can be given the opportunity to reach their full potential in life?

Nothing is beyond human ingenuity and wisdom if the will is there to achieve it.

We only have to look at the incredible advances in technology in the last century in science to see the amazing things which human beings can achieve when they set out to do so.

Even if the structure to begin with is imperfect, if an ever growing number of individuals have such an aim to achieve such a society, the right structures will without fail appear.

In the end it is up to us and those who believe in what we are trying to achieve, those who we need to teach what Nichiren Shoshu Buddhism is all about.

We must manifest the law of life of the universe in the actions of our daily lives as we transform ourselves and turn our own personal poisons into medicine.

Through this way we will gradually lead the way in every field of society.

Indeed it is amazing to think that three thousand years ago when Shakyamuni Buddha revealed and taught The Lotus Sutra, this is what he predicted.

That we would be the people who through the wisdom, compassion and courage of the Buddha state working in our lives would lead the way in society everywhere throughout the world. Some people say that religion is a matter for the inner self only and it is true that our prime concern is with our own inner self, through carrying out our practice of turning poison into medicine and transforming our inner lives but inevitably as a result of doing that, we in our actions outwards, will reveal the wisdom of that transformation happening within us, so that our thoughts, words and actions in every field of society will reflect that transformation within ourselves, then inevitably society is bound to change.

"It seems to me that when people are in this world they all fear what their lot will be in the life to come, so it is that some of them put their faith in heretical teachings, or pay honour to those who slander The Law, it distresses me that they should be so confused about right and wrong, but at the same time I feel pity that having embraced Buddhism, they should have chosen the wrong kind, with the power of faith that is in their hearts why must they vainly give credence to heretical doctrines.

If they do not shake off these delusions that they cling to, but continue to harbour false ideas, then they will quickly depart from the land of the living and fall into the hell of incessant suffering. Thus the Daijuku sutra says: "Though the ruler of a state may have for countless existences in the past practiced the giving of alms, observed the precepts and bided by the principles of wisdom, if he sees that my Law, The Dharma of The Buddha is in danger of perishing and stand idly by without doing anything to protect it, then all the inestimable store of good causes that he has accumulated through the practices just mentioned will be entirely wiped out.

Before long the ruler will fall gravely ill and after his life will come to an end he will be reborn in one of the major hells and the same fate will befall the rulers consort, his heir, the great ministers of the state, the lords of cities, village heads and generals, the magistrates of districts and the government officials."

Changing Poison into Medicine

Here, Nichiren Daishonin moves on to a new aspect when he says right at the beginning.

"It seems to me that when people are in this world, they all fear what their lot may be in the life to come."
In the Gosho, 'The Heritage of The Ultimate Law of Life,' Nichiren Daishonin says:

"Be resolved to summon forth the great power of your faith and chant Nam Myoho Renge Kyo with the prayer that your faith will be steadfast and correct at the moment of your death.
Never seek any other way to inherit the ultimate law and manifest it in your life, only then will you realise that earthly desires are enlightenment, and the sufferings of birth and death are nirvana."

Nichiren Daishonin says that much goes wrong with us because we fear our lot in the life to come.
This fear of death and a failure to come to terms with it inevitably has a very deep effect on our society.
The truth is that the riddle of death is not solved clearly or logically in other religions and in one way or the other this leads to either a feeling of apathy and resignation to one's lot in life, waiting as it were for heaven after death, or to great fear and superstition which lies very deep at the base of many people's lives.
Either way this fear of death and the unknown quantity that death is certainly breeds the three poisons of greed, anger and ignorance.
Other religions advise turning within yourself seeking only the inner self, in a sense ignoring reality on the grounds that it is an illusion, inevitably such practices become very passive and exclusive and indeed egocentric.
Nichiren Shoshu Buddhism on the other hand is simultaneously both inwards and outwards.
We generate the power of our inner state of self in order to develop ever greater creativity and positivity in our daily actions in the society and environment around us.
This is the practice known as Jigyo and Keta.
Furthermore Nichiren Daishonin's Buddhism explains the eternity of life, that death is in fact an essential phase of vigorous revitalization in readiness for the next life.
We all discover, having begun to understand the Buddhist teachings about death, that this removal of the fear of death from our lives happens in a gradual way.
Through this process we gain an insight and understanding of the functions and mechanics of life, and death's place in it.

Changing Poison into Medicine

This has an incredibly profound effect on all of us who practice Nichiren Shoshu Buddhism.

Somehow we find we are establishing a new set of basic values, things which were important no longer seem so important, things that were before less important become more important.

To take an example, a businessperson who really understands that life is eternal and who really understands the law of karma or cause and effect, will not pursue profit with ruthlessness and greed, perhaps killing themselves in the process and ruining others on the way, instead they will reach their targets through developing the full potential in their own life and in those who work for them and in their customers and as a result all will benefit.

This is just one small example, but you can see that an understanding of the eternity of life and the true place of death in the mechanics of life can in itself, on its own, change the whole world for the better.

"The Ninno sutra states that if a man does injury to the teachings of The Buddha, he will have no filial sons, no harmony with his close relatives and no aid from the heavenly deities.

Disease and evil spirits will come day after day to torment him, disasters will descend on him incessantly and misfortunes will dog him wherever he goes and when he dies he will fall into one of the three realms of hell, hunger or animality."

Nichiren Daishonin here is reiterating that erroneous, incorrect and inferior teachings can destroy the unity and harmony of not only society but also families, communities, nations and the whole world.

In the end it is a question of whether or not your life is in harmony or rhythm with the universal law of life which we call Myoho Renge Kyo.

For example, if we refuse to study the highway code we are more than likely to have a disastrous accident.

If we do study the highway code, we stand a much better chance of travelling with comparative freedom and safety, and if every single person driving a vehicle studies the highway code as well as us, we really stand a chance to be totally safe.

A happy society must always drive from the highway code or the ultimate truth of Nam Myoho Renge Kyo.

A happy society begins and ends with the smallest group within the social structure which is the family.

This is why families should be the foundation of a happy society, yet over the past hundred years this country has seen the total disintegration of the family as a happy unit.

Changing Poison into Medicine

Why is this?
Again it is because of erroneous, incorrect or inferior religious or philosophical teachings.
The family has become splintered and disintegrated, divorce ridden, and has no philosophical rock on which to base its growth and development, this really is another aspect of our national karma which we have to change through the wisdom deriving from the ultimate truth of life.
Through the power of Nichiren Daishonin's teachings and practices as taught by Nichiren Shoshu Buddhism we can create happy outward looking, creative families, each family as an open fortress of faith, each family strong enough to withstand attacks from the dark, devilish forces from outside and yet at the same time its doors are always open to those who come in friendship.
Let us hope that through this radical movement, amongst us all, each one of our families will become truly creative in which parents, sons, daughters, grandparents, uncles, aunts and all the rest of it are giving their own unique potential to the family as a whole.
This understanding of a truly creative and enlightened family, will spill out into our own families and into our society as a whole.
Gradually through this movement for Kosen Rufu we can overcome another sad aspect of our countries karma.

"Even if he should be reborn as a human being, he will be destined to become a slave in the army, retribution will follow as an echo follows a sound, or a shadow follows a form.
A person writing at night may put out the lamp, but he words he has written will still remain, it is the same with the destiny we create for ourselves in the threefold world.
The second volume of The Lotus Sutra says, 'One who refuses to take faith in this sutra and instead slanders it, will after he dies, fall into the hell of incessant suffering.' and in the Fukyo chapter in the seventh volume it says, 'for a thousand aeons they dwelt in the hell of incessant suffering and underwent great pain and torment.'
And in the Nirvana sutra we read, 'if a man separates himself from good friends, refuses to listen to the true law and instead embraces evil teachings, then as result he will sink down into the hell of incessant suffering, where he will experience indescribable torment.'

We live in the age of Mappo, it is not surprising that we are so effected by the state of the world today filled as it was predicted to be with what are known in Buddhism as the five impurities.

Changing Poison into Medicine

The five impurities are the three poisons, greed, anger and
ignorance plus conceit and doubt.
These impurities or poisons exist innately in everybody's life and if
they exist in many lives then obviously the state of society is also
impure and the state of the age is impure.
In the past people relied on morality in order to try to battle with
these poisons or impurities that exist innately in everybody, but
unfortunately moral codes cannot change human beings,
cannot change their karma, or purify their lives, they impose
something on top of life, but very little change occurs within its
depths.
Morality after all can even justify war.
Today now that there is no moral code virtually to speak of as no
one is following it anymore, people are beginning to worry.
The old christian morality has been rejected but nothing has
taken its place, the time is really ripe for people to understand the
ultimate truth of life.
This is why our efforts to Shakubuku cannot fail to succeed,
provided we make the effort to awaken and enlighten them.

"When we look at these wide variety of sutras, we find they all
stress how grave a matter it is to slander the Law, how pitiful that
all men should go out of the gate of the True Law and enter so
deep into the prison of these peverse dogmas, how stupid that
they should fall one after another into the snares of these evil
doctrines, remain for so long entangled in this net of slanderous
teachings, they lose their way in these mists and miasmas, and
sink down amid the raging flames of hell, how they must grieve,
how they must suffer.
Therefore you must quickly reform the tenets you hold in your
heart, and embrace the one true vehicle, the single good
doctrine of The Lotus Sutra, if you do so then the threefold world
will all become the Buddha land and how could a Buddha land
ever decline.
The regions in the ten directions will all become treasure realms
and how could a treasure realm ever suffer harm.
If you live in a country that knows no decline or diminution, in a
land that suffers no harm or disruption, then your body will find rest
and security and your mind will be calm and untroubled.
You must believe my words, heed what I say."

Nichiren Daishonin says that,
'You must quickly reform the tenets that you hold in your hearts
and embrace the one true vehicle, the single good doctrine of
The Lotus Sutra.'

Changing Poison into Medicine

This is Nichiren Daishonin's final exhortation at the end of this long thesis and he uses the word quickly.
We must get on with it.
We must get on changing our poison into medicine and the inner transformation of ourselves and we must get on with Shakubuku.

"Since the law is supreme, the person is worthy of respect, since the person is worthy of respect, the land is sacred"

We cannot make an impure land, pure through science and technology, through politics and economics, only the truth, the ultimate truth living in people's lives will achieve this.
This enables people to change their 'poison into medicine' and elevate their lives to the highest human state, that of awakened and enlightened Buddhahood.
This alone will change the land and avert the impending environmental climate crisis looming on humanities horizon.
Only people stopping themselves from slandering The True Dharma and destroying life can enable the land to become pure.
This is the message of Rissho Ankoku Ron and the manifesto of Nichiren Shoshu Buddhism.
Now the guest has his final say.
The guest said.

"Since it concerns both this life and the life to come, who could fail to be cautious in a matter such as this, who could fail to agree with you.
Now when I examine the passages you have cited from the sutras and see exactly what the Buddha has said, I realise that slandering is a very grave offence indeed.
That violating The Dharma is in truth a terrible sin.
I have put all my faith in one Buddha alone, Amida, and rejected all the other Buddhas, I have honoured the Three Pure Land sutras and set aside the other sutras, but this was not due to any distorted ideas of my own conception, I was simply obeying the words of the eminent men of the past, and the same is true of all the other persons in the ten directions who follow the Pure Land teachings but now I realise that to do so means to exhaust ones inborn capacity in this life and to fall into the hell of incessant suffering in the life to come.
The texts you have cited are perfectly clear on this point and their arguments are detailed, they leave no room for doubt.
With your kind instruction to guide me, I have been able, bit by bit, to dispel the ignorance from my mind.

Changing Poison into Medicine

Now I hope we may set about as quickly as possible, taking measure to deal with these slanders against the Law and to bring peace to the world without delay, ensuring that I may live in safety in this life and enjoy good fortune in the life to come but it is not enough that I alone should accept and have faith in your words.
We must see to it that others as well are warned of their errors."

It is quite clear that this document Rissho Ankoku Ron applies not to one country, not only to one race of people but to the entire world, the entire Planet, to the whole of humanity.
In the final line, the guest is determining to do Shakubuku.
Let us also hope that everyone who reads this book and understands it will feel the same.
We must Shakubuku without delay for all the great reasons that are explained in this amazing thesis of The Buddha of this Anthropocene Age, Nichiren Daishonin.
This thesis which has the answer to every single one of the problems of this world and the human problems that make this world up.
Please let us do Shakubuku and let us spread these amazing teachings and in that way change our own poison into medicine.
Change our own unhappy karma and change our society, change our nations unhappy karma and with our fellow Nichiren Shoshu Buddhists in the world to change the unhappy karma of this blue planet, humanities one and only home, called Planet Earth.

Kechimyaku.

"Kechimyaku" in Japanese and Chinese generally means a vein, a blood lineage, or a genealogy.
In Buddhism, it refers to the Heritage of the Law that is transmitted down through the ages from Master to Disciple and the order of succession of those who transmit the Heritage from one generation to the next.
As such, it is also called the lineage of a school or of The Dharma or Law.
In English, Nichiren Shoshu has traditionally called Kechimyaku the Heritage, and sometimes the Lifeblood, depending on the context.
Though 'Heritage' is closest in meaning, when Kechimyaku refers to that which is transmitted both 'Heritage' and 'Lifeblood' is probably fine so long as you understand the concept they represent as it is defined in The Nichiren Shoshu School.
Nichiren Daishonin teaches in the Heritage of the Ultimate Matter of Life and Death that:

"Without the Heritage, it would be useless to embrace The Lotus Sutra,"

And in The Essence of Shakyamuni's lifetime of Sacred Teachings, that:

"One cannot master this Sutra if one has not received the transmission from The Buddha."

Nichiren Daishonin is telling us that in Buddhist Practice it is fundamental to know of the Heritage and to exert oneself in faith under the direction of the person who has received the orthodox transmission of it.

In his preface to a book called the Bennaku Kanjin Sho, Sixty Fifth High Priest Nichijun Shonin wrote:

"Those who practice this Buddhism must pay heed to the path of the Master and Disciple, trace the orthodoxy of the Master's lineage to verify that the flow of the Law he transmits is correct, and only then partake of its pure water."

The historical rationale of this is that in the school of Nichiren Daishonin and his school called Nichiren Shoshu, it is as clear as the Sun is bright that the succession of The Transmission of The Law which began when the Sacred Founder, Nichiren Daishonin, transferred the Heritage of the Law to Second High Priest Nikko Shonin and willed that he be the Great Master of Propagation and continued when Third High Priest Nichimoku Shonin in turn succeeded Nikko Shonin has continued down through the ages to this day.

Thus, when one makes it a matter of principle to adhere to this relationship between the successive Master's and Disciples, one can intrinsically partake of the orthodox practice and faith. Thus, the Lifeblood of faith in Nichiren Shoshu lies in the Dai Gohonzon of the High Sanctuary and in Nichiren Daishonin's Heritage of the Law in the care of each of the successive High Priests.

ABOUT THE AUTHOR

Harvey Webb is the creator and founder of The Sun Lotus Recovery Movement where western science fuses with eastern Buddhist Dharma to create innovative and unique solutions for addiction disorders and has previously published Climbing The Mountain, The Complete Handbook of Buddhist Recovery which is the first publication of Sun Lotus Recovery and is currently working on a third publication to complete the triptych of works for the programme entitled 'Contemplations on The Gosho' to be published when the causes and conditions of life make it possible.

Sun Lotus Buddhist Recovery Programme

www.sunlotusbuddhistrecovery.com

sunlotusrecovery@gmail.com

Printed in Great Britain
by Amazon

77902062R00163